W9-BHD-974

GOVERNING SCOTLAND: PROBLEMS AND PROSPECTS

Governing Scotland: Problems and Prospects

The economic impact of the Scottish Parliament

Edited by
JOHN McCARTHY
DAVID NEWLANDS

Ashgate

Aldershot • Brookfield USA • Singapore • Sydney

Published by
Ashgate Publishing Ltd
Gower House
Croft Road
Aldershot
Hants GU11 3HR
England

Ashgate Publishing Company
Old Post Road
Brookfield
Vermont 05036
USA

British Library Cataloguing in Publication Data
Governing Scotland : problems and prospects : the economic
   impact of the Scottish Parliament. - (Urban and regional
   planning and development)
   1. Decentralization in government - Economic aspects -
   Scotland 2. Scotland - Economic conditions - 1973-
   3. Scotland - Politics and government - 20th century
   I. McCarthy, John II. Newlands, David
   330.9'411'0859

Library of Congress Catalog Card Number: 98-74508

ISBN 1 84014 570 6

Printed and bound by Athenaeum Press, Ltd.,
Gateshead, Tyne & Wear.

Contents

Contributors   vii

1   Introduction   1
    John McCarthy and David Newlands

Part I   Context

2   The economic impact of the Scottish Parliament: possibilities and   11
    constraints
    David Newlands

3   The Scottish Parliament and the European Union   25
    Peter Roberts

Part II   Financing

4   The fiscal arrangements for devolution   49
    David Heald and Neal Geaughan

5   Tax varying powers: the watchdog that will not bark   69
    Tony Jackson

Part III   Economic development

6   Economic development: the Scottish Parliament and the development   87
    agencies
    Mike Danson

7   Economic development: the Scottish Parliament and local government   103
    John Fairley

Part IV   Spatial impacts

8   The Scottish Parliament and the planning system: addressing the   121
    strategic deficit through spatial planning
    Greg Lloyd

9   Implications of the Scottish Parliament for urban regeneration   135
     John McCarthy

10   The local economic impact of the Scottish Parliament   149
     Ronald W. McQuaid

11   A policy agenda for the Scottish Parliament   167
     John McCarthy and David Newlands

Bibliography   171

Contributors

Mike Danson   Professor, Department of Accounting, Economics and Languages, Paisley University

John Fairley   Professor, Centre for Environmental Planning, Strathclyde University

Neal Geaughan   Teaching Fellow, Department of Accountancy, Aberdeen University

David Heald   Professor, Department of Accountancy, Aberdeen University

Tony Jackson   Senior Lecturer, School of Town and Regional Planning, Dundee University

Greg Lloyd   Professor, School of Town and Regional Planning, Dundee University

John McCarthy   Lecturer, School of Town and Regional Planning, Dundee University

Ronald W. McQuaid Senior Lecturer, Department of Economics, Napier University

David Newlands   Senior Lecturer, Department of Economics, Aberdeen University

Peter Roberts   Professor, School of Town and Regional Planning, Dundee University

1   Introduction

JOHN McCARTHY and DAVID NEWLANDS

1.1   The creation of the Scottish Parliament

The government introduced a Bill in December 1997 to create an elected Parliament in Scotland for the first time since 1707. The Bill is expected to become law in the summer or autumn of 1998. The Scottish Parliament and Executive will be created in 1999 and become fully operational in the year 2000.

The creation of the Scottish Parliament will have important implications for the pattern of regional governance in the UK and the conduct of regional and industrial policy. This book of edited papers discusses the potential economic impact of the Parliament. It seeks to introduce a more thoughtful, dispassionate and analytical tone to a debate which has been dominated by political rhetoric. The book consists of the revised versions of papers presented at a conference organised by the Scottish Branch of the Regional Studies Association in the City Chambers, Edinburgh on 27 February 1998.

This chapter gives a brief recap of the political background to the creation of the Scottish Parliament. It outlines the economic remit of the Parliament. Finally, it summarises the structure of the book.

1.2   The political background to the creation of the Scottish Parliament

The last parliament in Scotland was dissolved in 1707 following its union with the English parliament to create a Parliament of Great Britain meeting in London. However, Scotland retained its distinctive legal and educational systems. There was a Secretary of State for Scotland appointed in the first British government after 1707 but this appointment ceased after the Jacobite rebellion in 1745. A Secretary for Scotland was not appointed again until 1885. The post was enhanced to Secretary of State for Scotland in 1926. Then, in 1939, the functions of the Scottish Office in London were transferred to St Andrew's House in Edinburgh which became its new headquarters (Scottish Office, 1997a).

The Scottish Office gradually acquired more powers. The Highlands and Islands Development Board (HIDB), created in 1965, and a second development agency covering lowland Scotland, the Scottish Development Agency, created in 1975, were both answerable to the Scottish Office. A new Industry Department was created in the early 1970s to administer the Scottish Office's responsibilities in the industrial and economic development fields (Scottish Office, 1993a).

These developments were driven both by the belief that there were managerial or efficiency gains to be derived from decentralised government and by a broader political argument that decisions affecting Scotland should be made in Scotland.

In the 1970s, following the publication of the Royal Commission on the Constitution (the Kilbrandon Commission) (Kilbrandon, 1973), and in response to growing political support for the Scottish National Party (SNP), the Labour government put forward a proposal to create a Scottish Assembly. The Scotland Bill was introduced in 1977 and became law in 1978. The Scotland Act required that a referendum be held and an amendment carried during the Bill's passage through Parliament specified that, if less than 40 per cent of the electorate voted in favour, the Act would be repealed. That is precisely what happened. The referendum was held on 1 March 1979. 1,230,937 voted in favour of an Assembly, 51.6 per cent of those voting. However, given a turnout of 63 per cent, this represented only 32.9 per cent of the electorate. The Scotland Act was repealed on 26 July 1979.

It is worth noting at this point that there was considerable geographical variation in voting patterns in the referendum (Scottish Government Yearbook, 1979). In the Western Isles, 55.8 per cent voted to implement the Scotland Act. In Central Region, the figure was 54.7 per cent and, in Strathclyde Region, 54.0 per cent. In six Regional or Island Council areas, a minority of electors voted in favour of devolution: Tayside (49.5 per cent), Grampian (48.3 per cent), Borders (40.3 per cent), Dumfries and Galloway (40.3 per cent), Orkney (27.9 per cent) and Shetland (27.0 per cent).

Although a Scottish Assembly was not created in the late 1970s, one legacy of that period was the creation of a system determining public expenditure in Scotland (or strictly changes in the level of public expenditure) which survives to this day:

> The then Chief Secretary to the Treasury, Joel Barnett, devised a formula which ensured that any future changes in the Scottish or Welsh budgets should be calculated as a proportion of the changes in equivalent English spending. The formula allocated increases or decreases in public expenditure in Scotland, Wales and England in the ratio 10:5:85, the rounded share of GB population for the three nations concerned in 1976. This became known as the "Barnett formula" (Constitution Unit, 1996, p.66).

Renewed pressure for the creation of an elected Scottish Assembly or Parliament grew in the 1980s. This was in part due to the perceived rejection of Thatcherism by Scots. Until the 1960s, the Conservative share of the vote in Scotland was similar to its share in England. However, in 1979, the Conservatives gained 47.2 per cent of the vote in England but only 31.4 per cent in Scotland, a gap of 15.8 per cent. This gap increased further to 17.6 per cent in 1983 and 22.2 per cent in 1987 (although it narrowed slightly, to 19.8 per cent, in 1992) (Constitution Unit, 1996, p.16). Certain features of Conservative policy, notably the Community Charge or poll tax, were particularly unpopular in Scotland. There was a growing "democratic deficit" in Scotland.

There was also increasing interest in the experience of other countries. An elected tier of regional governments was created in both France and Spain in the 1980s while regional governments played an expanding role in the formulation and implementation of European Community regional policy.

From the late 1980s onwards, the cross party pressure for constitutional change in Scotland was led by the Scottish Constitutional Convention (SCC). All political parties in Scotland were invited to join the Convention. The Conservatives refused while the SNP were involved at the beginning but later withdrew. In addition, the SCC had representatives from local government, the churches, the Scottish TUC and business groups. It adopted its own Claim of Right by which "we, gathered as the Scottish Constitutional Convention, do hereby acknowledge the sovereign right of the Scottish people to determine the form of Government best suited to their needs".

In various reports, the SCC drew up a detailed scheme for the creation of a devolved Scottish Parliament (Scottish Constitutional Convention, 1990; Scottish Constitutional Convention, 1995; Lynch, 1996). The proposals of the SCC have been very influential. Many of its key proposals are to be found in the government's White Paper.

The Scottish Constitutional Convention proposed a Parliament of 129 members, part directly elected by the "first past the post" system, part drawn from a regional party list of additional members. There should be a Member of the Scottish Parliament for each of Orkney, Shetland and the Western Isles so as to ensure separate representation. The SCC urged that the political parties should select and field an equal number of male and female candidates for election.

The SCC argued that the Scottish Parliament and Scottish Executive should take over responsibility for the policy areas currently within the remit of the Scottish Office, including the financing and organisation of local government. The Scottish Parliament should be represented on UK delegations to the various organs of the European Union. The spending of the Scottish Parliament should be financed by the existing block grant system covered by the Barnett formula. However, the Scottish Parliament should also have the power to decrease or increase the basic rate of income tax levied in Scotland by a maximum of three pence in the pound, which Michael Forsyth, the then Secretary of State for Scotland, famously dubbed the "tartan tax".

Despite the Conservative government's continued opposition to the creation of a Scottish Parliament, there continued to be further measures of devolution of decision making powers to Scotland. With the creation in 1991 of Scottish Enterprise and Highlands and Islands Enterprise (from the merger of the SDA and the HIDB with the Scottish arm of the Training Agency) the Scottish Office gained greater responsibility over training policy in Scotland. Also in the early 1990s, oversight of the higher education system in Scotland passed to the Scottish Office with the creation of the Scottish Higher Education Funding Council. Thus, even under the Conservatives, while there may not have been legislative devolution to Scotland, there was very considerable administrative devolution.

Following the election of the Labour government in May 1997, a White Paper on the creation of a Scottish Parliament was published in July (Scottish Office, 1997a). The economic powers proposed in the White Paper are discussed in the next section. The proposals contained in the White Paper were confirmed in a two part referendum held on 11 September 1997.

Scottish electors were asked to vote on the principle of a Scottish Parliament and, separately, whether a Scottish Parliament should have tax varying powers. A substantial majority, 74.3 per cent, voted in favour of the principle of a Scottish Parliament while a smaller number, but still a significant majority, 63.5 per cent, voted in favour of a Scottish Parliament having tax varying powers.

There were considerable variations in the voting patterns across Scotland. There was majority support for the principle of a Scottish Parliament in every local authority area but within a range from 84.7 per cent in West Dunbartonshire to 57.3 per cent in Orkney. All the local authority areas in which there were very large votes in favour, of 80 per cent or more, were in West Central Scotland. Most of the local authorities areas with votes in favour of 65 per cent or less were in the Northern Isles or in rural areas.

A similar pattern emerged in voting on the second question, whether a Scottish Parliament should have tax varying powers. The highest vote in favour, 75.0 per cent, was in Glasgow. The other areas with substantial votes in favour, of 70 per cent or more, were also in West Central Scotland. Two areas, Orkney (47.4 per cent) and Dumfries and Galloway (48.8 per cent), failed to secure majority support for the second referendum question. These areas, and those in which there was only narrow majority support for tax varying powers, of 55 per cent or less, were again generally to be found in the Northern Isles and the rural areas of Scotland.

These patterns replicated those demonstrated in the 1979 referendum. The general argument has been that many people in the Northern Isles or in the rural areas of Scotland fear that devolution would simply involve the replacement of remote government from London by remote government from Edinburgh. Indeed, the situation might be worse to the extent that a Scottish Parliament dominated by Central Scotland interests operates in such a way that the concerns of the Northern Isles and rural areas of Scotland are more marginalised than ever.

1.3   The economic remit of the Parliament

The White Paper proposes the creation of a Scottish Parliament with legislative powers over a wide range of issues. A Scottish Executive headed by a First Minister will operate in a similar way to the UK government. The Scottish Parliament will consist of 129 members. 73 will be directly elected on a constituency basis (with Orkney and Shetland each having a member). 56 additional members (seven from each of the eight European Parliament constituencies) will be allocated between the political parties so that the overall result better reflects the share of votes gained by each party. Elections will be held every four years.

The Parliament will be located in Edinburgh. In January 1998, the government announced that the Parliament will be located on a site in Edinburgh's Royal Mile, close to Holyrood Palace. The Scottish Executive civil service will be drawn from, and continue to be part of, the UK Home Civil Service. By some estimates, the construction costs of the new Parliament building and the other buildings in the complex will be £100 million. The White Paper estimates the annual running costs of the Parliament to be between £20 and £30 million per year, about £5 per year per head of the Scottish population.

In outline, the areas of responsibility of the Scottish Parliament will include health, education, local government, economic development, the law and home affairs, the environment, sport and the arts. The Act setting up the Parliament will specify the powers reserved to the UK parliament. These include the UK constitution, UK foreign and defence policy, the UK's fiscal and monetary system, employment legislation, and social security provision. Relations with the European Union will remain the responsibility of the UK government but the White Paper proposes that the Scottish Executive should be closely involved in UK decision making on Europe.

The financing of the Scottish Parliament will be similar to the existing system of financing the activity of the Scottish Office through a block grant from the UK Exchequer. However, following support for tax varying powers in the referendum, the Scottish Parliament will also have the power to alter the basic rate of income tax set by the UK parliament (by up to the equivalent of three pence in the pound).

Considering the intended economic remit of the Parliament in more detail, as set out in the White Paper, the economic development and transport responsibilities which are identified are:

- economic development including the functions of Scottish Enterprise, Highlands and Islands Enterprise and the local enterprise companies;
- financial assistance to industry subject to common UK guidelines and consultation arrangements to be set out in a published concordat;
- inward investment including the functions of Locate in Scotland;
- promotion of trade and exports including the functions of Scottish Trade International;
- promotion of tourism including the functions of the Scottish Tourist Board;
- passenger and road transport covering the Scottish road network, the promotion of road safety, bus policy, concessionary fares, cycling, taxis and minicabs, non technical aspects of disability and transport, some rail grant powers, the Strathclyde Passenger Transport Executive and consultative arrangements in respect of public transport;
- appropriate air and transport powers covering ports, harbours and piers, the provision of freight shipping and ferry services, the activities of Highlands and Islands Airports Ltd and planning and environmental issues relating to airports; and
- inland waterways (Scottish Office, 1997a, pp.4-5).

In other areas, the Scottish Parliament will have responsibilities which are also relevant to economic development. In the area of education and training, the Scottish Parliament will be responsible for school education, further and higher education, science and research funding, training policy and lifelong learning, vocational qualifications, and careers advice and guidance.

In the area of local government and housing, the Scottish Parliament will be responsible for the system of local government (including local government finance and local domestic and non domestic taxation), housing (including the functions of Scottish Homes), area regeneration (including the designation of enterprise zones), and land use planning and building control.

In the area of the environment, the Scottish Parliament will have responsibility for environmental protection, water supplies and sewerage, and policies designed to promote sustainable development. The Scottish Parliament will also have responsibility for agriculture, forestry and fishing.

The means of financing the activity of the Scottish Parliament are also obviously relevant its potential economic role. The White Paper proposes that the Scottish Parliament should be financed largely by a block grant from the UK Exchequer, in a similar arrangement to the way in which the activity of the Scottish Office is currently funded. The Barnett formula will continue to operate, updated periodically to allow for population and other technical changes. In addition, the Scottish Parliament will be able to levy or reduce income tax for basic rate taxpayers in Scotland by up to around £450 million (the estimated revenue from a three pence income tax rate in Scotland). In spending its budget, the Scottish Parliament will have the maximum freedom to determine its own expenditure priorities.

1.4   Structure of the book

The book discusses the whole range of the economic powers, impact and potential of the Scottish Parliament under four themes: context, financing, economic development, and spatial impacts.

In part I, chapter 2, by David Newlands, discusses the lessons of economic theory and of the experience of other European countries for the economic potential of the Parliament. While recognising the available opportunities, it emphasises the considerable economic constraints on the freedom of action of the Parliament arising from Scotland being part of the British and EU political system and of increasingly integrated national, European and global markets. Chapter 3, by Peter Roberts, is another context chapter. It discusses the past relationship between Scotland and the European Union - with particular regard to the impact of Structural Fund spending in Scotland - and speculates whether the development of Scotland's relations with the EU under the Parliament could act as a model for the governance of small nations and regions elsewhere.

In part II, chapters 4 and 5 consider how the work of the Scottish Parliament is to be financed. In chapter 4, David Heald and Neil Geaughan discuss the balance of tax revenues and public expenditure in Scotland, and the operation of the Barnett formula. They argue that the plans for financing the Scottish Parliament do not constitute an enduring settlement since they do not involve a sustainable basis for determining the budget assigned to the Parliament. Chapter 5, by Tony Jackson, considers the tax varying powers of the Scottish Parliament, the so-called "tartan tax". Contrary to both supporters of tax varying powers, who suggest that such powers provide the Parliament with a valuable instrument of economic policy, and critics, who predict that any tax increases will have a number of adverse effects on the Scottish economy, Tony Jackson argues that the significance of tax varying powers has been greatly exaggerated. The likelihood is that they will be largely irrelevant to the economic policies pursued by the Scottish economy.

In part III, chapter 6, by Mike Danson, is the first of two chapters on economic development. It discusses the relationship between the Scottish Parliament and the development agencies and identifies four key principles - accountability, subsidiarity, sustainability, and integration/inclusion - to guide the debate about how the development agencies might be reformed. In chapter 7, John Fairley considers the history and practice of local government economic development in Scotland. He then assesses the possible impact of the Parliament: whether it will contribute to greater effectiveness, and stimulate new forms of partnership, in local economic development, and whether it will be a force for centralisation or decentralisation.

In part IV, three chapters consider the various spatial impacts the Scottish Parliament might have. Chapter 8, by Greg Lloyd, considers the implications of the Scottish Parliament for the planning process in Scotland. He argues there is a strategic deficit in the planning process, makes the case for a more robust strategic planning framework and outlines some of the arrangements by which the Scottish Parliament could construct such a framework. In chapter 9, John McCarthy considers the implications of the Scottish Parliament for urban regeneration. He reviews the development of urban policy in Scotland and then identifies a number of areas in which the Parliament might increase the capacity of urban policy to address the problems of urban decline, including the involvement of local communities and the use of experimentation for policy development. Chapter 10, by Ron McQuaid, discusses the local economic impact of the Scottish Parliament. It considers the likely income and employment impact on Edinburgh, and suggests a number of ways in which, depending on decisions made about physical infrastructure, organisational structures and public policies, the income and employment benefits of the Parliament could be spread beyond Edinburgh.

Finally, in chapter 11, John McCarthy and David Newlands present the major conclusions as to the opportunities which the Scottish Parliament offers to improve the governance of Scotland and of the UK and the economic constraints, problems and risks confronting the Parliament. In so doing, they contribute to the task - in which many others will share - of constructing a policy agenda for the Scottish Parliament for the first years of the twenty first century.

Part I

Context

2 The economic impact of the Scottish Parliament: possibilities and constraints

DAVID NEWLANDS

2.1 Introduction

This chapter discusses the possibilities of, and constraints on, the Scottish Parliament within the economic field. The architects of the Parliament have not been operating within a vacuum in seeking to determine its appropriate economic powers. Both economic theory and the experience of other countries which have created regional governments in recent years provide guidance as to the economic potential of the Scottish Parliament. This chapter seeks to identify the lessons which can be learned from economic theory and the experience of other European countries. It provides an overview of the potential economic impact of the Scottish Parliament but emphasises the economic constraints arising from Scotland being part of the British and EU political system and of increasingly integrated national, European and global markets.

Section 2.2 discusses the economic theory of the appropriate functions of regional government, including the debate about regional government versus regional administration. Section 2.3 considers developments elsewhere in Europe. The experiences of Germany, France, Italy and Spain and developments at the level of the European Union are considered. Section 2.4 summarises the potential economic impact of the Scottish Parliament and the principal economic constraints on it. Section 2.5 presents the key conclusions.

2.2 The economic theory of regional government

2.2.1 *The economic roles of government*

Much of the economic theory of the respective economic roles of the market and government derives from a neoclassical perspective in which intergovernmental relations are reduced to two levels, central and local. The neoclassical model is both incomplete and unconvincing but it provides a convenient starting point for an elaboration of the economic theory of regional government.

Neoclassical theory concedes three government economic functions which Musgrave (1959) terms the stabilisation, allocation and distribution functions. The stabilisation function refers to government's macroeconomic role. Market economies are subject to considerable fluctuations in output and employment. There is therefore a potential role for government to try to influence the level of macroeconomic activity. The allocation function arises because the conditions required by a market economy to ensure an optimal allocation of resources are very strict (Helm and Smith, 1989): individuals must be fully informed about the choices open to them; there should be no monopoly power; property rights must be perfectly defined and costlessly enforced; labour and capital should be perfectly mobile. The market fails to meet these stringent conditions and, as a result, government intervention may increase allocative efficiency. Neoclassical theory is principally concerned with efficiency and has therefore had much less to say about the distribution function. However, the market is unlikely to produce the desired distribution of income or of specific goods and services. At least in theory, therefore, there is a justification for government redistributive measures.

This threefold classification neglects another possible sphere of government activity which can be termed the growth function (Newlands, 1992). The neoclassical model is static, being concerned with the conditions necessary to ensure the most efficient allocation of a fixed volume of resources at a given point in time. While some economists have argued that market mechanisms also ensure the optimal rate of technological change and of economic growth (Solow, 1970), market failure may mean that government intervention will increase the dynamic efficiency of the economy.

There is general agreement that the stabilisation and distribution functions should be concentrated in the hands of national government or rather the highest level of the structure of government (King, 1984). While there is much controversy about the scope of government macroeconomic policy, it is accepted that there is no meaningful role for a subcentral government. The openness of local economies makes macroeconomic management impossible. Redistributive policies are most appropriately devised at the national or supranational level since it is important that a single level of government be assigned the role of determining the extent of income redistribution to avoid conflicts between different redistributive policies pursued independently by a number of levels of government.

2.2.2   Service provision

Since most of the stabilisation and distribution functions are reserved to central government, the main economic role of subcentral government according to neoclassical theory is the allocation function. The allocation function refers particularly to the collective provision of public goods characterised by non rivalness and non excludability which the market will under provide. While there are few pure public goods, many goods and services have a degree of "publicness".

The failure of market mechanisms to ensure an optimal allocation of resources provides a rationale for state intervention. However, the government's performance of the allocation function depends on its capacity to respond sensitively to individuals' preferences and its ability to obtain and process the required information. Decentralised government is likely to be better informed about individuals' preferences and better able to reflect those preferences. Thus, subcentral governments may use resources more efficiently than either central government or private providers in undertaking expenditure at the local level.

These arguments about economic functions have important implications for the financing of local government. They suggest that grants from central government to local authorities may play a number of roles. Firstly, there may be administrative economies to be reaped from central government collecting taxes on behalf of local government and then distributing these revenues as grants to finance the activities of local authorities. Secondly, grants are one means of recognising the legitimate interest that central government or people in other areas might have in specific aspects of a particular authority's spending - for instance, spending on education may need to reflect national priorities as well as local preferences. Thirdly, grants may be a means of addressing fiscally induced migration, of individuals and firms, if a suitable non mobile tax base cannot be identified. Finally, and most importantly, grants are a mechanism for the equalisation of differential needs and resources. All these arguments point to there being greater decentralisation of expenditure than of taxation.

The key insight of neoclassical theory, that the principal role of local government in a central-local government structure lies with the allocation function rather than the stabilisation or distribution functions, is of limited usefulness in explaining the appropriate role of a regional tier of government. Regional government is part of a more complex structure involving supranational government, such as the EU, national government, a regional tier immediately below national government, and smaller local authorities. However, the main flaw of the neoclassical model is that it exaggerates the effectiveness of market mechanisms and diminishes the economic role of government. This is true of the stabilisation, distribution and allocation functions which neoclassical theory concedes as legitimate roles of government. Moreover, the market model fails to recognise the potential for government to raise the dynamic efficiency and technological capability of the economy, what may be termed the growth function of government.

Before considering the growth function, it should be noted that the rationale for a regional tier of government, immediately below national government, also involves service provision, that is the allocation function. The same arguments about the provision of public services apply to regional governments as to the local authorities discussed in the neoclassical model but regions may be a more appropriate level for the provision of certain services than smaller local authorities, for several reasons.

Firstly, regions may be able to exploit administrative economies of scale and avoid complex externality effects while still maintaining the benefits of better information about local preferences. An example of a service for which the regional tier may be the optimal level of provision is further and higher education.

Secondly, regions face fewer constraints from migration than local authorities. Tiebout (1956) argues that differences in tax and expenditure packages between government jurisdictions will lead to migration but assumes that people can select and move to their preferred fiscal area relatively easily. In practice, the costs of moving are likely to be non marginal and will be greater for regions than local government areas and, hence, migration will pose a lesser threat to the region's tax base.

Thirdly, it may be that people are moving towards a greater uniformity of tastes and that the objectives and methods of public service bureaucracies are converging on increasingly uniform standards of provision with the result that distinctive patterns of individual preferences may be more readily identifiable at the regional rather than at the local level.

These arguments imply a different mix of assigned taxes and central government grants for regional authorities compared to local government. There need be less reliance on grants. Many regions will be large enough to be able to exploit economies of scale in tax collection. A regional scale of operation is more likely to internalise externalities. There will generally be less fiscally induced migration. While grants will still be required to equalise interregional differences, these are less marked than the disparities between local government areas. Nevertheless, grants to regional authorities from national or supranational government might still be justified for any of the above reasons.

2.2.3   *Economic development policy*

In addition to the allocation function, the other argument for a regional tier of government relates to the growth function, or economic development policy. Economic development policy occupies distinct ground between macroeconomic policy and service provision. On the one hand, macroeconomic policy is intended to achieve a more stable level of utilisation of the economy's productive capacity. In other words, macroeconomic policy is concerned with stabilisation around the trend rather than the trend itself. On the other hand, it is possible to view economic development policy as a public good, the benefits of which are largely non rival and non excludable, and thus include it under a service provision intended to achieve a more efficient allocation of given resources. However, this misses the point since it confines the argument to a mainly static framework while the importance of economic development policy is precisely as a means of increasing dynamic efficiency.

Economic development policies can be justified as a response to market failure to ensure optimal dynamic efficiency, arising from risk aversion, imperfect information, the existence of externalities, and so on. However, a positive role for national or supranational government in pursuit of the growth function does not necessarily imply any such role for local or regional government. Indeed, it has traditionally been considered that decentralised "economic development expenditures are purely diversionary 'zero sum' effects in a game which disproportionately burdens those localities which have the least resources to play the game" (Bennett, 1990, p.221).

More recently, there has been greater recognition of the contrary arguments, that regions can pursue economic development policies which reflect local knowledge and opportunities. The potential advantages of a decentralised industrial policy include: being closer to factor markets and thus able to switch priorities, for example between property development and labour training; better knowledge of local entrepreneurship and the barriers to its development; greater ease of identifying the targets of policy through local networks; greater openness to experimentation and innovation; a greater unity of purpose and sense of regional identity; faster response times given greater knowledge of local political and administrative structures; and greater flexibility in the implementation of central programmes (Begg, Lansbury and Mayes, 1995).

At the same time, decentralised economic development policy may be severely constrained by the active pursuit of distributional objectives, whether by central or subcentral governments. Drawing upon German experience, Zimmerman (1990) has argued that:

> distributional issues are easy to perceive and lend themselves to direct and visible remedy by public action. In contrast, growth (or at least sustained high level income) needs allocational instruments which work over a long time, are less visible, and imply present saving for future returns, which means no "public benefits" for a national government with a more short term political perspective. If this is true, the existence and safeguarding of strong subnational regional governments can be interpreted as an institutional provision to secure a share of resources for the national growth objective. Regional growth can shift to those regions which are able and willing to accommodate to the necessities of a growth orientation (Zimmerman, 1990, p.251).

The potential conflict between efficiency and equity concerns shows up again in the financing of regions' economic development policies. Some of the arguments for the use of grants to finance service provision may also be applicable to regions' economic development policies. Thus, other regions may derive an external benefit from the faster growth of any specific region. In addition, some regions may be judged not to have the resources necessary to finance economic development initiatives. However, in general, economic development policy should be self financing since it involves one region competing for gains at the expense of other regions.

2.2.4   *Devolved government versus devolved administration*

While economic theory provides a number of arguments for the decentralisation of government functions, it is much less clear whether such arguments imply that these functions should be carried out by regional government as opposed to the decentralised administration of central government.

The economic theory of the allocation function appears to constitute an argument for regional government rather than administration since the democratic process is a means, however imperfect, of revealing local preferences. By comparison with a devolved administrative structure, government is more likely to be able to gain consent for the pursuit of public welfare in all its inconsistencies and complexities.

The theoretical arguments of the growth function also provide a justification for regional government. To the extent that it is a question of reflecting preferences and of balancing conflicting claims upon resources as much as spotting profitable development opportunities, the key regional economic development role should be played by a directly elected authority.

However, these arguments are hardly very strong. Moreover, the very real political objections to quangos - of political appointments, secrecy and a lack of accountability - should not obscure the economic arguments for such arrangements, particularly in the economic development field. In more and more countries, separate arrangements are being made to promote and manage economic development initiatives at arms length from government, central, regional or local. The argument for quasi public agencies is that they are a means of avoiding bureaucratic inefficiency, injecting appropriate professional skills and of minimising the direct political influence on the process of economic development. Such organisations function according to market principles but, through funding mechanisms, board representation or seconded staff, it is intended that they act in the public interest and that they are ultimately accountable to the public.

There are other arguments for a broadening of economic development efforts beyond direct provision by regional or local authorities:

> Given the multi faceted character of local economic policy, success increasingly depends on the extent to which all actors can be mobilised and their resources and know how made available...the role of local government shifts from providing detailed strategies and implementation to a policy of working with other actors to coordinate and cooperate (Bennett and Krebs, 1991, p.171).

These arguments are revisited in chapter 6.

2.2.5 *Lessons for the Scottish Parliament from economic theory*

Economic theory confirms the sense of the arrangements contained in the White Paper and the Bill, outlined in chapter 1, by which powers over macroeconomic policy are not to be decentralised. The same is true of the main instruments by which government pursues redistributive policies. Social security policy remains with the UK government. It is true that some control over taxation is being decentralised but, as is explained at length in chapter 5, the principal argument behind the provision of tax varying powers concerns the raising of additional revenue for the Scottish Parliament rather than the redistribution of income within Scotland.

Economic theory also confirms the efficiency of the arrangements by which most of the spending of the Scottish Parliament will be financed - via a block grant - and of the greater decentralisation of control of public expenditure than of taxation.

In one sense, the lessons of economic theory for the economic development potential of the Scottish Parliament are encouraging. There is a growing acknowledgement that regions can fashion effective economic development policies reflecting their detailed knowledge of regional economic conditions and opportunities. However, this is primarily an argument for the decentralisation of economic development powers to Scotland - which has existed for many years in the form of the powers exercised by the Scottish Office and the two Scottish development agencies - rather than to an elected Scottish parliament as such.

2.3   Developments elsewhere in Europe

2.3.1   *Regional government functions in Germany, France, Italy and Spain*

The experience of countries elsewhere in Europe provides additional evidence concerning the appropriate division of state functions between the various tiers of government (Newlands, 1992 and 1995). This section briefly reviews the cases of Germany, France, Italy and Spain which - unlike the UK - all have a tier of elected regional authorities (at either levels 1 or 2 of the NUTS spatial classification system used by the EU). Its focus - on the economic powers of, and means of financing, regional governments in the four other large EU states - is narrower than in the discussion of devolution in Europe in the following chapter.

Germany has long had a well established system of powerful, constitutionally entrenched regional governments. In West Germany, there were eleven Länder and, following reunification, five Länder were recreated in the former East Germany. The responsibilities of the Länder include education, cultural affairs, and local government. In addition, the promotion of economic development has long been a decentralised area of policy in Germany. Thus, most Länder have their own regional programmes and, since the 1960s, have established industrial development agencies.

Despite the entrenched powers of the Länder, there has been a perceptible increase in the degree of centralisation of functions and finance (Jeffrey, 1997), largely as a result of attempts by the federal government to increase the extent of regional redistribution. The federal government has evolved a regional policy, mainly concerned with infrastructural improvements, which is operated in conjunction with the Länder. While there has been a strengthening of the regional policies pursued by the federal government, the principal means of redistribution in Germany, as in other federal countries, is the fiscal system. The Länder only have complete control over a few relatively minor taxes but they also receive assigned revenues from a number of taxes, including income tax and VAT. Reflecting and reinforcing the trend towards more centralised decision making, there has also been an element of financial centralisation. An equalisation fund financed by the federal government and the richest Länder was established in 1969 to provide another source of income for Länder in need of extra resources. With reunification, the five new Länder have been included in the regional policy system but the reunification process is placing enormous strain on the equalisation fund and the other mechanisms of redistribution between the German Länder.

The twenty two regions in France were created in 1955. At first, their only function was as the framework for the regional dimension of the National Plan. They had few effective powers and, until 1972, had no budgets. They have only been elected bodies since 1986. The regional councils play an essential role in the elaboration of regional development plans. In addition to this planning role, the French regions have a number of other functions in the encouragement of economic growth. They have responsibility for vocational training and adult education. They are empowered to finance or guarantee loans, provide industrial sites, and arrange business advice. Some regions have even established offices abroad to canvass for inward investment.

While there has been some genuine and significant decentralisation of government functions in France, "the larger economic environment, the structural shifts in the regional economy and intraregional differences have a bigger impact on regional performance than the initiation of formal regional government" (Budd, 1997, p.191). Moreover, central government continues to largely determine regional development policies, not least by means of its tight control of regional finances. Regional governments can levy certain minor taxes and receive the revenues from a car registration tax but are largely dependent on central government grants. The system has the potential to be redistributive, from rich to poor regions, but the extent of any redistribution appears to be small (Prud'homme, 1990).

Regionalism has always been strong in Italy and many of the present regions were independent states prior to unification. The 1948 Constitution provided for five "special" regions and fourteen (later increased to fifteen) "ordinary" regions. While the special regions were created in 1948, the ordinary regions were not formed until 1970. Apart from social and cultural provision, the Italian regions' powers mainly concern economic development policy and physical planning although these are only exercised within guidelines set down by central government.

Regional governments in Italy have no independent taxation powers. There is legal provision for a local income tax surcharge but this has never been implemented. The yield from several taxes is transferred to the regions but contributes less than 5 per cent of their income. Almost all regional finances are state grants. In terms of their redistributive impact, while the allocation of funds has generally favoured the poorer regions in the South, the relative economic advantage of the Northern regions has largely persisted. Nevertheless, the stability of the structure of regional government in Italy has been threatened in recent years by the rise in strong regionalist feeling in the North and growing resentment of what is perceived to be special treatment of the South.

Over the last twenty years, Spain has created a system of regional government. Partly in response to deep seated cultural differences, especially in the case of the Basques and the Catalans, and partly in reaction to centuries of extreme centralism, culminating in the Franco period, decentralisation was viewed as an essential element in the return to democracy after the death of Franco. In 1979, the Basque country and Catalonia became the first two Autonomous Communities created under the new Spanish Constitution of 1978. Fifteen other Autonomous Communities were created between 1981 and 1983. The exclusive powers of the Spanish regions cover a wide range including cultural affairs, social welfare, housing, town planning, and environmental protection. Economic development policy is among the powers shared between the central and regional governments.

While the Spanish Constitution recognised the right of the regions to financial autonomy, this is exercised within the overall framework of taxation laid down by central government. The regions retain the revenues from certain taxes levied by central government and also derive income from their own local taxes, rates, and surcharges on state taxes. However, the revenue from all of these is comparatively small. Thus, in practice, the regions are heavily dependent on tax sharing grants from central government. The state also controls the Interregional Compensation Fund. On the other hand, there is evidence that the fiscal system is a powerful means of redistributing income in Spain (Castells, 1990).

2.3.2 *Developments at EU level*

The "regionalisation" of a number of EU member countries is mirrored and reinforced by developments at EU level. The European Commission seeks an increased role for regional and local governments in the formulation and implementation of EU regional policy. The most recent major reform of EU regional policy greatly expanded the size of the Structural Funds in recognition of the fact that the likely effects of the completion of a single market would be to widen income and employment disparities. There was a switch from financing individual projects to programme finance based on regional development plans which - in most EU countries - are drawn up by regional governments.

The principal argument for the increased involvement of regional governments is similar to that derived from economic theory, that the greater direct involvement of regional and local authorities means a better understanding of local needs in the formulation of development plans (Council of Europe, 1990). However, there are also other, more pragmatic, considerations. Any measures which have been agreed with regional governments are more likely to command their support at the implementation stage. Moreover, by channelling funds directly to regional and local authorities, the Commission hopes to ensure that EU funds are truly additional to national funds.

There are still a number of serious barriers to the building of an institutional framework within which regional governments can be involved in EU regional policy. Not all member states have established regional government structures. Furthermore, at present, Belgium and Germany are the only two countries which have a formal machinery for involving regional authorities in the EU decision making process (Haynes et al, 1997). Moreover, not all regional development plans are drawn up by the regions themselves.

There remains opposition in many member states to proposals to grant the regions more powers (Commission of the European Communities, 1991). Nevertheless, the role of the regions emerged strengthened from the Maastricht summit, in particular with the creation of a Committee of the Regions. This may yet form the institutional foundation for a future "Europe of the Regions".

2.3.3 *Lessons for the Scottish Parliament from developments elsewhere in Europe*

There are several lessons to be learnt from the experience of other European countries. As economic theory also predicts, the economic powers of regional governments largely concern service provision and economic development policy. However, despite significant decentralisation in France, Italy and Spain, central government in all three countries exerts considerable control over the economic activities of subcentral government. Regional (and local) authorities are heavily dependent on central government grants. Indeed, not even all the opportunities to give regions more fiscal autonomy have been taken. Thus, as noted, the legal provision for regions in Italy to levy an income tax surcharge has never been implemented. Despite all the controversy about the "tartan tax", the same may yet turn out to be true of Scotland. Even in Germany, there is more decentralisation of powers over expenditure than over taxation.

The reforms in France and Italy suggest that significant decentralisation may take some time and require several different stages. The changes in Italy and Spain have involved a significantly different array of powers being available to different regions. France too has made exceptional provisions in the case of Corsica. Decentralisation in these countries has not therefore required all regions to move at the same pace or indeed to be involved at all in every stage of change although, only in Italy, have arrangements designed to meet the demands of a small number of regions not been followed relatively quickly by a structure encompassing the whole country. This implies that the Scottish Parliament (and indeed the Assemblies in Wales and Northern Ireland) can evolve distinctive economic policies and reap economic gains without awaiting the regionalisation of England.

The other important conclusion concerns the conflict between efficiency and equity concerns. While a regional structure of government may bring several efficiency gains both in the provision of public services and in the operation of planning and economic development policies, it does not necessarily ensure an equitable distribution between what remain different parts of the same political structure. If anything, decentralisation may exacerbate regional inequality. As the cases of Germany and Spain demonstrate, it is possible to design and implement effective redistributive mechanisms but these constrain the autonomy of regions and may threaten the efficiency gains of a regional structure. The redistributive mechanisms of the UK fiscal system, and possible changes which might threaten the fiscal position of the Scottish Parliament, are considered in chapter 4.

2.4   The potential economic impact of the Scottish Parliament

2.4.1   *Constraints*

Adoption of the appropriate economic policies by the Scottish Parliament opens up the possibility of increasing the rate of economic growth in Scotland and improving the competitiveness and productivity of the Scottish economy.   Not that the Parliament will necessarily bring about any automatic improvements.   It is very difficult to justify sweeping claims such as that:

> the removal of decision making from Scotland has had a damaging effect on the economy and the establishment of a Scottish Parliament will lead to a reversal of this trend (Scottish Constitutional Convention, 1989, p.7).

The freedom of action of a Scottish Parliament, as of any regional government anywhere in the world, is limited.   Income and employment levels in Scotland are primarily determined by levels of demand and the competitiveness of private business. The integration of the Scottish economy into the British, European and world economies means that distant economic events over which no actor in Scotland has any control, such as the collapse of stock markets in Asia, may have much greater effects on demand levels in Scotland than any actions which the Scottish Parliament might undertake.   The openness of the Scottish economy is such that attempts to stimulate economic activity in Scotland by reducing income tax rates or to depress economic activity by raising income tax rates are largely doomed to failure.

To the extent that government action makes a difference to demand levels in Scotland, it is action taken at the UK government level or, increasingly, at the European Union level which counts.   It will be the actions of the UK Chancellor of the Exchequer and the Monetary Policy Committee of the Bank of England, and developments surrounding the move towards a single European currency, which will determine interest rates and tax levels in Scotland.   The Scottish Parliament will not have powers over monetary policy and only very limited powers over fiscal policy.

The economic policies pursued by the Scottish Parliament will also be constrained by the revenues available to it.   As explained in detail in chapter 4, the best the Parliament can realistically expect is to be established with a block grant no smaller than that currently received by the Scottish Office.   Moreover, the importance of the power to increase revenues by raising the basic rate of income tax has been enormously exaggerated.   The use of tax varying powers might have a number of adverse administrative and wider economic consequences - considered at length in chapter 5 - but perhaps the greatest problem would be that the burden of public expectation is so great that £450 million, which is the additional annual revenue which the full increase of three pence in the pound would raise, could not even begin to meet the competing demands upon it.   Such a sum would enable a doubling of the spending of Scottish Enterprise but constitutes only some 3 per cent of the existing Scottish Office budget.

Throughout the world, disillusionment with demand side policies has led to greater concern with supply side issues, factors which affect costs of production, business competitiveness, and the creation and adoption of technologically advanced methods of production. Business competitiveness depends on a whole number of factors including firms' strategy and organisation, the degree of competition between companies, the quality of physical infrastructure, and levels of human capital. A regional government like the Scottish Parliament can devise supply side policies which will deliver improved competitiveness, in ways which are discussed in more detail throughout this book. It should be stressed, however, that little can be achieved in the short term. Changing business and institutional conditions is inevitably a very long term project.

The economic possibilities of the Scottish Parliament, for better or worse, will depend on its impact upon the rate of economic growth and development in Scotland. Scotland has long had an economic development policy which has been determined within Scotland by Scottish institutions (Danson et al, 1990). The records of both the Highlands and Islands Development Board (HIDB) and the Scottish Development Agency (SDA) in the 1970s and 1980s were generally reckoned to be in credit. The subsequent reconstitution of the HIDB and SDA in 1991 as Highlands and Islands Enterprise (HIE) and Scottish Enterprise (SE) might have been expected to increase their effectiveness. HIE and SE took over the training functions previously exercised in Scotland by the Training Agency while there was a further decentralisation of economic development and training responsibilities to Local Enterprise Companies throughout Scotland. However, there have been doubts as to the direction of economic development policy. The creation of the LECs may have taken decentralisation too far, with the loss of a central strategic overview of the problems of the Scottish economy and a multiplication of the problems of coordination, between the various LECs, between HIE and SE and the LECs, and between the whole HIE and SE structures and the economic development efforts of Scottish local authorities.

Highlands and Islands Enterprise and Scottish Enterprise might not look very different as and when they are under the control of the Scottish Parliament. However, given that the success or otherwise of regional development agencies depends upon their local knowledge and their ability to put together packages which draw upon the contributions of a wide range of actors in the private and public sectors, the creation of a directly elected Scottish Parliament which is seen to more closely reflect the preferences of the Scottish people may lead to more effective and imaginative economic development partnerships (Begg, Lansbury and Mayes, 1995). The relationship between the Scottish Parliament and the development agencies in Scotland are discussed in detail in chapter 6.

The issues of technology policy, innovation, new firm formation and the ownership of industry are all closely connected and provide one of the prime examples of the way in which the Scottish Parliament could in the long term increase the dynamic efficiency of the Scottish economy (Danson, Lloyd and Newlands, 1990). The attraction of inward investment to Scotland which has been a major concern of the Scottish Office and Scottish Enterprise (and their joint agency Locate in Scotland) might not be such a priority under the Scottish Parliament.

While inward investment has been a means by which Scotland has acquired new technology, new investment and new management skills, a number of commentators have argued that the increase in the external ownership of Scottish industry has had a number of detrimental effects upon the Scottish economy:

> In an externally controlled enterprise strategy, purchasing, sourcing, basic research and development, product development, marketing, financial and professional services, will all be determined on the basis of corporate interests, not on the basis of the needs of the local economy (Standing Commission on the Scottish Economy, 1989, p.47).

The consequences are far reaching. The "branch plant syndrome" is a major explanatory factor in Scotland's low rates of innovation and new firm formation, and its under representation in high technology growth sectors.

It is neither realistic nor desirable that a Scottish Parliament should seek as a general policy to limit or reverse the growth of external ownership of Scottish industry but it could change the priority given to the attraction of inward investment and the nature of negotiations with potential inward investors. For example, it could seek to secure the transfer of more senior management and research posts, and an opening up of corporate recruitment, sales and purchasing procedures.

2.4.3   *The effectiveness of policy making*

The credibility and effectiveness of a Scottish Parliament will depend on a number of factors. One is the Parliament's representativeness. Here, the initial signs are encouraging. A form of proportional representation has been agreed for elections to the Parliament. The three main island groups will each have their own Member of Scottish Parliament. The Labour and Liberal Parties have agreed to adopt selection procedures which will aim to ensure equal gender representation among their MSPs.

Credibility and effectiveness will also depend on the quality of MSPs, the Parliament's civil service and the pool of economic advisers upon whom the Parliament can call. The electoral system may lead to MSPs being drawn from beyond the realms of existing political activists but this is as yet to be demonstrated. The Parliament's civil service will be drawn primarily from those who currently work in the Scottish Office. This would provide valuable continuity in the first years when the Scottish Parliament is being established but, beyond that, the value of the civil service would probably be determined by its ability to help formulate and execute *different* economic policies. There are not a lot of economists in Scotland, in academia or elsewhere, interested in the Scottish economy. Nevertheless, there is probably sufficient economic expertise to support the work of the Scottish Parliament. A greater handicap is the poor quality of data on the structure and performance of the

Scottish economy. At modest cost, the Parliament could increase the effectiveness of policy making by investing in the improvement of the statistical base.

2.5 Conclusions

Economic theory provides arguments for the regional decentralisation of government functions, arising from the ability of regional authorities to identify and act upon distinctive regional preferences. However, there is the possibility that decentralisation will lead to competitive behaviour between regions and thus a zero (or even negative) sum game. Moreover, it is often difficult to distinguish general arguments for regional *decentralisation* from specific arguments for regional *government*.

The experience of the other large EU states, each of which has an elected tier of regional governments, confirms most of the predictions of economic theory. Thus, as economic theory would predict, the economic powers of regional governments largely concern service provision and economic development policy although, in all four countries, there is greater decentralisation of powers over expenditure than over taxation.

Adoption of the appropriate economic policies by the Scottish Parliament opens up the possibility of an increase in the rate of economic growth in Scotland, the increased adoption of new technology, and a higher rate of new firm formation. The Scottish Parliament could therefore succeed in raising the dynamic efficiency of the Scottish economy. However, nobody should be under any illusions that it is anything other than a long term project since, given the existing considerable array of decentralised economic development institutions, the growth function is already being vigorously pursued in Scotland.

3 The Scottish Parliament and the European Union

PETER ROBERTS

3.1 Introduction

This chapter offers a European perspective on the challenges and opportunities associated with the establishment of the Scottish Parliament. The analysis presented in the chapter combines a consideration of matters of constitutional and operational significance with a discussion of issues of a more mundane nature. In addition, a perspective is provided on the symbolic importance of the first significant breach of the long-standing territorial uniformity that results from the government of the United Kingdom as a unitary state. The consequences of the move towards the establishment of an intermediate level of government are also examined, including the likelihood that this experience will provide a model that may assist in the formulation of future adjustments to the system of government elsewhere in the UK.

Any analysis of this kind is inevitably selective and speculative. The White Paper (Scottish Office, 1997a) and the Scotland Bill (published in December 1997), contain a blend of specific proposals and more opaque suggestions with regard to the extent of the powers that will be granted to and exercised by a Scottish Parliament. On European matters the position is, on the one hand, relatively clear - Scotland will enjoy a limited degree of discretion on certain aspects of European representation and administration. On the other hand, although the majority of European matters will in the first instance be determined in London, this position may change over time. In such a situation, the best that can be offered by way of analysis is to develop and review a number of alternative scenarios, and to evaluate the advantages and disadvantages associated with each option for the distribution and discharge of power and responsibility.

The following sections of the chapter consider three topics. Section 3.2 discusses the context for the "Scottish experiment" provided by the experience of intermediate or mesolevel government in other European Member States. Unlike chapter 2, which had a narrow focus upon the economic powers of mesolevel government and the way in which it is financed, the discussion here centres on broader constitutional matters and issues of governance. Section 3.3 considers the past experience of Scotland with regard to the European Union, including the organisation, operation and impact of European Union Structural Fund and spatial policies. Section 3.4 discusses the significance and implications of the establishment of the Scottish Parliament in relation to Scotland's role and influence in Europe, including the possible future evolution of Scotland's relations with Europe as a model for the governance of small nations and regions elsewhere. This selection of topics reflects the experience and interests of the present author - no doubt another author would select different topics - and it is intended to illustrate, rather than to define fully, the changing institutional geographies and new structures of governance that have recently emerged in many of the regions of Europe, and which may emerge in Scotland.

3.2   Mesolevel government in Europe

Mesolevel government has a long and distinguished history in Europe, and this history represents a degree of political and cultural continuity that has frequently eluded the large nation-state (Quintin, 1973). For example, some of the Länder of Germany have survived, almost unchanged, despite successive transformations in the form of the nation-state. From Prussia, through Bismarck's German unified state and the Federal Republic, to the re-unification of Germany, the Länder mesolevel represents the inheritance and tradition of past governance and government. However, this important characteristic and distinctive outward manifestation of the mesolevel is not universal. Some independent nations have been absorbed fully into larger nation-states and have lost their individual identity, whilst other nations have been assimilated into larger territorial units only to re-emerge at a later date (Ventura, 1963). The break-up of the former Soviet Union provides evidence of the latter tendency and, whilst not suggesting that constitutional change in the United Kingdom will result in such cataclysmic events, it is illustrative of the way in which "sleeper" nations can re-emerge following a long period of central domination and the seeming invulnerability of the great nation-state. The clearest illustration of these tendencies is the re-emergence of the stateless nations of Spain in the 1970s and 1980s (Balcells, 1996), but this analysis can also be extended to other territories that are currently stateless (McCrone, 1994; Roberts, 1997a).

Sharpe defines the mesolevel as "an intermediate level of government between the centre and the basic municipal or communal level" and observes that it is a "near-universal phenomenon over the last twenty years or so in the Western European state" (Sharpe, 1993, p.1). The meso is seen by Sharpe to provide a more appropriate level for certain kinds of decisions and policies than either central or local government; this is a role that is clearly in accord with the theory of subsidiarity. This intermediate level of government has emerged in various guises: as administrative regionalism; as reorganised or strengthened local government at a regional scale; as a new elected regional tier of government; or, exceptionally, as the creation of new nation-states. The regionalisation and subsequent division of former Czechoslovakia provides an example of the final case.

As late as 1994, Harvie described the British scene as one in which "most Westminster politicians looked at federalism and sulked patriotically", but which also contained within it a number of "stateless nations" - Scotland, Wales and Northern Ireland (Harvie, 1994, p.1). It appeared at this time that the European regional project had failed to take root in Britain; indeed central government policy still emphasised the acquisition of power by the centre and the fragmentation or control of the powers of local government. Furthermore, despite assurances to the contrary, the promises that a future Labour administration would pursue a policy of devolution of political power to Scotland, Wales and the English regions was treated with a degree of suspicion that reflected the failure to deliver such a policy commitment in the late 1970s. In hindsight it can be argued that the failure of the 1970s, whilst delaying the establishment of mesolevel government, provided the basis for the more mature form of devolution that is now on offer.

The greater maturity evident in the design of the current devolution package reflects a number of formative influences. Some of these factors are domestic in origin, including the desire to redress the democratic imbalance between the centre and the local/regional level. This imbalance has existed for many decades, though it was exacerbated as a consequence of the abolition of the metropolitan county authorities in England, the regional councils in Scotland and the county councils in Wales. Another set of factors that has influenced the form and content of the present devolution package reflects the outcome of political and policy developments that can be broadly described as European in origin. First, and most frequently quoted, are the models and examples of devolution offered elsewhere in Europe. Second, more subtle and, perhaps, more influential in terms of their eventual impact, are the various strands of theory and policy that have developed in relation to the structure of each level of government and governance within the European Union. Third, are the lessons gained and the greater confidence instilled from British participation in European networks and exchange arrangements.

3.2.1   *European models of devolution*

In the search for a possible future role for Scotland, the most obvious models, at least at first sight, can be identified in the recent histories of the creation of autonomous or semi-autonomous mesolevel governments elsewhere in the European Union. Although parallels, including the creation of the Spanish autonomous communities and the state reform of Belgium in the early 1990s, appear to provide general insight and guidance as to the future evolution of Scotland, there are dangers in assuming that devolution in the UK will proceed along a similar pathway. In the case of Belgium, a major difference is that devolution established a federal structure that allocated a wide range of competences to the sub-national level (Kerremans and Beyers, 1997). Included among these competences was the ability of sub-national authorities to conclude international agreements in those policy fields in which they possessed exclusive competence; this is a matter currently excluded from the powers to be granted to the Scottish Parliament.

The Spanish case provides more fertile territory in the search for models. During the Franco era the degree of autonomy enjoyed by sub-national government had been subject to extensive erosion culminating in a high level of centralisation of power. Since the death of Franco in November 1975 the country "had to face two great problems: transition to democracy and the transformation of an authoritarian and unitary state into a decentralised one" (Khatami, 1991, p.173). Progress towards the first objective has been much faster than the resolution of the second problem. Whilst not wishing to imply that past regimes in the UK have resembled the centralised state imposed on Spain by Franco, lessons for Scotland can be gleaned from a study of the reforms brought about by the establishment of the 1978 Spanish Constitution. As is likely to be the case in Scotland, the Spanish reforms of 1978 failed fully to clarify the position with respect to the division of powers to the various levels of government. The Constitution is a hybrid system which is "neither Federal nor regional but based on the principles of the unity of the Spanish nation and the autonomy of the nationalities and regions which constitute it" (Morata, 1992, p.188). In establishing the autonomous communities, the Spanish model adopted a quasi-federal approach that allowed for the distribution of competence through a complex process of negotiation between the Spanish Parliament and the communities. Devolution has resulted in a heterogeneous pattern of mesolevel government with some communities enjoying a wider range of competence than others.

While there are parallels between the situation in the UK and that in Spain - a heterogeneous pattern of devolution is emerging in the UK with different levels of power allocated to Scotland, Wales, Northern Ireland and the English regions - there are also important differences. The most significant of these differences are that, at least at present, the UK model is not quasi-federalist in character (Bradbury and Mawson, 1997) and that the present intentions that have shaped the Scotland Bill are more limited in scope.

However, while there are limits to the search for immediate parallels between the Scottish situation and the experience of either Belgium or Spain, it is apparent that the process of devolution, having started, is unlikely to be a once and for all settlement. Irrespective of the differences in the legal structure and status of the model used to introduce devolution, the very establishment of mesolevel government releases dynamic forces that may result in further reassignments of competence between central government and the mesolevel.

Less bold and ambitious programmes of devolution have taken place elsewhere in Europe, and these models, whilst appearing to offer fewer competences to the mesolevel than is claimed for the present Scottish proposals, represent alternative pathways that merit study. The present author has discussed elsewhere (Roberts, 1997b) the gradualist approach adopted in France. In this case administrative devolution - similar in some respects to the current situation in Scotland - established a system whereby the regional prefect was advised by a representative commission drawn from local and regional authorities and interest groups (Hansen, 1968). A more substantial regional capability subsequently emerged, and the regionalisation of central government functions led eventually, in 1982, to the establishment of directly elected regional authorities as a "territorial collective".

Other models of devolved government are less readily applicable to the Scottish case. Quite clearly the German Länder enjoy a much wider range of powers than is intended for Scotland, whilst the Dutch system employs a matrix form of organisation of competence that, although offering many useful lessons on operational matters, is not easily equated to the arrangements likely to be established in Scotland. Regional structures in Italy and Austria broadly follow one or other of the models introduced earlier, whilst devolution in other Member States, such as Ireland and Finland, is at an early stage.

3.2.2 The lessons of devolution elsewhere

While the precise degree of fit between the proposed Scottish model and the characteristics of mesolevel systems elsewhere is important, of greater concern are the lessons that can be used to help to position both the range of powers to be discharged by the Scottish Parliament, and the structure and extent of Scottish competence with regard to the establishment of direct political relationships with the European Union and other Member States. The latter point is a matter of considerable significance and much present contention (see, for example, the report by Booth, 1997, in *The Scotsman* on the day following the publication of the Scotland Bill).

Various attempts have been made to analyse and categorise the competences exercised by mesolevel governments. Among the most comprehensive of these studies are those undertaken by Wiehler and Stumm (1995) and by Savy (1996). The evidence assessed in these research projects helps to position Scotland, both now and after the establishment of the Scottish Parliament, in relation to mesolevel government elsewhere. Wiehler and Stumm (1995) categorised the arrangements for mesolevel government in four groups, as follows:

- *Group 1* - Regions with wide-ranging powers (elected regional parliament, budgetary powers, legislative power, right to levy taxes, and so on) including the German Länder and Belgian provinces.
- *Group 2* - Regions with advanced powers (elected regional parliament, limited right to levy taxes and limited budgetary power) including the Spanish autonomous communities and Italian regions.
- *Group 3* - Regions with limited powers (elected regional parliament, limited right to levy taxes, limited budgetary powers and substantial financial transfers from central government) including the French regions, Dutch provinces, Scotland, Wales and Danish amtskommuner.
- *Group 4* - Regions with no powers (no elected parliament, no right to levy taxes, no budgetary power and all financial resources transferred by central government) including the Greek nomoi, Portuguese planning regions, Irish counties, English counties and Northern Ireland.

While this categorisation does not satisfy all of the criteria that could be applied, the resulting overview provides a sense of the relative position of Scotland as a European mesolevel. On this categorisation it can be argued that, strictly speaking, the proposed new powers for Scotland do little to enhance the relative status of its mesolevel government. Rather, the establishment of an elected parliament simply confirms the position of Scotland in Group 3. However, given the tendency for pressure to emerge to extend the powers exercised at the mesolevel following the initial devolution, it is reasonable to expect Scotland eventually to achieve a status similar to those areas listed in Group 2.

Savy's (1996) analysis examines the situation from the perspective of the current and future challenges that face mesolevel government. His central argument is that the effective and efficient operation of European cohesion policies can only be assured by the full application of subsidiarity. This involves the notion of territorial cohesion, and his conclusion points to the importance of reinforcing the competence of sub-national government in order to combat the forces of political disintegration (seen especially in central and eastern Europe) and globalisation (experienced throughout Europe). On this basis, the establishment of the Scottish Parliament represents a move towards greater territorial cohesion.

A final point of detail to be considered is the possible nature of the new relationships that Scotland will be able to establish with the various institutions of the European Union and with other Member States. Although the detailed structure and content of these relationships is discussed in the section 3.4, it is apparent from the experience of other mesolevels that the ability to design and conduct "foreign policy" is considered to be a characteristic of genuinely autonomous sub-national government. Despite the fact that the current Bill considers foreign policy, including relations with Europe, to be a reserved matter, it is possible, although unlikely, that this position may soften during the passage of the Bill or may be relaxed subsequently.

Learning from the experience of the establishment of mesolevel government elsewhere in the European Union, it is apparent that:

- each national system of devolution is unique, reflecting the particular constitutional, cultural and historical traditions of a country and its constituent regions;
- most national systems of devolution distribute an even package of competence to all sub-national governments, though there are examples of the asymmetrical distribution of competences;
- once started, the process of devolution continues to strengthen - the creation of an elected parliament would appear to help to consolidate existing competences and exert pressure to extend the portfolio of mesolevel government;
- the characteristics typical of sub-national government with wide-ranging powers include the presence of an elected parliament, budgetary, tax raising and legislative powers and the right to participate in or conduct "foreign policy";
- more restricted forms of devolution can provide a basis for the establishment or extension of powers at an intermediate level and the reassignment of competences between the mesolevel and national or local government.

3.3   European Structural Funds and spatial policies

The two policy areas discusses in this section are the characteristics and performance of the regional programmes supported by the European Structural Funds and, much more briefly, the significance for Scotland of the recent upsurge of interest in European spatial policy. These topics are of particular importance for Scotland and they demonstrate the potentials for change in the nature and operation of a specific policy regime that are inherent in the proposal for devolution.

3.3.1 *The Structural Funds and regional development*

The significance of the Structural Funds in Scotland is related to both the financial contribution made by the Funds to the process of regional development and to the influence exerted by the Funds on the emergence and growing maturity of collaborative arrangements for regional management. While cash has been considered to be more important than institutional capacity in the past, the present changes related to the future allocation and management of the Funds suggest that the non-financial benefits of participation in the programmes may be more enduring over the long-term.

The current importance of the Structural Funds to Scotland is illustrated by Table 3.1. During the current round of programmes the gross value of the main regional programmes supported by the Funds is calculated to be in the order of MECU 2,322, the contribution made by the Funds is MECU 859 and the national public sector element is MECU 1,130. At present the main regional programmes supported by the Funds cover an area containing some 85 per cent of the Scottish population. The programmes are generally considered to represent the most significant additional spatially-determined source of public expenditure in Scotland and they also provide a range of economic, social and other benefits that may not otherwise have materialised (Bryden, 1997).

This suggests that both the lessons of past practice and the prospects for the future are of considerable interest to any organisation or individual involved in the processes of regional planning, development and management.

Table 3.1   Current Structural Fund regional programmes in Scotland

	Total Expenditure MECU	Total Structural Funds MECU	Total National Expenditure MECU
Objective 1			
Highlands and Islands	1,012	311	406
Objective 2			
Eastern Scotland	292	121	171
Western Scotland	660	286	374
Objective 5b			
Borders	76	30	38
Central Scotland/Tayside	63	25	34
Dumfries and Galloway	124	47	60
Grampian	95	39	47

Source: Commission of the European Communities, 1997a

3.3.2 *Lessons from the past*

Several recent studies of the operation of the regional programmes in Scotland have highlighted a number of important lessons that are of particular significance, given the changes that are likely to occur in the operation of the Structural Funds after 1999 (Danson et al, 1997; Roberts and Hart, 1996; Turok, 1997). These lessons relate to the procedures employed in the formulation and approval of programmes, the formation and operation of partnerships and the arrangements for programme management.

Regional programmes have evolved in various ways in the different regions of Scotland, and this varied pattern of programme formulation both reflects the very different geographies of the areas involved and the inheritance of previous eras of strategic planning. While the first round of regional programmes proved to be difficult to construct, due in part to the absence of the necessary institutional infrastructure, the current set of strategies were easier to design. Although it is difficult, and often dangerous, to generalise about the ability of partnerships to develop and agree a programme, it is evident that the experience of working together has allowed for the establishment of a greater sense of common purpose and that this corporate perspective has allowed for the agreement of objectives and programme detail. The emergence of intertwined institutional arrangements, with, for example, the East of Scotland European Partnership having overlapping membership and interests with the East of Scotland European Consortium (Sutcliffe, 1997), has allowed for and reinforced experiential learning and has created a broad base of strategic agreement on what measures are required and how they can best be designed and implemented.

Learning from the lessons of the pre-1994 programmes, the partnerships - at this early stage, chiefly the regional and local partners and the Scottish Office - were able to construct strategies and programmes that reflected the requirements of their regions. It was at the approval stage that difficulties were encountered, and this introduces one of the questions that the creation of the Scottish Parliament might be expected to address. The approval of the negotiated programmes introduced two additional groups of actors into the process: the European Commission and UK central government. Difficulties were experienced, due in part to the short period of time available for negotiation. These difficulties concerned the extent of conformity of the Scottish programmes with the view of UK central government about the nature and structure of programmes, and with the Commission with respect to the content and programmes, their detailed internal organisation and the extent to which they reflected the (often unwritten) views of the Commission as to what a programme should seek to achieve and how these objectives should be expressed. Despite such obstacles, the programmes were eventually negotiated and approved. Notwithstanding the additional problems resulting from the reorganisation of local government in Scotland, the "mid-term" reviews of the programmes, which took place in 1996, were also successful. This recent experience demonstrates the growing maturity of partnership arrangements and the value of the foundations of collaborative strategic working that were established during the earlier rounds of partnership activity.

The experience of the formation and operation of regional partnerships reflects many of the above points and, in addition, it indicates the value of having a special unit within the Scottish Office that can prepare and present a Scottish corporate view of the programmes. Networking and inter-institutional arrangements in Scotland both reflect the relatively small size of the Scottish policy community and the longstanding tradition of organisational collaboration (Danson et al, 1997). In comparison with the often fragmented institutional structures found in the English regions, the strength of the Scottish arrangements can be seen to have conferred a greater sense of permanence and confidence in the partnerships. The House of Lords Select Committee on the European Communities commented that "this sense of partnership between the Scottish Office and the local organisations was appreciated" (House of Lords, 1997, p.15).

This is not to suggest that all aspects of partnership have been trouble free. The selection of partners was frequently a matter of contention, and in some partnerships it continues to be so, as was the degree of freedom regarding operational matters that was given to regional and local partners by the Scottish Office and the European Commission. Questions related to the selection and role of partners somewhat dominate this debate, especially the vexed matter of the exclusion of elected local authority members from partnerships. Here again, this was an issue that resulted from a UK national decision on the interpretation of the Regulations governing the operation of the Structural Funds (Commission of the European Communities, 1996). These Regulations state that the arrangements made for the involvement of partners should be set within a framework that reflects national rules and practices with regard to such matters. The UK government, at the time of the establishment of the partnerships, determined that some of the social partners, such as trade unions and certain private sector organisations, and local authority members, should generally be excluded from the partnerships.

Other issues related to the formation of partnerships included a number of difficulties in determining the roles that partners should perform. Partnership has many meanings; in the early days many European partnerships were marriages of convenience and "had the air of impermanent alliances forged for almost opportunistic purposes" (Roberts and Hart, 1996, p.29), but by the early 1990s this was no longer the case in most Scottish partnerships. The participation of private and voluntary sector partners was not always easy to secure, and private sector representation was sometimes atypical of the business sector. A final difficulty was experienced in ensuring that the partners acted as the custodians of the programme rather than as potential recipients, but this tendency generally diminished, and during the current programme round it would appear that most partners support the strategic objectives of the programme as a whole.

Programme management in Scotland has also matured and, in particular, has benefited from the existence of more adequate and independent administrative support than is the case in England. Again, the presence of a special unit in the Scottish Office helped to create a sense of strategic purpose and has allowed the Scottish partnerships to avoid many of the inter-departmental divisions experienced in England. In addition, a major success in Scotland has been the creation of the Programme

Executives. These bodies operate at arm's length from any individual partner and perform a number of crucial roles including: the servicing of committees; the administration of project application approval and monitoring procedures; the monitoring, evaluation and review of the programme; and, most importantly, they act as the guardians of the agreed regional strategy (Colwell, 1997).

Thus, generally, the operation of the regional programmes in Scotland has proved to be a positive and beneficial experience. This is certainly the case when the Scottish experience is compared with certain other UK regions (Bentley and Shutt, 1997; Roberts and Hart, 1997), and clearly reflects the existence of a prevailing culture of collaboration and territorial common purpose. Many of the difficulties encountered in relation to the development, approval, partnership formation and management of the programmes originated from UK national arrangements. Clearly there is considerable scope to improve further the operation of the programmes, and this should be possible under the devolution proposals. However, the operation of the Structural Funds is unlikely to remain a steady-state policy field and, before commenting in detail on the new possibilities for improved programme management that might follow the establishment of the Scottish Parliament, it is essential to understand the dynamics that are driving the current review of Structural Fund policy and to appreciate what this process might mean for Scotland.

Two processes are at work here. The first is the establishment of the Scottish Parliament and the second is the current review of the Structural Funds. Both issues are currently the subject of much speculation and, while the debate on the latter issue has been somewhat protracted, there would appear to be little or no relationship between the duration of the debate and the extent of policy clarity or agreement.

3.3.3 Review of the Structural Funds

Although a number of reviews of the purposes and content of the Structural Funds have taken place during the past ten years, the majority of these exercises have focused on either the extension of the coverage - territorial and financial - of the Funds, or on relatively minor matters. Any serious attempt at reform has been deflected or fudged. However, these regular and modest changes to the policy regime supported by the Funds have failed to tackle a number of underlying problems, partly because any attempt to review the Funds in isolation from associated areas of policy would be unlikely to be successful, and partly due to the inherent difficulty in withdrawing financial support from regions that have become dependent upon it. Furthermore, and there is considerable support for this overall conclusion, the Structural Funds as currently configured have proved to be capable of absorbing new tasks, accommodating the requirements associated with new areas of policy and assisting in the induction of new members into the Union (Bachtler and Turok, 1997). Having stated the case for leaving well alone, it is clear that the prospect of further enlargement and the intensification of certain of the problems associated with the current operations have combined with other structural, budgetary and political pressures in order to provide the basis for a more fundamental review of a range of European Union policies.

The Agenda 2000 process commenced in July 1997 (Commission of the European Communities, 1997b) with the publication of the Commission's position on the broad perspectives for the development of the Union beyond the year 2000. This document represents the response of the Commission to the request made by the Madrid European Council, held in December 1995, that it should submit opinions on the applications for membership of the European Union made by a number of central and eastern European states, and undertake an analysis of the Union's financing system. The document provides a variety of perspectives on a range of policy issues, and one of the areas given special attention is the future of the Structural Funds.

Agenda 2000 proposes that the operation of the Structural Funds should be subject to simplification and concentration with the overall objective of improving efficiency and effectiveness. In order to achieve these aims, it proposes that the present Structural Fund Objectives should be consolidated into three new Objectives: two regional Objectives and a horizontal Objective for human resources. Figure 3.1 summarises these proposals. The anticipated spatial consequence of the proposed reform is that the percentage of the population of the Union of 15 covered by the new Objectives 1 and 2 should be reduced from 51 per cent to 35-40 per cent. Special measures of transitional support will be introduced to assist those regions that cease to be eligible under the new arrangements.

Figure 3.1   Old and new Structural Fund Objectives

New Objectives	Purpose	Old Objectives
1	Assisting lagging regions	1 and 6
2	Economic and social restructuring	2 and 5b
3	Redevelopment of human resources	3 and 4

As might be expected, there has been much debate and speculation on the consequences of the Agenda 2000 proposals. Some elements of the debate are concerned with attempting to influence the overall philosophy that underpins the proposals, whilst other elements are focused on the likely eligibility criteria, the arrangements for transitional support, and the future allocation, approval and management structures envisaged under Agenda 2000.

At the time of writing, there is little indication of the likely outcome of the Agenda 2000 process and it is, therefore, not intended to rehearse all of the possible scenarios herein. However, a number of issues can be identified that are of importance for

Scotland, including the likelihood that the post-1999 Structural Fund regime will strictly apply the 75 per cent of Community average GDP per capita threshold as the eligibility criteria for gaining access to the new Objective 1, the considerable reduction envisaged in the extent of the areas eligible under the new Objective 2 and the possibility that the new Objective 3 will be regionalised. All of these suggestions carry with them implications for particular regions of Scotland. The status of the Highlands and Islands as an Objective 1 region may be in doubt, although salvation may be granted through boundary redefinition, the low density of population or the high level of unemployment. The current Objective 2 regions - Eastern and Western Scotland - and the Objective 5b regions will have to wait for some time before any clarity regarding the eligibility criteria emerges from the present round of discussions between the Commission and Member States, although there are justifiable fears that some regions will lose their status as eligible areas. In addition, it is likely that those regions that retain their status will be much reduced in spatial extent; in future, Structural Fund assistance will be more concerned with "spot cleaning" rather than dealing with the wider range of restructuring problems evident in the regions in which these challenges occur.

3.3.4 *Implications of the Scottish Parliament*

In a number of respects questions reflecting the likely consequences of a greater degree of Scottish control and influence over the future content and management of Structural Fund programmes are linked to the outcomes of the Agenda 2000 process. However, this evolving relationship can be considered to be more about the management of the outcome of a process in which the dominant force is still UK central government, than about the establishment of a unique Structural Funds package tailored to meet the precise requirements of the Scottish regions. Given the considerable degree of autonomy on issues related to programme management that is currently exercised by the Scottish Office, it is likely that the future operational control of the Structural Funds will remain essentially a Scottish matter. But what will be available to be managed and what influence will the Scottish Parliament have on the content and direction of the future programmes?

The importance of the debate on Agenda 2000 is reflected in the current level of joint activity engaged in by various Scottish organisations and interest groups that have a stake in the outcome of the negotiations. A joint exercise involving the Scottish Office, the Convention of Scottish Local Authorities (COSLA), Scotland Europa and Scottish Enterprise is attempting to influence the Agenda 2000 process. Although it is by no means clear if this initiative will be successful, the intention is to ensure that a specific Scottish case is presented. Among other matters, advocacy is currently focused on:

■ demonstrating the benefits gained from the past and current use of the Structural Funds in Scotland, including an invitation to the regional Policy Committee of the European Parliament to visit the various programmes;

- arguing the case for the various regions in Scotland and attempting to influence the choice of eligibility criteria in order to ensure the maximum coverage of eligible areas;
- as a fall-back position, attempting to ensure that any transitional support is available for the maximum possible period;
- using the subsidiarity argument in order to ensure that the Structural Fund programmes remain a regional matter;
- resisting any suggestion that a single Scotland-wide programme should be established.

Assuming that these representations are successful and that the majority of the present programmes are renegotiated and approved, what adjustments in the operational management of the programmes might occur following the establishment of the Scottish Parliament? Two convergent trends can be observed: the creation of the Scottish Parliament and the move at a UK level more generally to emphasise regional requirements. These trends suggest that, in future, Structural Fund programmes will be better integrated with other aspects of spatial development, including the activities of local authorities, Local Enterprise Companies (LECs) and national policies related to transport, the environment and economic development. In addition, it is clear that the Scottish Parliament will wish to take a stronger role in ensuring accountability through overseeing the progress of the programmes and helping to resolve any difficulties experienced by the programmes on various issues, such as relations with the European Commission and ensuring the availability of matching funding (Colwell, 1997). Moves such as these would do much to overcome the criticisms, voiced by a number of observers, that the present programmes suffer from a lack of democratic control and are weakly integrated into their regional economies (Danson, 1997; Keating, 1995).

In the short to medium term it is likely that a strengthened version of the current arrangements for the management of the programme in Scotland will be established. Under such a regime it is reasonable to suggest that the Programme Executives may play a stronger coordinating role, especially given the current absence of any proposals to re-establish regional councils. The Executives have enjoyed a considerable degree of success in providing an arm's length secretariat for the programmes and maintaining a strategic overview of the evolution of individual regions. Building on this record of achievement and working within the spirit of the view expressed in the White Paper that the establishment of a Scottish Parliament should not result in the accumulation of "new functions at the centre which would be more appropriately and efficiently delivered by other bodies in Scotland" (Scottish Office, 1997, p.19), the Executives, under strengthened democratic control and expanded in size, could help to ensure the spatial integration of the various sources of funding.

In the longer term, and certainly within the lifetime of the new programmes, the current arrangements could well evolve to enable a far greater degree of control to be exercised over the programmes within Scotland. Even in those regions that enjoy only a limited degree of devolution, such as in the Netherlands, a considerable degree of autonomy is exercised regarding the negotiation and management of Structural

Fund programmes. A recent study of the operation of the Friesland 5b programme demonstrates the merits of a considerable degree of regional independence in the process of programme negotiation and management, including the benefits, in terms of directness and clarity, that result from the province maintaining a direct financial relationship with the Commission (Roberts et al, 1997).

3.3.5 *Spatial policy*

The second European policy area examined in this section is of more recent origin, but it demonstrates the potential for Scotland, with its long tradition of strategic spatial planning, to play an active role in future in relation to issues of spatial policy formulation and implementation. What is suggested here is an interchange of experience and skills, with Scotland benefiting from the greater emphasis placed by the European Union on spatial policy, and the other Member States gaining insights and understanding from the Scottish experience. The coincidence of the proposal for the establishment of a Scottish Parliament with the publication of the draft European Spatial Development Perspective (ESDP) provides a basis for Scotland to exercise leadership over the further refinement of European spatial policy.

In June 1997 the draft ESDP was published (Ministers Responsible for Spatial Planning, 1997). The document carries forward a work programme which started in November 1993, and it represents the first consensus statement on spatial policy. It is the intention of the British Presidency to complete the draft by June 1998, although it is unlikely that this will complete the process. The starting point of the ESDP is that the three fundamental goals of economic and social cohesion, sustainable development and the balanced competitiveness of the European territory, are very different in nature and could conflict. By recognising this potential for conflict and establishing a basis for action to be taken at various levels of government - EU, national, regional and local - the intention is to seek to achieve balanced progress towards these objectives.

The stated intention of the ESDP is to develop and pursue spatial policy in order to provide for a better balance between competition and co-operation. Although the language employed differs from that used in relation to the National Planning Guidelines (NPG) and National Planning Policy Guidelines (NPPG) system in Scotland - discussed in chapter 8 - the intentions are broadly similar. The Scottish approach to guidance on matters of spatial policy has produced a number of benefits, including the ability of individual local authorities to position their priorities and plans in a national context, the setting of national and sub-national priorities, and the early identification of potential conflicts and planning pressure points (Lloyd, 1994). This strong sense of strategic leadership and guidance has permeated other aspects of spatial policy in Scotland, such as the greater sense of integration that is evident in rural areas.

While not intending to imply that present practice in Scotland cannot benefit from the innovations introduced through the ESDP, or that Scotland should isolate itself from these important transnational developments, it is clear that the current European spatial initiative reflects many of the elements of best practice that have been evident in Scotland since 1974. In addition, and there is much contained in the ESDP that is not discussed here, there are a number of specific areas for attention and possible action by the Scottish Parliament including:

- actions to stimulate complementarity and co-operation between towns and cities - the common interests of Scottish urban areas could be better served by the further elaboration of national spatial policy;
- measures to enhance sustainable development of the urban and rural system;
- encouraging greater partnership between towns and the countryside;
- enhancing accessibility both within Scotland and between Scotland and the rest of the European Union - a clear priority in a peripheral area of Europe;
- providing better non-physical communication;
- encouraging the greater diffusion of knowledge and innovation;
- enhanced management of natural and cultural resources.

All of these issues are already matters of interest and policy attention in Scotland, but the ESDP moves them to centre stage and, additionally, it promotes transnational co-operation and the exchange of experience related to their further development. While the completion of the ESDP may lack the immediate attraction of the funding opportunities that are associated with the debate on the future of the Structural Funds, it espouses aspirations that provide support for a renaissance of strategic thinking and action on matters of spatial policy in Scotland. Over the long haul the ESDP may prove to be the more enduring of the two policy systems that have been discussed in this section.

3.4 Scotland's future relationship with Europe

The final section of this chapter takes stock of the messages and lessons that can be gleaned from the previous two sections, and it also considers a number of additional aspects of Scotland's future relationship with the European Union, including the influence that Scotland may be able to exert on the building of regional competences elsewhere.

3.4.1 Taking stock and looking to the future

When viewed from a European perspective, the move to establish the Scottish Parliament can be seen as the belated adoption of the "normal" structures of government and governance within the wider application of the principle of subsidiarity. The "Europe of the Regions" debate has largely been ignored in the UK during the past twenty years, partly due to the dominance of an ideology that has emphasised central control over the powers and functions of government, and partly because other matters, such as the almost endless process of local government reorganisation and the creation of new quangos have tended to deflect the attention of advocates of devolution. However, the recent resurgence of the devolution issue has drawn strength from these examples of the "democratic deficit", especially from the proliferation of extra-governmental organisations (Weir and Hall, 1994), and this has resulted in the current moves to devolve power to Scotland, Wales, Northern Ireland and the English regions. Too late, but perhaps not too little, the present proposals in the UK offer an opportunity to introduce an model of devolution that initially distributes power to the most appropriate tier of government and which then keeps this distribution under review to ensure that any imperfections are identified and rectified.

This introduces the first set of lessons and observations that are likely to be of importance in defining Scotland's relationship with Europe. Reflecting the conventions of an era prior to the inception of the European Union's regional project, the Council of Europe sought to establish an appropriate distribution of competences to the various levels of government. In a background paper, Strassoldo argued that historically, the nation-state "has concerned itself mainly with self-assertion, armed forces and war", while the region has strived for "co-operation, administration and planning" (Strassoldo, 1973, p.13). This distinction between the purposes and perspectives of the nation-state and those of the mesolevel offers a positive prospectus for the Scottish Parliament. Co-operation, sound administration, planning and, one might add, territorial integration, are all features which can be identified in modern mesolevel government. By implication, co-operation suggests both the sharing of competence with lower tiers of government and the establishment of channels of discourse and negotiation between the mesolevel and national or supranational governments. In addition, co-operation can, and increasingly does in Europe, take the form of transnational co-operation between sub-national units of government - regions, provinces and other territorial governments below the level of the Member State. In order to help affirm and consolidate its new found powers, the Scottish Parliament will wish to establish or reinforce direct links with other equivalent tiers of government and also to participate fully in transnational organisations. Three aspects of the links between Scotland and Europe are considered here: formal relationships, representation and networking activities.

The formal dimension of these links is defined by the powers assigned to the Scottish Parliament. On this issue the current Bill, while reserving relations with the European Union to the UK central government, does provide for Scottish participation in various processes, especially legal matters, and for Scottish representation in a number of European Union fora. On the subject of European law, it is the Member State that is bound by treaty to accept inter alia the primacy of European law over national law, and it is the case that although there will be a transfer of powers to Scottish Ministers with regard to subordinate legislation under clause 49 of the Bill, the appropriate UK Secretary of State will retain the overall responsibility to direct and ensure proper implementation of European law in Scotland. Schedule 5(6) of the Bill sets out the reserved matters related to the European Union and notes that, while Ministers of the Scottish Parliament could not represent the whole of the UK in international decision making, this does not prevent the Scottish Parliament from observing and implementing obligations under European law. In addition, it allows Scottish Ministers to assist Ministers of the Crown and to be involved in European legislative processes. Although this is a lesser role than that exercised by mesolevel government ministers in certain other Member States, and despite the fact that it represents little more than the formalisation of current practice, it provides a platform for future progress. Concern has been expressed that Scotland's role in Europe might be diminished since Scottish Ministers would no longer be able to attend the Council of Ministers by right - a point made, somewhat surprisingly, by a Conservative spokesman (Ancram, 1997) - but it has been stated by a Scottish Office Minister that the future Scottish Ministers "will have full powers to observe and implement European law...and they will be able to play a role in negotiations with European partners" (McLeish, 1998, col.248-249).

Despite the fact that the Bill as currently worded restricts the right of Scottish Ministers to act independently of UK Ministers, or to act on behalf of the UK as a whole, as is the case in Germany and Belgium (in these countries ministers from sub-national government frequently represent the Member State), in practice the situation could arise when on a specific topic a Scottish Minister is the most appropriate person to represent the UK case. The absence of clarity in the Bill on this point could result in confusion and the issue will need either to be addressed directly or to be tested in relation to a specific issue.

Questions of representation relate both to the European Parliament and to formal European Union Committees. Scotland currently has eight members of the European Parliament and there are no suggestions in the Bill that this representation should be adjusted. Despite the restrictions placed on the role of Scottish Ministers, there is no specific discussion of the nature of the relationship between MEPs and the Parliament. It can be assumed that the Parliament will wish to devote considerable time to the debate and scrutiny of European matters as they affect Scotland, and that Scottish MEPs will both be involved in such arrangements and will act as an interface between the Scottish and European Parliaments, perhaps through a dual mandate. Scotland has five out of the UK's 24 members of the Committee of the Regions - a delegation larger than originally intended (Roberts, 1997b) - and it is not proposed to alter this representation. It is recognised by COSLA that the Scottish Parliament may wish to be represented on the Scottish delegation to the Committee of the Regions, and it is proposed by COSLA that this could be achieved through joint working to ensure an equitable split in the delegation between local government and the Parliament (Colwell, 1997).

Two other questions related to representation require attention. First, at present the UK maintains a Permanent Representation in Brussels (UK REP), and there is usually at least one Scottish Office official seconded to this body. The White Paper suggests that the Scottish Parliament may wish to establish its own office in Brussels, although UK REP would continue to represent the interests of the UK as a whole. This suggestion is in keeping with the representations maintained by other mesolevel governments. However, a bolder, though unlikely, step would be for the Parliament to follow the example set by some other mesolevels and to create a "ministry" of external or foreign affairs with, perhaps, the first "embassy" established in London. The second issue relates to the future role of Scotland Europa, which has achieved considerable success in providing a focal point in Brussels for Scotland's relationships with European Union institutions. Scotland Europa represents a variety of Scottish interests - local authorities, Scottish Enterprise, universities, colleges and others - and is likely to continue to do so. There is the possibility that the Parliament's representation in Brussels could be co-located with Scotland Europa.

The third issue to be considered relates to Scotland's networking activities and to other less formal means of representation in Europe. This is a matter of considerable importance because it provides an opportunity for Scotland to strengthen its position alongside other mesolevel governments, both in the European Union and in the wider Europe. Many local authorities and other organisations in Scotland already engage in such fora. For example, a number of the former regional councils were leading members of the Assembly of European Regions (AER) and collaborative arrangements have allowed such participation to continue, while other authorities are members of the Association of European Regions of Industry and Technology (RETI) or of the Council of European Municipalities and Regions (CEMR). In addition to those quasi-formal structures, which are generally the result of collaboration between elected sub-national governments, there are many other informal, professional and academic networks that provide the opportunity to develop or present a Scottish perspective on a variety of relevant matters.

There are many links between these less formal bodies and the formal structures of the European Union. Many of the bodies have overlapping membership - especially the Committee of the Regions and the AER - and, therefore, the opportunities for the interchange of views and the exercise of influence are considerable. As Dehousse and Christiansen (1995) note in the Preface to their review of the Committee of the Regions, many of the functions and operational objectives of the Committee were decided in advance of its formation through collective lobbying by mesolevel governments. In addition, there are countless opportunities to engage in transnational projects on specific topics and individual spatial themes both through European Union initiatives and under the auspices of the quasi-formal organisations. These opportunities will increase as a result of the ESDP work programme and as the competences of the European Union are extended further. In all of these opportunities it will be vital to ensure the most effective use of resources and the Parliament, alongside COSLA and other co-ordinating bodies, will have an important role to play in this respect.

Finally, there is the issue of the internal management of European activities within Scotland, especially in relation to the Structural Funds programmes and other key areas of policy such as agriculture and fisheries. To date, the Scottish Office, COSLA and other bodies have taken an active role in such matters, and it is to be expected that the level of engagement will increase in future, especially if the Parliament wishes to reinforce the existing distinctive Scottish style of territorial planning and management. In relation to the Structural Funds, notwithstanding the outcome of the Agenda 2000 process, the new Scottish Executive will wish to ensure the most effective use of the resources available and it is likely that this will result in a strengthening of the current approach to strategic spatial management. By maintaining the present structure of the regional programmes in Scotland and linking them more directly to other aspects of regional development, including the activities controlled by local authorities, the LECs, Scottish Natural Heritage and other agents of spatial development, it should then be possible to enhance both the individual and cumulative effects of such actions. A neglected but highly appropriate model for future regional development in Scotland is provided by the experience elsewhere in Europe of the application of the concept of ecological modernisation (Roberts, 1996a). This approach could prove to be a distinguishing feature of the regional programmes after 1999. While there is limited experience of the application of this model in Scotland, such evidence as is available demonstrates the benefits associated with this approach (Jackson and Roberts, 1997).

As was noted in the previous section, the Programme Executives potentially have a major role to play in ensuring the development and delivery of a strengthened system of co-ordinated regional planning and management. This strengthening of the administrative basis for regional planning and management could also involve other existing agencies. In addition, it is clear that the creation of the Parliament provides an opportunity to re-think the fundamental nature and structure of a range of organisational relationships both within Scotland and between Scotland and other mesolevel, national and supranational governments and organisations. The exchange of experience, the dissemination of lessons from different styles of operation and the provision of support for mutually beneficial policy initiatives is a two-way process, with the individual mesolevel both gaining from and contributing to the further development of a Europe-wide capacity to manage and govern territorial development. These more subtle consequences are most clearly seen in federal systems, where the dynamic nature of power sharing between the various levels of government is kept under review. In such systems the implications and consequences of enhanced interaction between the "subcentral" level of government and all other levels of government, including other mesolevels, national governments and the European Union, have generally been seen as positive (Goetz, 1993).

3.4.2 Scotland's contributions to mesolevel government

The final elements to be considered in this chapter are the extent to which the "Scottish experiment" will add to our collective knowledge and understanding of mesolevel government, and the contribution of more immediate operational assistance that Scotland can make to the organisation and implementation of regional government elsewhere in Europe and worldwide. Both these issues are considered in the light of the evidence presented in the previous sections and on the assumption that at least some of the applicant nations of central and eastern Europe will eventually join the European Union.

Any longer term contributions made by Scotland to the collective store of knowledge will be conditioned by the extent to which the Parliament exercises its powers fully and by the willingness of the Parliament to challenge and extend the range of competences initially allocated to it. As noted in section 3.2, once established, most mesolevel governments have demonstrated a tendency to expand their portfolio of powers. There may be disruptions to this trend as a consequence of the centre attempting to recapture devolved powers - the experience of the UK during the 1980s and Spain at present provide examples - but such setbacks are normally only temporary aberrations.

While the range of the powers to be conferred on the Scottish Parliament are not as extensive as those distributed in other recent cases, such as in Spain, Belgium or Italy, the process of devolution is occurring at a point in time when the implementation of the principle of subsidiarity is strengthening throughout Europe, and when the opportunity to demonstrate that devolution can work in a mature unitary state will carry considerable weight. Specific elements of Scottish devolution may be of particular importance. These include the projection of the impression that Europe is an important factor in determining the constituencies of MSPs; seven regional members shall be returned for eight regional constituencies, which are the same as the constituencies used for the election of MEPs. Other elements are the expressed willingness of those likely to hold senior ministerial office to enter into agreement with Scottish local government on the structure of the delegation to represent Scotland at the Committee of the Regions, and the opportunity to extend the arrangements that have been successful in generating and implementing the regional programmes supported by the Structural Funds to other aspects of regional planning and development. If those opportunities are grasped, then Scotland will have demonstrated its ability to use its new found competences in a manner that supports the wider European regional cause.

The acid tests of the value of the Scottish contribution in a European context will, on the one hand, be the extent to which the Parliament engages in a positive manner with both the formal institutions of the European Union and with the other Member States and mesolevel governments. On the other hand, of equal importance will be the style of that engagement, both in terms of the degree of creativity, collaboration and enthusiasm that is employed in reaching solutions to common problems, and the process through which the Parliament works with the regions and localities of Scotland to establish the strategy and the substance of the Scottish stance on European affairs.

In the short term Scotland should continue to contribute to the enhancement of regional capability elsewhere in Europe. Scottish experience has demonstrated that a distinctive approach to policy making and the development of a source of strategic common purpose can both overcome the submersion of a former nation-state and defeat the "fear and ignorance of nationalism in Scotland (and Wales) on the part of the political centre in London" (Kellas, 1991, p.93). Furthermore, Scotland has also demonstrated the importance and value of working with other mesolevel governments in the European Union to press the regional cause, and the desirability of developing a sub-national perspective on both European Union and national policies, such as EMU and international trade (Colwell, 1997).

Scotland's experience of working to establish devolved government within a unitary state is of particular value to other sub-national and regional groups that aspire to have a greater say in controlling their own affairs. This experience may help to guide reforms in other European Union Member States and in the nations of central and eastern Europe. Although many of the countries of the former Soviet bloc continue to experience considerable difficulty in implementing and adjusting to recently established national reforms, there are also considerable pressures in such nations for the process of democratic reform to extend to a sub-national level. Scotland can assist this process by demonstrating how a "stateless nation" can emerge from a long period of central domination. Collaboration, information dissemination and mentoring is already under way at both Scotland-wide and local levels - COSLA, for example, in recent months has assisted partners from Poland, Hungary and the Czech Republic, while Dundee City Council participates in a number of transnational schemes that include partners from central and eastern Europe - and these and other activities could usefully be extended in the future.

3.5   Conclusions

This chapter has reviewed the past and present experience of a number of key aspects of Scotland's relationship with Europe and has attempted to look forward to the contribution that Scotland might make to the extension and reinforcement of the general capability of mesolevel government. One issue that should not be overlooked in all of this is the psychological impact of devolution. In order to avoid the Balkanisation of British politics it is essential that the benefits and opportunities of devolution are not frittered away on a display of Scottish nationalism. Rather, effort should be focused on establishing new or strengthened alliances both within and outwith Scotland. Perhaps the Scottish model can even provide a basis for the devolution of political power to the English regions!

Part II

Financing

4 The fiscal arrangements for devolution

DAVID HEALD and NEAL GEAUGHAN

4.1 Introduction

The United Kingdom is embarking upon a path of asymmetric quasi-federalism. This might more plausibly be denounced as a constitutional outrage were it not for previous experience of such arrangements during the 1921-72 period of devolved government in Northern Ireland and also the various 1979-97 Conservative Government plans for Northern Ireland (Crick, 1995).[1] Reviews of international experience (for example, Hesse and Wright, 1996) in federal-like structures of government have shown that the preconditions for making these both workable and acceptable relate to the building of mutual trust and not to the availability of technical options. The United Kingdom, much remarked upon for its highly centralised polity and fiscal system, faces a sharp learning curve both in terms of digesting technical desiderata and of modifying political and fiscal styles.

This chapter contends that the plans currently being implemented for devolution in Scotland, Wales and Northern Ireland do not embody a fiscal settlement. The word "settlement" conveys the sense of something considered and intended to be enduring. Key features of such a settlement are, in fact, missing, notably a sustainable basis for determining the assigned budget and therefore public expenditure relatives. What are in place are fiscal arrangements, of unknown durability.

On several important issues, what has transpired has rather been a succession of high-level political compromises, sometimes with limited insight into the policy problem. There has been a misguided belief - viewed as a pretence by some commentators - that there can be a continuation of the past. In part this reflects a failure of policy development, in part a set of political calculations: for example, the issue of cross-border spillovers (drawing the attention of middle-England voters to the direction and size of territorial transfers) seems to have been the motivation for Labour's insistence in 1995 that the Scottish Constitutional Convention abandon its 1990 proposal for assigned revenues (Heald and Geaughan, 1996).

Intriguingly, the commitment to have referendums resulted in the Scotland and Wales devolution White Papers being campaigning - rather than reflective - documents. Whereas the two-question referendum in Scotland was widely suspected to be designed to kill off devolved taxation powers, the combined impact of the decisive general election and referendum results in Scotland ended substantive opposition to devolution. In the event, the lack of preparation regarding finance has not created the vulnerability which would have resulted had serious opposition remained.[2] A remarkably rapid transformation means that the year 2000 will bring "Home Rule All Round", with elected bodies in Belfast, Cardiff and Edinburgh. On a political level, there is undoubtedly "safety in numbers" for the devolved administrations, giving protection which an isolated Scottish Parliament would not have enjoyed. Paradoxically, there are now opportunities which better Whitehall-led preparation might have closed off. An important task of this chapter is therefore to explore the options available.

For reasons which were entirely predictable and understandable, the pre-referendum debate about the financial aspects of devolution concentrated heavily upon the "tartan tax" and the possible repercussions upon the Barnett formula. The Scotland Bill is itself non-specific about many important financial issues, preferring to leave them to be tackled through administrative mechanisms. The effect of seeking to avoid sensitive issues may be to stoke up unnecessary trouble for the future. Devolutionists, such as ourselves, who draw attention to this are likely to be criticised for rocking the boat. However, such a reaction reflects excessive complacency, as ought to have been clearly signalled by the tone of both the Treasury Committee (1997) evidence session on the Barnett formula and that of the campaign for the Mayoralty of London (Archer and Livingstone, 1998). The nature of fiscal debates will be heavily conditioned by the way in which London-based and Scotland-based newspapers - in some cases, editions of the same newspaper - play to the prejudices of their readerships.[3] Moreover, there are some complex agendas being played out in sections of the Scottish press; Marr (1998) observed that *The Scotsman*, which had kept the flag of devolution flying through periods of adversity, "is now being driven by Unionism and Nationalism working hand-in-hand against Labour". Whether intended or not, the effect is to destabilise preparations for implementing devolution.

The chapter is structured in the following way. Section 4.2 broadens the horizon from current UK developments to review certain theoretical predictions about decentralised government. Section 4.3 examines territorial public expenditure relatives and the role which the Barnett formula has played. Section 4.4 reviews the interface between devolved administrations and local government; in Scotland and Wales, though not in Northern Ireland, a large proportion of devolved expenditure will actually be disbursed by local authorities. Finally, section 4.5 charts some of the challenges which lie ahead.

At several points in the chapter, references are made to other papers for detailed support for particular arguments. The case for devolved taxes is made in Heald and Geaughan (1996), whilst a sympathetic exposition of the tartan tax is provided by Heald and Geaughan (1997)[4] - chapter 5 presents a less favourable treatment. A discussion of the fiscal consequences of devolution for the United Kingdom appears as Heald and Geaughan (1998). An overview of the issues involved in financing UK devolution can be found in Heald et al (1998). What differentiates the present chapter is its direct focus on the issues which have to be addressed after the referendums but before vesting. Inevitably, this means that parts of this chapter are speculative in nature.

Fiscal decisions are political in several senses: for example, in the straightforward party sense of a left-right spectrum on desirable levels of public expenditure; in terms of conflicts within the machinery of government; and in terms of electoral spillovers from decisions made at different tiers of government. One obvious origin of "New" Labour's highly centralised party management was the damage perceived to have been done in the early 1980s to the Labour Party at UK level by local authorities caricatured in the media as the "loony left". Accordingly, it is not just the formal tiered structure of government and intergovernment financial relationships which need to be studied, but also the links between tiers which are forged by political parties.

4.2   Propositions about decentralised government

In terms of the substantive effects of UK devolution on public expenditure and public service delivery, there is a marked disjuncture between the expectations of many who have supported devolution and the conventional wisdom of the economics literature on fiscal federalism.[5]   Many writers explicitly link decentralised government to smaller government:[6]

> Considering all the federations there have been in the world, I believe that federalism has been a significant force for limited government and hence for personal freedom (Riker, 1996, p. 20).

> The extent of decentralization also depends, to some extent, upon the desired magnitude of the role of government in the economy. Typically economists who prefer a smaller role for the government would also favor more decentralization (Jha, 1998, p.466).

In contrast, the UK constitutional reform agenda, in which devolution features prominently, has been mounted largely by those generally hostile to the Thatcherite agenda of free markets and smaller government.

The closest UK counterparts to those - especially in the United States - who view federalism as a protection against big government are the journalists Andrew Neil and Michael Fry. Ever since it became likely that devolution would occur, they have consistently run the argument that the Scottish Parliament should raise all its own money and not be dependent on the UK Exchequer via a block grant. In essence, they have argued for a scheme analogous to that contained in the Government of Ireland Act 1920. Scotland would therefore receive all tax revenues generated in Scotland and would make a contribution for reserved services, but would have no access to UK revenues.[7] Such an arrangement would be expected to lead to expenditure reductions in any jurisdiction with a below-average taxable capacity and above-average inherited level of expenditure. The fiscal history of devolved government in Northern Ireland (Lawrence, 1965; Gibson, 1996) certainly indicates that expenditure was held at a much lower level than would have been likely under fiscal integration with Great Britain.

The substantive expenditure effects of asymmetric quasi-federalism in the United Kingdom are ambiguous, and likely to be contingent upon the dynamics of party competition. On the one hand, Neil (1997a) has denounced the financing basis for the Scottish Parliament as "a system tailor-made for exploitation to Nationalist advantage". On the other, Adonis (1998) emphasised that the hitherto implicit territorial transfers are likely to be flushed out and exposed to public gaze. Blow et al (1996) also questioned the extent to which existing patterns of territorial transfer would survive the glare of publicity consequent upon greater transparency. "Political muscle" might either reinforce pressures for lower territorial transfers or attenuate them.

Smith (1996) distinguished between "decentralisation of administration" and "decentralisation of choice" - the same distinction as that between devolved administration and devolved government which was discussed in chapter 2. This is a useful way of conceptualising the transition from administrative devolution (Scottish Office, Welsh Office, Northern Ireland Office and Departments, all headed by Cabinet-rank Westminster politicians) to political devolution (territorial Executives accountable to territorially elected bodies). A move to more local electoral control will have complex effects on expenditure levels, some stimulating and some depressing, therefore leaving doubts about the net effect. However, if the budget constraint is perceived to be harder, there would be more incentive to confront certain politically difficult decisions; an obvious example is school closures in response to excess capacity, which were not made on the necessary scale by Scottish local authorities in the early 1990s, partly to avoid confrontations with local pressure groups. Moreover, when local authorities did attempt to establish school closure programmes, Scottish Office ministers actively encouraged parents to invoke opt-out procedures, thereby generating paralysis and undoubted inefficiency. Elected territorial bodies such as the Scottish Parliament and Welsh Assembly may possess more political muscle, in relation to both the UK Government and local interest groups.

Political debates about the territorial dimensions of public finance do not take place behind a veil of ignorance; the various actors are only too aware how particular arguments and mechanisms affect their interests. Consequently, it should be recognised that there are two levels of discourse which often become intermingled; first, an attempt to specify a set of general principles as to how a system of decentralised public finance should operate; and, second, intense political conflict, often characterised by blatant opportunism, about actual or proposed fiscal arrangements. The effects are to sow public confusion, to make it difficult to hold to transparent ground rules, and to make empirical work more difficult to conduct.

A crucial matter of contextual background is that the UK constitutional reform agenda is in part a reaction against the "free market, strong state" dimension of Thatcherism (Gamble, 1994). The two OECD countries which have most enthusiastically and successfully implemented the free-market agenda have been New Zealand and the United Kingdom, both countries in which there are no effective counterweights to a determined central government. In contrast, policy in Germany has been more tentative and consensual, for which the federal nature of Germany must be a significant explanatory factor. Political resources play a substantial role in shaping fiscal outcomes. For example, Keating (1998, p.184) observed that:

> in Germany the revenue-sharing agreement is negotiated with the Länder and must be approved by the Bundesrat, which represents the Länder governments. This gives the Länder collectively more control over taxation and spending than any other subnational governments in Europe and its adoption in Britain, with its implications for Treasury dominance, would represent a far more radical step than conceding independent tax powers to regional governments.

Moreover, a relevant qualification to Riker's (1996) view of the effects of decentralisation can be detected in another of his propositions:

> Governments that are not federations can reorganize the local units at will, destroying old regional units and creating new ones. But in federations the constituent units have agreed with one another that each will retain its identity and its unique functions. [The whole point of federalism is] the tiered structure cannot arbitrarily be revised, or even revised to adjust for changed conditions (p.10).

In the United Kingdom, the Greater London Council and the metropolitan councils were abolished in 1986 and Scottish regional councils in 1996, all by a central government whose party could not win control of these bodies. Such constraints on the power of central government as suggested by Riker would represent a very significant change. Across the UK political spectrum, there is now recognition that the state needs relegitimation, and that forms of democratic participation at subnational level will have a role to play in this (Jenkins, 1995; Select Committee on Relations between Central and Local Government, 1996).

Extending the focus beyond UK developments draws attention to several interesting parallels and differences. There are signs of a new generation of theoretical work on the internal structure of the state, evidenced, for example, by recent work by Tirole (1994) and Seabright (1996). To a considerable extent, this should be interpreted as extending recent developments in the theory of the firm, notably with regard to principal-agent relationships in a world of incomplete contracts, to the analysis of governmental structures. This new work is interesting, not least because the field had become relatively unfashionable since the synthesising work of Oates (1972), who built upon the insights of Musgrave (1959). Some of the factors stimulating such renewed theoretical interest can readily be discerned.

First, the collapse of the centralised economic systems of the Eastern bloc has often been accompanied by dramatic reconstructions in both the configurations of states and their internal organisation. Undoubtedly, this is the principal reason why the International Monetary Fund (IMF) has taken so much interest in intergovernmental fiscal structures during the 1990s (Tanzi, 1996; Ter-Minassian, 1997). In several cases, it really has been a question of redesigning state structures and fiscal systems from scratch.

Second, rapid developments towards European Monetary Union (EMU) raise a plethora of economic, fiscal and monetary issues (Eichengreen, 1997). Crucially, EMU is going ahead with less economic convergence than had been posited as prerequisite and without the enlarged European Union (EU) budget foreseen at the time of earlier deliberations about fiscal structure after deeper integration (MacDougall, 1977). Inevitably, these circumstances have provoked discussions about the mechanisms for securing budgetary adjustments at member-state level following asymmetric macroeconomic shocks.[8] In turn, the absence of territorial fiscal transfers, both extensive and automatic in all existing federations, has been attracting attention to both sets of circumstances.

Third, there has been a veritable outburst of initiatives in connection with fiscal transparency. On a global level, the International Monetary Fund (IMF) (1998) has proclaimed a code on fiscal transparency, supported by a research study (Kopits and Craig, 1998). This appears to have been prompted by fears about the instability of the world financial system, and the way in which this might be exacerbated by sudden fiscal crises beyond the capacity of the IMF to handle. At the UK level, Gordon Brown, Chancellor of the Exchequer in the Labour Government elected in May 1997, has published *The Code for Fiscal Stability* (Treasury, 1998b) which will be given a statutory basis through the 1998 Finance Act. An obvious, though unmentionable, motive for these UK developments has been the desire to blame the previous Conservative Government for the severity of the last UK economic cycle and for the extent of desynchronisation with the rest of the EU cycle.[9] There is a curious juxtaposition between vogueish enthusiasm for transparency and the pervasiveness of news management and spin doctoring.[10]

Broadening the fiscal canvas beyond the United Kingdom proves useful in two ways. Comparative material brings home the diversity of arrangements and emphasises the importance of making fiscal systems work in particular political and institutional settings. Of perhaps greater importance in the UK context, it shows that most of the troublesome issues confronting UK devolution have their counterparts elsewhere.

4.3   Territorial expenditure and the Barnett formula

Turning to the mechanisms for territorial expenditure allocation as these have evolved in the United Kingdom, the starting point must be to recognise that this is an arena which combines technical obscurity with high political salience.[11] Quite apart from the difficulty of establishing a coherent account of either process or outcome, interpretation entails considerable problems. For example, one might ask whether the obscurity is simply a regrettable defect in the system, or whether it has been instrumental.

Midwinter et al (1991) attributed Scotland's "advantage" in public expenditure terms to three factors: social needs; political muscle; and "classical incrementalism".[12] They characterised the territorial public expenditure system, as it affected Scotland in the 1980s, in the following way. Conservative Secretaries of State for Scotland continued to fight the Scottish corner, not taking on board the disrepute in which much of the

Cabinet held public expenditure: "The whole process was conducted with discretion to avoid arousing the jealousy of English ministers and MPs" (Midwinter et al, 1991, p.110).

Nevertheless, Scotland's position had begun to attract hostile attention from the Conservative Government's own backbenches:

> The growing gap between the power bases of the major parties has thus added a territorial dimension to the old ideological disagreements over the merits of public expenditure (p.98).

> Conservative backbenchers in the late 1980s began to intervene regularly in discussions of Scottish public expenditure, portraying the Scots as "force-fed" with public expenditure and the victims of a "dependency culture", while the Scottish Office budget is described as a "slush fund"...The assault is thus two-pronged, an ideological attack on high levels of public spending and territorial attack on the privileges enjoyed by ungrateful Scots (p.110).

In these circumstances, it was not surprising that the Scottish Office valued the retention of the Barnett formula because it curtailed debate about public expenditure relatives.[13] A marked difference between the Secretaryships of George Younger and Malcolm Rifkind, and those of Ian Lang and Michael Forsyth, can be seen in the way in which the latter pair simultaneously identified higher levels of public expenditure as a policy problem yet flaunted this as a benefit of the Union. This constituted a "scorched earth" policy which was bound to leave many hostages to fortune.[14] In future, the harshest political criticism of the Barnett formula is likely to come from the Labour Government's backbenches.[15]

For accounts of how the Barnett formula has worked, the reader is referred to Heald (1992, 1994), Bell et al (1996), Treasury (1997b,c) and Twigger (1998).[16] A considerable amount of media and political comment seriously misrepresents the formula. Indeed, a considerable proportion of media coverage should be viewed as either government spinning or news invention by journalists to provide a peg for editorial pronouncements.[17] In particular, the formula cannot properly be described as needs-based. However, it plays a crucial role as a regulating mechanism within a system which embodies a commitment to the territorial matching of needs and resources. Accordingly, the 1978 decision to use the formula for governing changes in the Scottish block, with the expectation that this would lead to some degree of convergence of per capita expenditure, was based upon the implied view that Scotland's expenditure relative exceeded its needs relative. Recourse to the Barnett formula, later extended to cover Wales and Northern Ireland, signalled a desire for convergence, without having to decide how much convergence. It is therefore part of a broad-brush fiscal arrangement, contrasting markedly to the fine-grained, highly disaggregated and complex systems used for the distribution of Revenue Support Grant (RSG) to local authorities and purchasing budgets to health authorities.[18]

The fundamental point about the future of the Barnett formula is that it will be transformed from a mechanism *internal* to one government to one used for regulating the transfer of money *between* tiers of government. The intensity of recent political and media interest, together with the extent of both misunderstanding and misrepresentation, gives some indication of what the future holds. Such a non-statutory mechanism, functioning in the absence of an independent body such as a Territorial Exchequer Board (Heald, 1990), will depend entirely upon ministerial discretion. The announcement by the Chief Secretary to the Treasury (Darling, 1997), on 9 December 1997, that there would be annual upratings of population from 1999-2000 was a spoiler to head off the expected critical report from the Treasury Committee.[19]

Two interesting insights can be drawn from the Treasury Committee's evidence session on 17 November 1997 (Treasury Committee, 1997). First, Lord Barnett placed great emphasis upon relative income per head as the underpinning for the 1978 adoption of the formula. This contrasts with what has hitherto been drawn from governmental statements. A possible explanation is that Lord Barnett was recounting how this new arrangement was made politically acceptable to the then Labour Cabinet, rather than the reasoning why the Treasury and Scottish Office promoted such a mechanism. Second, academic and media commentators on territorial aspects of public finances had expected that a commitment to devolution would lead to a much more thorough account being placed in the public domain as to how the Barnett formula has worked over 20 years. The answers provided by Treasury witnesses and the inadequate data later provided in a Treasury (1998a) memorandum suggest that such expectations might be ill-founded.[20]

There is an important sense in which the incessant attention in the 1990s to the mechanics of the Barnett formula has begun to damage what its spirit was intended to achieve. The purpose behind such territorial formulae is to avoid repeated annual controversies about changes in expenditure; once a formula is set it should hold for a number of years. The danger of repeated conflict is that this both undermines the purpose of the formula and raises a set of divisive yet irresolvable territorial controversies.

The crucial point is that the long-term, general equilibrium effects of the structure of government are impossible to pin down authoritatively. Any attempt to quantify these will involve assumptions which are inevitably vulnerable to challenge by those who do not like the conclusions.[21]

In the view of the present authors (Heald et al, 1998), the direction of *current* territorial transfers within the United Kingdom is clear, though there is some scope for argument about size. The "territories" spend considerably more than the UK average and the best available evidence indicates that they generate less than the UK average in revenues; the net flow is therefore from England (Scottish Office, 1997b; Welsh Office, 1997).[22]

However, this is a conclusion about the territorial pattern of public finances given the historical development of UK government and the way it has influenced the territorial distribution of economic activity and population. The highly centralised nature of the British state has resulted in London being dominant in almost every aspect of British life. The United Kingdom is atypical in the close mapping of industrial, financial, political and governmental activity; this is resented especially, though not exclusively, in the territories. This pattern is markedly different from what occurs in federal states such as Australia, Canada, Germany and the United States. If the United Kingdom had not existed in its highly centralised form, the geographical pattern of economic activity in the British Isles would have been markedly different. One telling statistic is that the non-England share of the population of the United Kingdom plus Republic of Ireland fell from 46 per cent in 1801 (the year of the first modern census) to 21 per cent in 1991 (Heald, 1992, p.43). Over the same period, England's share of GB population rose from 76 per cent to 86 per cent. Under different governmental scenarios, both the structure of population and the pre-tax and benefit distribution of income in the United Kingdom would probably have been very different. As was dramatically shown by the geographical pattern of voting in the Welsh devolution referendum, the west-east links connecting Wales with England in both north and south markedly differentiate the context of Welsh from Scottish devolution. There is international evidence that frontiers affect economic development and population trends; obvious examples concern Belgium, Germany and Netherlands, and Canada and the United States. If Wales and England had been separate states, the situation now would probably be quite different; for example, one would speculate that there would have been a markedly different configuration of Welsh transport investments, emphasising the internal cohesion of Wales.

The impact of UK devolution, still more so a fragmentation of the United Kingdom into four independent parts, would be highly uncertain. This allows those on all sides of these constitutional issues to visualise outcomes favourable to their viewpoint. One argument, which has been seized upon by Alex Salmond, Leader of the Scottish National Party, is that the remarkable recent economic performance of Ireland might serve as a model for an independent Scotland within the European Union. In other words, the types of calculation discussed above would be dismissed as largely irrelevant; and the frame of reference would be rejected as the wrong starting point and as misrepresenting the relevant dynamics.

Turning to the case of Northern Ireland, Gibson (1996) used Kornai's (1980) notion of the soft budget constraint as a vehicle for analysing the public finances of Northern Ireland during the periods of devolution and direct rule. The implementation of the financial provisions of the Government of Ireland Act 1920 severely disadvantaged Northern Ireland. Even in the absence of measurement, it clearly suffered from higher-than-GB expenditure needs and lower-than-GB taxable capacity. The Northern Ireland Government was not in a position to provide GB-comparable services after paying the first-charge "Imperial contribution" to the UK Treasury. Complicating matters further, Northern Ireland was not only separated from the Republic but also disengaged from Great Britain in both psychological and financial senses. The realities of the territorial financial system were concealed, and the Northern Ireland Government faced an extremely hard budget constraint. Even when successively relaxed (Gibson, 1996), this remained harsh if compared with the notional position of a "poor" GB region. Moreover, the rigidities of the financial system simultaneously undermined the substance of devolution and created potentially serious economic distortions.[23] A prime reason for the lack of resolution of these issues has been the contested status of Northern Ireland, and the way in which all developments have been subject to dual interpretation, resulting in ossification. Direct rule from 1972 dramatically relaxed the budget constraint, leading to a remarkable period of expenditure growth as the UK Government expected GB standards of provision to apply. A damaging aspect of these arrangements is that access to the UK Exchequer protected Northern Ireland from the costs of political violence.[24] In the long term, the transparency which is likely to accompany devolution might bring back a harder budget constraint.

Perhaps the most significant "lesson" to be derived from the historical experience of Northern Ireland is that long-term effects are extremely difficult to predict. First, one would expect that labour markets would encourage migration from low-income to high-income regions. Such a response to earnings differentials is likely to be intensified by fiscally induced migration if "poor" jurisdictions have to balance their budgets without any equalisation payments for below-average resources and/or above-average needs. As well as securing higher labour earnings, the migrant will receive a higher level of public services for any given tax payment. Solely from an economic perspective, policymakers may doubt whether such trends are wholly beneficial, especially if migration is concentrated among more skilled workers and if there are congestion effects in receiving regions. Second, the political effects of migration can be equally complex and highly contentious in a society marked by sharp cleavages. In Northern Ireland, prolonged political violence has exerted differential effects on migration; most notably, a significant number of students from Protestant households study at GB universities and do not subsequently return. Migration has affected the religious balance of Northern Ireland, just as it has drastically altered the population distribution of the United Kingdom. Third, a lasting peace which brought greater economic prosperity would have complex effects. For example, lower unemployment and an increase in wages in Northern Ireland towards the UK level would bring substantial benefits to the working class in both communities. In the long run, there would be downwards pressure on the real incomes of middle-class households (especially those benefiting from GB-pegged wages and low house prices), though in the short run this would be masked by the windfall capital gains as prices rose in response to higher confidence and stronger GDP growth. Fourth, a sustained peace in Northern Ireland would give the Northern Ireland Executive substantial political muscle in UK deliberations about territorial expenditure. During the referendum campaign, the Chancellor of the Exchequer announced a £315 million package (Northern Ireland Information Service, 1998a); Richard Branson chipped in with the promise of more Virgin megastores and cinemas if there were a Yes vote (Northern Ireland Information Service, 1998b).

4.4   The interface with local government finance

Although this chapter has concentrated upon the Scottish Parliament's relationship with Westminster, it is essential to have some discussion about the interface with local government. However, this discussion is not intended to be comprehensive, but instead focuses attention on key issues. In recognition of the salience of this relationship with local government, the Secretary of State for Scotland has appointed a Commission on Local Government and the Scottish Parliament; its remit includes "effective relations" between the two but regrettably excludes finance. The Commission, which is now consulting widely (Commission on Local Government and the Scottish Parliament, 1998), has been tasked to present its final report to the First Minister when that person takes office.

Throughout the United Kingdom, local government was seriously damaged during the 1979-97 Conservative Government (Jenkins, 1995). The reasons were complex. First, as a major service provider, local government was inevitably caught up in the Thatcherite project of not only redrawing the boundaries between the market and the state but also of reconceptualising the state as an enabler. Second, there was a partisan motive, especially as the Conservative Party's success in winning four successive UK general elections was accompanied by dramatically reduced local government representation.

Although the change of government in May 1997 was widely expected to lead to a strengthening of local government, the opposite has so far been observed. Because these developments are new, the reasons are just beginning to emerge.

First, and much discussed elsewhere, the "New" Labour project is highly centralist both in substance and in style.

Second, during the 1979-97 Conservative Government, opposition parties in Scotland protested interminably about Scotland being badly done by at RSG settlements when the evidence was clearly to the contrary. Such has been the opacity of the local government financial system that it has been possible to choose a number favourable to one's argument, run that in a misleading way, and then shrug one's shoulders if the number is challenged, secure in the knowledge that few will understand anyway. The opportunity for a serious dialogue about why Scottish local authority expenditure is much higher than that in England and Wales was missed because of bad feeling between Ian Lang, Secretary of State from 1990 to 1995, and the Convention of Scottish Local Authorities. The unilateral commissioning by the Scottish Office of a study by Coopers & Lybrand and Pieda (1997) compounded matters; the context within which the study was commissioned and conducted allowed its findings to be dismissed as politically motivated.[25]

Third, Scottish local government now seems to have been more damaged than previously realised. The 1996 reorganisation was widely condemned as an abuse of central government power,[26] though a consensus-minded Secretary of State for Scotland would have been able to take advantage of the widely held view that devolution would be accompanied by a switch to single-tier local authorities. There seems to have been a strong reluctance among the devolutionist majority to criticise local authorities when they were under explicit attack from the abrasive and media-astute Michael Forsyth (Secretary of State for Scotland, 1995-97). Paradoxically, the change of government put Scottish local authorities into the political spotlight: an attack on alleged local authority sleaze and incompetence is a proxy attack on the Labour Secretary of State. Moreover, local authority accountability has been diminished by intensified central government controls, and their legitimacy has been undermined by the distorting effects of the first-past-the-post voting system in a four-party context. Notwithstanding institutional differences, many of the concerns articulated by Emmerson and Hall (1998) extend to Scotland. An effective agenda for revitalising Scottish local government would have to address both the electoral system (a move to proportional representation in local government seems an inevitable consequence of its adoption for the Scottish Parliament) and the financial system (where the key issue is not the proportion of local authority expenditure financed by grant, but rather the ability of local authorities to take decisions on expenditure levels).

The toughness of the questions now being asked of UK local authorities confirms that they were treated gently by the Lords' Select Committee on Relations between Central and Local Government (1996).[27] In the case of Scottish local authorities, the issues are rendered more urgent by the integral links between the finances of the Scottish Parliament and those of local authorities. Aggregate External Finance (AEF)[28] represents in 1998-99 approximately 38 per cent of the Scottish block; a further 4 per cent is accounted for by local authority capital expenditure. Indeed, when health expenditure (33 per cent) is added, the combined proportion of the Scottish block for local government and health is 75 per cent (Scottish Office, 1998, p.15). Moreover, AEF per head of population in 1998-99 is 35 per cent higher in Scotland than in England. A consequence is that the formula consequences (that is, 10.66 per cent) of increases in AEF in England inevitably produce a lower percentage increase in AEF in Scotland, thereby necessitating either a higher rate of council tax increase or a lower rate of expenditure growth. Moreover, there is a warning in the Scotland Devolution White Paper (Scottish Office, 1997a) that an "excessive growth" in Local Authority Self-Financed Expenditure (LASFE) in Scotland relative to England might be scored against the assigned budget.[29] The public expenditure target of successive UK governments has been some variant of General Government Expenditure (GGE), which scores total local government expenditure and not just the part supported by central government.

4.5 The challenge ahead

The overwhelming impression is that there has been a sudden releasing of constraints and that, on a wide range of constitutional and fiscal issues, there is a remarkably open agenda. On some key issues, there is latent consensus across a broad political spectrum and considerable harmony between academic and practitioner perspectives. This should not be obscured by the inevitably raucous noise of party competition. Five issues will be briefly reviewed in this concluding section.

First, the institutions of governance need to be relegitimated. Notwithstanding opposing assessments of the substantive direction of the Conservative Government's local government reorganisation, there is widespread concern about the damaged fabric of local democracy. Equally, necessary repairs to that fabric must address both the financial system (81.8 per cent of local authorities in England and Wales budgeted in 1997-98 within 0.1 per cent of their provisional capping limit) (Emmerson and Hall, 1998) and the electoral system (the distorting effects of first-past-the-post were magnified by the cumulative impact on Conservative local government representation of four successive general election victories). In Scotland, key sections of the media have switched their campaigning from quangos (which had been characterised as full of Conservative Party ciphers) to Labour-controlled local authorities (from whose cupboards skeletons have alarmingly tumbled). The election on the basis of proportional representation of devolved bodies in all three territories, each with financial responsibility for local government, creates opportunities for wide-ranging reform.

Second, much more transparency about territorial fiscal matters is now inevitable. Indeed, that inevitability adds pragmatic backing to the principled argument for transparency; if documents will, in any case, be selectively leaked or spun, it is advisable to place the information in the public domain in an orderly and comprehensible manner. This will require cultural change within the territorial departments, which have tended to justify their monopoly of key fiscal data on the basis that secrecy allowed them to protect territorial interests by stealth. Whether or not this was a genuine or merely self-justifying argument, there will be much greater transparency to both those within, and those external to, the territories. Territorial civil servants and public managers will in future be caught up in a public glare which they have so far in large part avoided. This will often be uncomfortable and sometimes unedifying; however, remedying the democratic deficit must bring greater exposure for holders of such posts to "locally elected" politicians.[30]

Third, it is the "newness" of the institutions which creates a fleeting window of opportunity before the new political system beds down. Whatever their democratic rhetoric, or what they said in opposition, politicians in government view the control of information flows as a key source of power, maximising their areas of policy discretion. Number generation is not a neutral business; not least, it allows those in office to ridicule the expenditure and tax proposals of others. Although there are complex technical matters for which specialist knowledge is required, the key features can usually be explained in accessible language. Accordingly it is immensely important that the initial budgetary documents presented to the newly elected territorial bodies take advantage of the current enthusiasm for transparency to establish the precedent of openness, clarity and accessibility. Significant gains sometimes come because of timing and individual initiative; for example, Russell Hillhouse, then Principal Finance Officer at the Scottish Office, published the first Commentary on the Scotland Programme (Scottish Office, 1983) when there was doubt about whether the Committee on Scottish Affairs would hold a public expenditure hearing with the Secretary of State for Scotland. In time, this innovation was copied in Northern Ireland and Wales, and was a precursor of departmental reports (which have been published for all UK departments since 1991).[31]

Fourth, though this is a matter which requires more extensive discussion elsewhere, the working assumption behind the design of financial procedures for devolved bodies should be to maximise the delegation of in-year financial discretion to the devolved Executives in return for effective participation in the process of priority formation and prompt disclosure of relevant financial information in a coherent form. Such arrangements are essential because the assigned budgets must be effectively managed in aggregate and because they feed a vast array of public, quasi-public and private organisations whose own planning and budgeting will affect Value-for-Money.

Fifth, there are several new Treasury initiatives which will affect the territorial fiscal system. For example, the operation of the Barnett formula will certainly be affected by the introduction of Resource Budgeting, under which there will be two aggregates: the resource budget (accruals) and the total financing requirement (cash). Moreover, the introduction of three-year expenditure planning within the new fiscal framework (Treasury, 1998b,c,d) is likely to have (predictable and unexpected) effects on the dynamic properties of the formula.[32] It will be essential to voice the fundamental proposition that the extent of fiscal equalisation must be decoupled from the choice of system of government within the United Kingdom (Quigley, 1996). Having established that principle, the devolved Executives will have to develop sufficient technical expertise to sustain their cases in arguments with the Treasury, especially in the absence of buffer institutions such as a Territorial Exchequer Board.[33]

Notes

1. Moreover, the Conservative Government would "reaffirm that they will uphold the democratic wish of a greater number of people of Northern Ireland on the issue of whether they prefer to support the Union or a sovereign United Ireland" (Northern Ireland Office, 1995, p.27). This contrasted markedly with the attitude taken towards the proposals for devolution developed by the Scottish Constitutional Convention (1990, 1995) and the Scottish National Party's plans for independence.
2. Indeed, the Government has made a virtue out of necessity, convening the broad-based Consultative Steering Group (CSG) chaired by Henry McLeish, Minister of State at the Scottish Office. The Financial Issues Advisory Group (FIAG) is one of the sub-groups reporting to CSG.
3. On 15 April 1998, the *Scottish Mirror* ran a front-page story, "You want £2bn from Scotland? Get Lost! Fury over cash demand from man who would be Mayor of London" (Fletcher, 1998), supported by an inside article and an abrasive editorial ("Ignore the rantings of one silly man"). The main edition of the *Daily Mirror* ignored the story.
4. Those papers set out why, notwithstanding the comparatively small revenue yield of the "tartan tax", it was extremely important that the commitment to devolved taxes held firm.
5. It should be recognised that, for many of the key policy propositions derived from the fiscal federalism tradition within public economics, there are counter propositions derived in the public choice literature (Jha, 1998, p.464).
6. Notwithstanding such theoretical arguments, the empirical evidence is mixed. Anderson and van den Berg (1998, pp.183-84) concluded that "our results offer no evidence of a link between fiscal centralization and government size, within the forty-five countries covered in our world sample".
7. Heald et al (1998) explicitly rejected this view. It is important to recognise that there can be two variants of this argument. In the first, the United Kingdom keeps control of tax rates, so that the Scottish Parliament would have to adjust its expenditure downwards in order to balance its budget. In the second, control of all tax rates would also be devolved, meaning that there would be a trade-off between expenditure reductions and Scottish tax increases.
8. Goodhart and Smith's (1993, p.443) closing of their retrospective on the MacDougall Report is worth quoting: "it is arguable that [it] provided all the necessary and appropriate analysis on Community stabilization issues. The fact that the Report has been pigeon-holed, with none of its recommendations implemented, is not a commentary on its economic analysis, but perhaps, on two failures. The first was a failure to distinguish sufficiently between stabilization and redistributive measures, and the second, crucial, failure was its inability to address the political, and also some of the economic, problems that any such redistributive transfers would involve".
9. This motivation is at its most blatant in the Treasury's (1997a) analysis of UK public finances during the last economic cycle.
10. Although it is not fashionable to have public doubts about the desirability of transparency, it is clear that attitudes in practice are ambivalent. There seems to be a presumption in some Finance Ministries, most notably in the New Zealand Treasury, that greater transparency will lead to lower spending. Moreover, it is difficult to take

the UK Treasury's new-found enthusiasm for transparency at face value when there is so much pressure to use the Private Finance Initiative as a vehicle for off-balance sheet finance. Furthermore, the effect, so far, of the Comprehensive Spending Review has been to bring even more obscurity to public expenditure numbers (Heald, 1995, 1998).

11. However, there is a marked asymmetry in that territorial allocation is hugely important for the territorial departments but much less important for the Treasury, as even the three territorial blocks constitute a relatively small part of total public expenditure. Indeed, Barnett's (1982) autobiographical account of his work at the Treasury does not mention the Barnett formula.

12. Of course, these three factors are not necessarily mutually exclusive; for example, it might be that territorial political muscle and classical incrementalism were factors working against attempts to reduce expenditure relativities, whether or not the expenditure differentials had justifications in differential needs.

13. How particular commentators interpret these events depends crucially upon their substantive policy preferences. Whereas Midwinter (1997) viewed them as evidence of a more effective defence of public services in Scotland, Neil (1997b) considered them as yet more evidence of the "out-of-date collectivist consensus" which he believes inflicts severe damage upon Scotland.

14. McLean (1997, p.80) remarked: "the Forsyth plan is to warn the Scottish electorate that, once these numbers become generally known, they will be unsustainable. By bringing them into the open, devolution will bring Scotland's favourable treatment to an end (Note the Forsyth plan depends on the English not reading what he writes for Scottish eyes)". This assumption that the Secretary of State did not intend others to read his words is a serious misinterpretation of events.

15. Questioning Lord Barnett at the Treasury Committee evidence session on 17 November 1997, Brian Sedgemore (Labour MP for Hackney South and Shoreditch) asked: "whether you think I would be correct in thinking that, as applied to the current situation, this means that the Government is in fact ruled by a Scottish hegemony that English Cabinet ministers cannot smash, and that is replicated in the Treasury because the Chancellor, the Chief Secretary to the Treasury and the Economic Secretary to the Treasury are all Scottish MPs. Does that not sum it up? Is that not why this is something that is going to be pushed into the long grass?" (Sedgemore, 1997, Q.7).

16. Briefly, the formula provided that increases in public expenditure in Scotland and in Wales for specific services within the territorial blocks would be determined according to the formula consequences of changes in equivalent expenditure in England. Initially, Scotland received 10/85ths and Wales 5/85ths of the change in England. A parallel formula allocated 2.75 per cent of the change in equivalent expenditure in Great Britain to Northern Ireland. The essential distinction is between base expenditure (whose current levels are carried forward) and incremental expenditure (which is determined by the formula). Under this arrangement, block expenditure relatives would in the long run converge on the UK per capita average. However, the intention was to seek a better alignment of expenditure and needs relatives, not full convergence (Mackay, 1996). In practice, convergence has been substantially frustrated by formula bypass, and in Scotland by relative population decline. In 1992, the formula was recalibrated (10.66:6.02:100.00 and Northern Ireland 2.87 per cent) in recognition of the results of the 1991 population census.

17. A comment in *The Herald* (Dinwoodie, 1998) about the previous day's lead story (MacMahon et al, 1998) and editorial in *The Scotsman* (1998) illustrates the general point well: "[Mr Dewar] hated this week's headlines about big spending to come, not just because *the figures were essentially manufactured* but because as a lawyer he realised that in months to come they would be taken down and used in evidence against him" (Dinwoodie, 1998, emphasis added). It is a matter of guesswork whether this particular instance of manufacturing was done by Scottish Office spin doctors or journalists.

18. Heald (1990) set out the advantages of using a broad-brush formula such as Barnett, in the traditions of the Goschen formula (announced in 1888 and of which use was still made in the late 1950s). There are powerful arguments against drawing the territories into a UK-wide annual needs assessment exercise such as that used for the distribution of RSG in England. In the territorial context, needs assessments should be periodic, and then used to inform the calibration of the territorial formula for the next period.

19. The effects of annual upratings of population are likely to be minimal, as these will effect only the increment. The significance of Scotland's relative population decline is that it offsets the convergent properties of the Barnett formula: it is always actual population in that year which is used as the denominator in calculations of per capita expenditure. Apart from the danger of being seen to politicise the mid-year population estimates, this change will heighten the political sensitivity of relative population trends.

20. It seems unlikely that systematic information about the past operation of the Barnett formula will ever become available. Replying to questions about English equivalent expenditure to Scottish and Welsh block expenditure, Treasury witnesses made the following observations: "We do not have the information collected anywhere. If you are asking for figures going back for 20 years, it would be quite a major exercise" (Gieve, 1997); and "We can do it [current figures] but it is not a trivial exercise, and if you are talking about a note next week, the answer is no. If you are talking about something maybe in a month or two, yes" (Ritchie, 1997). The Treasury (1998a) provided data which make possible the calculation of the following per capita figures in 1995-96 for English equivalent expenditure in relation to each of the territorial blocks: Scotland 132 (England = 100); Wales 125 (England = 100); and Northern Ireland 132 (England = 100). However, the indexes cannot be compared across the territories because the compositions of the blocks differ. At this level of aggregation, the new numbers are not particularly helpful.

21. There is another danger, illustrated by debates over Economic and Monetary Union: the less secure is economic knowledge, the more strident are pronouncements.

22. The data on identifiable expenditure should always be read with awareness about the impact of non-identified expenditure on services such as defence. Debates about the territorial pattern of defence expenditure are a telling reminder that political concerns are as often about inputs (hence employment effects) as about outputs. When the focus is upon both expenditure and revenue, tax expenditures (for example, on owner-occupied housing) cancel out because regional revenue is correspondingly depressed. Historically, North Sea oil revenues (which are attributed to the UK Continental Shelf which is part of the United Kingdom but not part of any region) have been large. The Scottish National Party's argument that Scotland subsidised the United Kingdom by £28 billion during the years 1978-79 to 1994-95 is discussed in

Heald et al (1998). Whatever view is taken about the past, oil revenues have much less significance for the future. Some of the income tax figures are puzzling, possibly reflecting issues of sample size and methodological changes. The present authors believe that recent Scottish Office work provides a reasonably robust picture of Scotland's public finances. In 1995-96, the General Government Borrowing Requirement in Scotland is estimated as 12.5 per cent of GDP, compared with 5.25 per cent for the United Kingdom (Scottish Office, 1997b).

23. On the former, the financial incentives for the Northern Ireland Government to follow GB policy acquired overwhelming importance. On the latter, Gibson (1996, p.45) posed a series of questions: "A critical question which seems to have gone unanswered was the effect parity of services, especially cash social services, would have on the functioning of the regional labour market, where average earnings were substantially lower and per capita income barely 70 per cent of that of the UK...Might the pursuit of parity, through the provision of better public services and by effectively putting a floor to wages, inhibit certain forms of economic development, accentuate some types of unemployment and affect migration? And might it also lead to the concentration of unemployment amongst the unskilled and relatively deprived members of society? With many of these to be found in the Nationalist community might it exacerbate social divisions?" However, parity of cash benefits with Great Britain acquired a symbolic importance as a sign of membership of the United Kingdom. Like many other public expenditure issues in Northern Ireland, it would have been interpreted in terms of which community was most affected. Moreover, a breach of parity in cash benefits in the case of Northern Ireland would have been predicted by low-income GB regions to have repercussions for themselves.

24. "...of especial importance to Northern Ireland is the soft budget constraint and the costs of violence; security costs, compensation for destruction of property, loss of business, human injury and loss of life...who bears security and related costs may be highly significant for how a society responds to violence" (Gibson, 1996, p.81). The costs of the conflict in Northern Ireland were extremely unevenly spread over the population; those unaffected had no fiscal incentive to take these costs into account, either in their voting behaviour or in their decisions about whether to participate in the political process.

25. There had been discussion about the possibility of a study being jointly commissioned by the Scottish Office and the Convention of Scottish Local Authorities (COSLA). Consequently, the unilateral issuing of tender documents by the Scottish Office was viewed by COSLA as a hostile move. The terms of reference bizarrely "expressly prohibited the appointed consultants from involving local authorities or local authority associations in England and Wales or to collect information from them" (Coopers & Lybrand and Pieda, 1997, Appendix 1). Inevitably, these circumstances made likely a hostile reception for the report when it was published in February 1997 on the eve of the general election. Following the change of government in May 1997, the second phase of the study, which had been recommended by the contractors, was cancelled. Nevertheless, the expenditure differentials calculated in the study have been widely quoted.

26. Midwinter (1993, p.53) described Scottish Office policy, including the local government review, as "narrowly partisan and lacking in adequate diagnosis and understanding of the current system".

27. These circumstances have left local authorities ill-prepared for the aggressiveness of the attacks which are now being made on their role. The journalist, Andrew Neil, consistently returns to his theme: "A revolution in Scottish local government - whose general efficiency is currently on a par with a steel mill in Stalinist Russia - would be a crusade worth launching. However, the Government has no stomach since it is unwilling to upset its friends on the Labour-controlled Convention of Scottish Local Authorities, a cosy cartel which represents the interests of the complacent, comatose and the corrupt" (Neil, 1998). The fact that such extravagant language is not matched by evidence is not necessarily the point; the Major administration was mercilessly and unfairly caricatured as "sleaze-ridden".

28. AEF is defined as the "envelope of external support for local authorities which are also funded from the council tax. It comprises Revenue Support Grant, payments from the yield of non-domestic rates, and certain specific grants" (Scottish Office, 1998).

29. "Should self-financed expenditure start to rise steeply, the Scottish Parliament would clearly come under pressure from council tax payers in Scotland to exercise its [capping] powers. If growth relative to England were excessive and were such as to threaten targets set for public expenditure as part of the management of the UK economy, and the Scottish Parliament nevertheless chose not to exercise its powers, it would be open to the UK Government to take the excess into account in considering the level of their support for expenditure in Scotland" (Scottish Office, 1997a, para.7.24). There is no guidance on what would constitute "excessive" growth.

30. On technical financial issues, Committees of the devolved bodies should, when appropriate, take evidence from officials separately from ministers; ministers give political answers and their presence often inhibits officials' efforts to explain the technical issues.

31. Some of the possibilities for technical improvements to improve clarity are obvious: a better alignment of PES and Estimates coverage; transparent treatment of European Union funds; clearer exploration of External Financing Limit controls; and transparent accounting for Private Finance Initiative assets.

32. An excellent example of how changes in the public expenditure control system can affect the results of formula operation can be found in the conversion from volume planning to cash planning in 1982-83 (Heald, 1994, p.163). This change reinforced the convergence effect.

33. An obvious issue is that LASFE in the territories, and expenditure financed by the "tartan tax", will be included within the Treasury's new category of "Annually Managed Expenditure", separated from the Departmental Expenditure Limit (now labelled "Scottish Office" but presumably soon to be relabelled "Assigned Budget") (Treasury, 1998c, pp.30-31).

5 Tax varying powers: the watchdog that will not bark

TONY JACKSON

5.1 Introduction

In some respects, the decision to provide a Scottish Parliament with tax varying powers could be viewed as a decisive acknowledgement of the current Labour administration's commitment to genuine devolution, involving real decision-making authority. The Scottish Council Development and Industry (SCDI, 1997), in a review undertaken before the publication of either the administration's White Paper (Scottish Office, 1997a) or its Bill (Scotland Bill, 1997-98) on the Scottish Parliament, commented that supporters of this tax varying capacity believed parliamentary legitimacy "would only come with a tax varying power" (p.11). At the same time, the Scottish Council also observed that those critical of proposals for a Scottish Parliament believed the possibility of Scotland's economy becoming an uncompetitive business location compared to other parts of the United Kingdom "specifically caused by the proposed power to vary the income tax rate by up to 3p in the pound" (p.3) was the main disadvantage.

In the subsequent debate on the White Paper, the Scottish Secretary argued that this aspect of the government's proposals gave the Scottish Parliament trust and accountability since

> it asks the Scottish Parliament to face real financial choices and makes it, in a sense, more directly accountable to the people it represents. The important point is that we are trusting the people of Scotland to make choices on their own behalf. After all, Scots elected to the UK Parliament and to local government are trusted in that way and the new Parliament should be as well (House of Commons Debates, 31 July 1997, c.465).

A similar estimate of the importance of tax varying powers had already been provided by Donald Dewar's Conservative predecessor, Michael Forsyth, when commenting on the Scottish Constitutional Convention's proposals (SCC, 1995) which first set out the formula eventually adopted. On 30 November 1995 - St. Andrew's Day - the then Scottish Secretary in giving the third Richard Stewart Memorial Lecture, characterised this element as a "tartan tax", an epithet which stuck over the subsequent campaign.

This chapter will argue, despite such a background, that when viewed in the light of the actual powers being proposed, much of the debate on this aspect of Scottish devolution has been misconceived. Far from offering the thin end of the wedge for full independence and for an uncompetitive Scottish business sector, as critics argue, or providing a macroeconomic boost to the Scottish economy, as well as helping to establish a mature and accountable parliament, as supporters claim, in its present form the proposals for tax varying powers amount to little more than political tokenism. Moreover, this tokenism has effectively distracted attention from other aspects of the arrangements for devolution which are much more critical to the political and economic welfare of Scotland in the foreseeable future.

Because the exercise of these powers will remain tightly under UK Treasury control, leaving a Scottish Parliament executive only an emasculated role in fiscal management, which will be confined almost wholly to incremental elements of Scottish expenditure, the proposals for tax-varying powers are likely to become a watch dog that will not bark. Many of the real future battles to determine the scale and pattern of Scottish expenditure and its financing will leave this animal quiescent, and lull the Scottish electorate and taxpayers into a false sense of security that their interests are being safeguarded by a mechanism which will be largely irrelevant to the management of the Scottish economy.

5.2   The proposals

The Scottish Secretary, presenting the White Paper to the House of Commons, stated that the proposals gave a Scottish Parliament the right to

> approve spending decisions that are fully in accordance with Scottish needs and priorities. As an integral part of these financial arrangements, the control of local government expenditure, non-domestic rates and other local taxation will also be devolved to the Scottish Parliament, with appropriate safeguards to protect all UK taxpayers. The Government's objective is to ensure that Scotland's spending decisions are taken in Scotland, in the light of Scottish circumstances (House of Commons Debates, 24 July 1997, c.1044).

Chapters 4 and 7 respectively consider the impact on Scottish public expenditure and Scottish local government of these proposals for devolution, and test whether they match up to the objective of ensuring that spending decisions are taken in Scotland, in the light of Scottish circumstances. In this chapter, the validity of the Government's avowed objective is tested against its proposals for tax varying powers.

The relevant clauses for tax varying powers in the Scotland Bill 1997-98 are clauses 69 to 75 and clause 98. These permit the Scottish Parliament to pass a "tax varying resolution". Any such resolution must be proposed by the Scottish executive and cannot vary the basic rate of income tax by more than 3p in the pound. Savings and dividend income are exempted from any supplementary levy (these are at present taxed at 20 per cent and 40 per cent, so conveniently do not get taxed at the basic rate). Those liable to such a levy will be taxpayers normally resident in the United Kingdom for whom Scotland is the location with which they have closest connection, generally determined by a person's principal place of residence. Clause 71(2)(c) extends this definition to cover members of the Scottish Parliament and those representing Scottish constituencies at the UK and European Parliaments.

The power is reserved to the UK Treasury to propose amendments to the Scottish Parliament's tax varying capacity in the event of any reshaping of the UK tax system which would result in a tax take out-of-line with what such powers would presently generate in the way of real gross income for Scotland (currently estimated at around £450 million for a levy of 3p on the standard rate of income tax). Proceeds from any supplementary tax levy of this nature would be placed in the Scottish Consolidated Fund, net of costs of collection incurred by the Inland Revenue. Equally, losses incurred in revenue from a reduction in basic rate for Scottish taxpayers would be taken from the Scottish Consolidated Fund to make up the shortfall to the Inland Revenue. Finally, any consequent expenses incurred by the UK social security system in meeting claims to beneficiaries for means tested and income-based allowances arising from variations in rates of taxation between Scotland and the rest of the UK would similarly be met from the Scottish Consolidated Fund.

On careful inspection, what are termed tax varying powers amount to a tightly circumscribed authority for an elected Scottish parliament to vary its expenditure on Scottish services by a maximum sum of £450 million in each direction, net of the costs incurred by the UK tax and benefits systems in doing this. The 1998-99 Scottish Office budget amounts to £14.6 billion, so this power amounts at most to the capacity to vary 3 per cent of current Scottish Office public expenditure. The Scottish Office has published official estimates of government expenditure and revenue in Scotland for 1995-96 (Scottish Office, 1997b). These indicate that general government expenditure in Scotland in 1995-96 amounted to £30.9 billion. The use of these powers would, on this measure, amount to the capacity to vary overall government expenditure in Scotland by 1.5 per cent.

The scale of this power is enshrined within the Bill, which gives the UK Treasury the responsibility for placing before the UK Parliament such amendments to ensure that in real terms (taking account of inflation) an equivalent sum will be available to the Scottish Parliament in 2000-2001, when it is first convened. Clause 72(5) states that in exercising this right the potential impact on taxpayers cannot be significantly different to that of earlier years.

The Scotsman, in an editorial (13 December 1997), observed that a reading of this part of the Bill revealed far less than the devolution of tax varying powers to a Scottish Parliament since

> It transpires that the Treasury is to retain control over the tax-levying powers of the Scottish Parliament...more power is to be reserved at Westminster, and greater restraints placed on Edinburgh, than we were led to believe.

Moreover, a Scottish Parliament cannot exercise any right to undertake significant budgetary demand management of the Scottish economy through the use of these powers. Any reductions in tax for basic rate Scottish income tax payers will immediate result in a loss of spending power, with the Inland Revenue being compensated for the loss of tax take through reductions in the Scottish Consolidated Fund. In other words, attempts to reduce the tax burden on Scottish income tax payers (a realistic possibility if the political complexion of the Scottish Parliament differed from that in Westminster) could only be realised by foregoing expenditure on Scottish services. In response to a House of Lords debate on this question, Lord Sewel on behalf of the Government stated

> Clearly, if you reduce taxation, you have to pay for it...Reductions in expenditure must be made...If the parliament decided to increase tax, the Inland Revenue would collect the extra tax, which would be paid over to the Scottish Parliament by the UK Government. If the parliament decreased tax, then the Inland Revenue's overall tax take would be reduced. To reflect that, the overall level of resources passed to the Scottish Parliament by way of block grant would be reduced accordingly (House of Lords Debates, 1 July 1997, c.150).

Equally, any resolution from a Scottish executive to levy taxes would not be considered kindly by the UK government if it did not relate to specific expenditure proposals, but merely resulted in a budgetary surplus or an additional subsidy to Scottish local taxpayers. In the words of the Scottish Secretary in the House of Commons debate on the White Paper,

> It is important to recognise that the power may be used to deal with some special project or difficulty. I do not expect that it would simply be added to the block-and-grant formula sum that is negotiated as a continuously available additional revenue support. I believe that that would constitute a misuse of the power (House of Commons Debates, 31 July 1997, c.465).

This relegates the tax varying powers of the Scotland Bill to an instrument largely confined to minor incremental variations in the level of expenditure on Scottish public services. The variation in public expenditure permitted would be equivalent to the discretion currently allowed Scottish local authorities, as Table 5.1 illustrates. This provides a comparison for both Scotland and England and Wales of recent excesses in aggregate local authority budgeted expenditure over central government needs assessment levels, on which the block grants are based. In this context, it should be noted that the current take of council tax levied by Scottish local authorities amounts to £1.3 billion, three times the maximum permitted to the Scottish Parliament.

Table 5.1   Comparison of local authority budgets and government needs assessments

Year	England and Wales % excess	Scotland % excess
1990-91	9.6	5.4
1991-92	0.3	2.5
1992-93	0.9	1.2
1993-94	2.5	2.2

Source: Midwinter and McGarvey, 1995, p.18

Table 5.2 is derived from work commissioned by the Scottish Office to compare expenditure on local public services in Scotland with England and Wales. This confirmed that for all but police services, Scottish expenditure on local public services was running above levels south of the border, on average by 23 per cent in 1994-95. A gross yield of £450 million in tax from a 3p in the pound increase in the basic rate of income tax would permit just under £88 additional spending per head. If such a sum were devoted purely to local public services, it would provide 4.6 per cent of the amount spent on these in Scotland in 1994-95. So tax varying powers devolved to a Scottish Parliament could not realistically be expected to compensate for any attempt by the UK Treasury to reduce the gap in spending on these services between Scotland and England through revisions of the block grant formula for the UK annual public expenditure settlement.

Table 5.2   **Expenditure per head on local public services in Scotland and England, 1994-95**

Services	Expenditure per head, 1994-5 (£) Scotland	Expenditure per head, 1994-5 (£) England	% difference in expenditure per head, Scotland - England
Education	427.5	347.2	+23.1
Social work	191.9	164.9	+16.4
Roads/transport	102.3	71.8	+42.5
Environmental services	61.8	44.4	+39.2
Leisure/recreation	54.9	29.6	+85.5
Libraries/museums	23.2	17.3	+34.1
Planning/economic development	35.7	20.2	+76.1
Police	122.9	124.4	-1.2
Fire/civil defence	31.4	27.2	+15.4
Health	860.0	706.0	+21.8
OVERALL	1,911.6	1,553.0	+23.1

Source: Coopers and Lybrand/Peida, 1997

Apart from variations in public expenditure levels around the margin of what has been determined by the general formula governing the UK allocation, the only element of fiscal demand management potentially left open to a Scottish Parliament through the exercise of its tax varying powers is the limited instrument of a balanced budget multiplier, which is considered in more detail below.

5.3   Broader fiscal implications of tax varying powers for a devolved Parliament

The basic principles governing the arguments for the granting of a tax varying capacity to a devolved assembly were well-rehearsed by the Royal Commission on the Constitution (Kilbrandon, 1973), otherwise known as the Kilbrandon Report. This paved the way for an earlier Labour administration attempt to establish devolved assemblies in Scotland and Wales, which subsequently failed, bringing down the government in the process. Kilbrandon identified two alternative principles on which devolved finance might be based: the revenue or the expenditure basis.

Were devolution fully to follow federal principles, Kilbrandon argued that the revenue basis would be more appropriate. This would entail devolving to a sub-national assembly certain sources of revenue, from which devolved services would have to be funded. It would be up to the devolved assembly to manage its affairs so as to establish the level of taxation required to fund the desired level of expenditure. Under such an approach there would be no guarantee that the level of taxation, the level of expenditure or the level of service provision for these devolved services within Scottish boundaries would match the rest of the UK. Clearly, such an approach, although perfectly logical, would make little sense unless devolution of powers were to be applied throughout each part of the United Kingdom, which neither the earlier nor the current proposals have contemplated.

By contrast, devolution of services on an expenditure basis would entail pre-determination of the needs of the area served by the assembly, applying national criteria of service provision. Expenditure provision would be made available so as to maintain one of the basic precepts of a unitary state, that each person, no matter where resident in the UK, should as far as possible have equal access to a similar level of provision. On this basis, Kilbrandon argued, it was sufficient simply to allocate a devolved assembly funds through a nationally negotiated annual settlement to enable the assembly to fund devolved services on an equal footing. No requirement for tax varying powers need be met. Given an expenditure based approach to devolution, the devolved assembly could determine different priorities in the mix of public expenditure allocated to it and in the share financed by council tax and business rates, but not variations in its overall capacity to fund or to provide public services.

The expenditure basis was chosen as the means of financing devolution by the Callaghan administration, with the arguments set out in a White Paper (HMSO, 1977b). At the same time, the method which had been used by the UK Treasury with minor variations since the time of Goschen for allocating the pre-determined level of public expenditure provision between the territories of the United Kingdom was up-dated and re-named the Barnett formula, after the Treasury Minister charged with establishing an appropriate system for funding Scottish and Welsh needs after devolution, as was explained in more detail in chapter 4.

In essence, this still remains the basis for the proposals to fund both Welsh and Scottish devolved services, albeit with the provision of additional marginal capacity for the Scottish Parliament to vary expenditure through limited supplementary powers of taxation. In a newspaper article the Minister for home affairs and devolution in the

Scottish Office, Henry McLeish, stated the case in explicit terms, grounded in an assertion of the unitary concept of government provision:

> In your editorial of 9 December, you...said "simplicity and justice suggest...that parliament raise its own revenues". This repeats the notion...that retention of Scottish taxes would be a preferable option to retaining the Barnett formula for determining the finances of the Scottish parliament. But I believe that supporting an assigned revenue system would still result in some form of block grant being required and with a greater need for negotiations. The current system results in Scotland receiving more expenditure from central Government than it contributes in terms of revenue. This is based on the sound principle that Government expenditure in the UK should not be based on where taxes are raised, but rather on where the demand for service requirements lies...If Scotland were to be assigned its revenues then, after paying its fair share for centrally-run services like defence and overseas aid, it would have insufficient funds left to provide its own services at a similar level to the rest of the UK. In this case, either the Scottish parliament would simply have to accept cuts in funding...or a top-up grant would need to be negotiated with Westminster (*The Scotsman,* 12 December 1997).

The Minister's comments suggest the UK Treasury view of the purposes and scope of devolution prevails as much now as it did in the earlier attempt to pass a Bill for a Scottish assembly twenty years ago. Given the acceptance of a philosophy of unitary government, it follows that spatial differences in levels of service provision should be limited to the minimal necessary to assuage marginal political differences in priorities that might arise between an elected UK and an elected Scottish Parliament. The real power to determine the funding for public service provision in Scotland will remain with the Treasury, both in terms of its control over the scale of these tax varying powers and, much more importantly, through its influence in the determination at Cabinet level of revisions to the Barnett formula for calculating the appropriate level of expenditure needed by Scotland to provide service provision comparable with the rest of the UK.

This places the tax varying powers of a Scottish Parliament in an analogous position to local authorities, for which an annual settlement is determined by central government on the basis of various formulae designed to identify non-discretionary spatial differences in need and in the cost of meeting these. The annual settlement is designed to even out such variations, while leaving local government with limited scope for varying provision by setting local property taxes accordingly (Rowett, 1980; Bennett, 1982; Jackson, 1989).

This is certainly not the stuff of fiscal federalism (Tiebout, 1956 and 1961; Musgrave, 1961; Rothenburg, 1970; Oates, 1972 and 1977; Atkinson and Stiglitz, 1980). Tax instruments suitable for fiscal federalism would be designed to promote a spatially optimal distribution of public service provision across a nation by making voters sensitive to the fiscal implications of their choices, and willing to vote with their feet to obtain a desired level of provision. Sub-national assemblies would be sensitive to and constrained by the potentially damaging implications of factor mobility in determining their levels of service provision, without the need for sanctions from a centrally-determined budget.

In contrast, the fiscal instrument needed to deliver an expenditure based form of devolution should have precisely opposite characteristics. It should combine ease of collection and low administrative cost with lump sum characteristics designed to minimise any allocative distortions on the UK tax system. In a recent study, Blow, Hall and Smith (1996) reviewed the options available on this basis before expressing a preference for the proposal advocated by the Scottish Constitutional Convention and subsequently included in the Bill since

> it is least likely to lead to major locational distortions (especially if the regional power to vary tax rates is confined to the basic rate), and because it is more transparent in its burden and incidence than either a regional sales tax or regional business rate would be, and hence might promote accountability (p.60).

Confined as it is to the basic rate, the maximum a Scottish income tax payer could currently face from the full levy with current allowances amounts to £660 per annum. Given the exemption proposed for savings and dividend income, which is much more sensitive to variations in the basic rate of income tax, such a level of taxation on labour incomes is unlikely to produce significant tax-induced migration impacts, particularly since the higher marginal rate of taxation will remain unaffected. As discussed below, some anomalies will still arise, and Scottish pensioners and rentiers receiving such income will remain subject to the possibility of higher basic rates of taxation.

5.4   Criticisms of the tax varying proposals

Criticisms of the tax varying powers proposed for the Scottish Parliament have ranged across a wide spectrum, from fundamental concerns about the economic and political integrity of the United Kingdom, to more detailed examinations of administrative complications. In what follows, it can be seen that many of the more alarmist apprehensions about these powers relate to the prospect of a Scottish Parliament exercising the kind of fiscal federalism that it is now apparent the current proposals could not entertain. It is equally the case that the potential benefits that might conceivably stem from giving a Scottish Parliament fuller revenue raising powers will not be realised by the current proposals.

5.4.1   *Administrative feasibility and the cost of collection*

Aside from the more fundamental considerations rehearsed by the Kilbrandon Report, the impracticality of administering tax varying powers was a clinching factor in leading to rejection of such proposals in the 1977 White Paper (HMSO, 1977b). This argued that the costs of combining a supplementary income tax with PAYE would be prohibitive. Prior to computerisation, the Inland Revenue would have had considerable problems in establishing the residence of any taxpayer, given that it was the location of the employer's payroll office which determined for the majority of income tax payers which office dealt with their affairs, regardless of residence.

The strength of this objection has been lessened by recent changes in the administration of income tax. Computerisation has allowed self-assessment to be introduced for a large proportion of higher income workers, with liability assessed on a current year basis. Nonetheless, even with improved systems, present indications suggest that the additional costs of tax varying powers remain significant. These costs can be divided up into the setting up and administrative costs for the Inland Revenue, and the costs falling to employers through the PAYE system, which will require the use of additional schedules.

The costs to the Inland Revenue of establishing the mechanism for tax variation are currently estimated at around £10 million, with additional collection costs expected to run at some £8 million per annum (Seely, 1998). In addition, the financial memorandum to the Scotland Bill indicates that should a Scottish Parliament decide to exercise its powers to vary the basic rate of income tax, additional costs to the UK social security system would arise through the administration of income-based payments and maintenance arrangements. The extra public expenditure incurred in this respect, estimated to run at up to £5 million per annum, would be added to the Inland Revenue's costs and netted from the proceeds accruing to the Scottish Consolidated Fund, leaving the costs to be borne by the Scottish executive in the form of a lower tax yield. Finally, there could also be costs associated with the provision of public sector pensions, which are provisionally estimated to amount to £4 million, including setting up costs, which would similarly be charged to the Scottish Consolidated Fund. Taken together, these costs falling to the public purse can be annualised at some £15 million per annum, or just over 3 per cent of the estimated maximum yield.

To this should be added the additional costs borne by employers through the PAYE system. The White Paper (Scottish Office, 1997a) puts a figure of £50 million on the setting up costs borne by employers, and a range from £6 million to £15 million in their additional operating costs. The annualised sum to business is thus estimated to be of the same order as that incurred by the public purse. If the public costs are netted off the tax yield, this amounts to an overall administrative cost, ignoring any other tax-related costs borne by the taxpayer, of some 7 per cent of the maximum net tax take. Because most of these costs would remain the same whatever the supplementary levy charged, the costs of administering the proposals could rise to more than 20 per cent for a tax take restricted to 1p in the pound, a not inconsiderable cost (and one which argues in favour of the exercise of the full tax raising powers).

Interestingly, the above estimates are very much in line with those given in the 1977 White Paper. This argued that a supplementary income tax "seems an attractive candidate at first sight because of its high yield and broad coverage" but then went on to rule it out, primarily because such a tax

> would impose a heavy new burden on the PAYE system and would reduce its efficiency as the Government's main revenue collector. Furthermore, because a

marginal tax would be at a low rate, the cost of collection could represent as much as 20% of the yield (HMSO, 1977b, p.6).

5.4.2 *The impact of liability on migration and inward investment*

The proposed tests for liability to a Scottish income tax regime, which will apply to those resident in the United Kingdom for income tax purposes who in any tax year spend at least half the time in Scotland when in the UK, or whose principal home is in Scotland, are unlikely to prove straightforward. A report in *The Scotsman* based on a briefing paper produced by a major firm of accountants suggests the net has been cast wider for these proposals than for previous UK tax legislation (10 February 1998). The simple arithmetic test to determine whether a taxpayer's "closest connection" is with Scotland counts the number of days spent in Scotland, with liability to a Scottish tax regime if the number spent in Scotland equals or exceeds the number spent elsewhere in the UK in the same year.

There are, however, two further aspects of the proposals which may catch a wider number of people than such a test would imply. The first is designed to apply to those who only spend part of the year in the UK, who have a principal home in Scotland which they use as a place of residence, and who spend at least as much time in Scotland as their principal home as time spent elsewhere in the UK. Applying this test, those who spend a quarter of the year in Scotland, a quarter in the rest of the UK, and up to 182 days outwith the UK would render themselves liable for the Scottish income tax regime as long as their main place of residence was Scotland.

The second is the way in which it is proposed to calculate days spent in Scotland. Only days spent wholly outside Scotland would be ignored, whereas any part of the start or end of the day in Scotland would count. Thus, a commuter flying from Scotland to London on Monday for three days' work and returning on Wednesday would be counted for the purposes of calculating liability to these tax varying powers as having spent only one day outside Scotland.

A substantial number of workers commute across the Scottish border, and the experience of North America suggests that anomalies will take time to resolve. Workers on North Sea oil rigs provide an obvious test case in establishing the extent to which those employed in a Scottish offshore location but normally resident outwith Scotland would be exempt from variations in the basic rate of income tax after applying these rules. Other workers commute across the Scottish border on a daily basis, with their place of work and place of residence potentially subject to differing tax regimes, which will complicate the affairs of the self-employed liable to income tax on the profits of unincorporated businesses. Will liability for members of the armed forces be determined by the location of their current posting? Will Scots on overseas postings, who remain normally resident for tax purposes in the UK, be affected? How will the test of closest connection in clause 71(1) be applied in such cases?

Given these points, some concern has been expressed about discouraging young executives from accepting posts in Scotland, faced with the possibility of liability to higher basic income tax rates. However, this concern seems misconceived. The sums involved are minimal, and tiny in comparison to other existing differences affecting net executive remuneration, many of which tend to offset each other. These include house prices, for which Scotland offers a much cheaper regime than the South East of England, and the burden of council tax, which is far higher north of the border for housing priced at the same level. A more general concern in attracting both executives and small and medium sized businesses to Scotland is evidence of the limited scope for career and business development available to rapidly growing companies within Scotland compared to the business environment in the South East (Keeble, Bryson and Wood, 1991; O'Farrell, Hitchens and Moffat, 1992).

Applying the same logic, the belief that variations in basic rates of income tax *per se* might directly influence the rate of emigration from Scotland also appears implausible. Rates of migration of people of working age are most sensitive to differences in rates of unemployment between Scotland and the rest of the UK. During the most recent recession, when Scottish rates of unemployment fell for the first time below the average for Great Britain, Scotland experienced for a period a net gain from migration. As is argued later, any effect tax varying powers may have on migration are more likely to show up through impacts on the Scottish economy and Scottish unemployment rates.

Similarly, there is no evidence to support a belief that tax varying powers of such limited scope would become a key influence on footloose investment decisions and hence on the ability of Scotland to continue to attract foreign inward investment. Over the period 1984 to 1994 the number of overseas-owned manufacturing plants in Scotland rose 4 per cent, with their associated employment rising by 15 per cent. The United States accounts for the largest share, owning 45 per cent of such plants. Overall more than 12 per cent of Scottish manufacturing plants was in overseas ownership in 1994, providing almost 28 per cent of Scottish manufacturing employment, as measured by the Scottish Register of Employment. In 1992, net capital investment by these plants accounted for more than 29 per cent of total manufacturing investment in Scotland (Scottish Office, 1995c).

Hill and Mundy (1992) found that two-thirds of the variation in regional shares of UK inward investment new jobs, and almost four-fifths of variations in shares of new inward investment projects could be explained by financial incentives such as regional assistance and by infrastructure improvements which improved accessibility. Scotland's ability to market itself on the basis of the availability of skilled labour, access to good sites, and the effective delivery of financial incentives will be influenced far more by post-devolution arrangements for regional policy mechanisms, the share Scotland gains of UK public sector expenditure settlements, and the willingness of a Scottish executive to devote funds to this end, than the existence of tightly constrained tax-varying powers. In a review of the impact of devolution on inward investment, Hood (1995) concluded "there is no *prima facie* case for claiming that devolution as currently proposed will have a negative effect on Scotland's position for either inward investment attraction or development" (p.75). The analysis on which Hood based this conclusion was tested on a number of business and public sector leaders in Scotland, who broadly concurred. The largest intangible is the effect devolution will have on confidence in Scotland as a place of investment. In this respect, tax-varying powers appear to operate adversely if at all by raising fears in the minds of investors about the possibility of high taxing, high spending public sector programmes in Scotland out of line with those elsewhere in the country. This is not a feasible option under current proposals, although it may be necessary to deflate expectations held by some who favour such an approach in case this does implant unnecessary uncertainties in the minds of potential investors. As Hood suggests, both foreign direct investors and those from within the UK are much more likely to be sensitive to macroeconomic variables, such as the exchange rate, European Monetary Union and the single currency, and the evolution of regional policy instruments for the UK as a whole relative to the rest of the European Union.

5.4.3   Fiscal autonomy and fiscal federalism

Many of the most vehement critiques of the concept of a "tartan tax" have been founded on the threat to the integrity of the UK as a common economic and monetary union, or the distorting effects variations in national tax rates would create for this union. The strength of these arguments rests on the extent to which the tax varying proposals are based on a desire to provide a Scottish Parliament with a measurable degree of fiscal autonomy through the exercise of revenue raising powers.

The present proposals indicate this is far from being the Government's intention. The Scotland Bill retains within the control of Westminster both the capacity to levy supplementary taxes in Scotland, and the extent to which this can be exercised. Moreover, the Government has clearly indicated that it desires a system of devolved services founded on retention of the principle of similar access to a comparable level of service provision for all its residents, wherever located in the UK. It has indicated that this will be achieved, not through the exercise of tax varying powers, but by a block and formula mechanism agreed by the UK Cabinet for sharing any agreed level of public expenditure equitably across the constituent territorial parts of the union. This will leave the Scottish Parliament with less flexibility in determining public expenditure and service provision than its local authorities (which derive up to 20 per cent of their funding from local taxation) presently enjoy. Few would claim that the degree of fiscal autonomy exercised by local government in the UK is tantamount to fiscal federalism or a threat to the economic and monetary union.

The only cogent case to which the Government has paid heed on these grounds is that put by the Scottish financial sector, worried about the integrity of UK capital markets and the disincentives to Scottish life assurance and fund management companies from any possible variation in income taxed at source on savings interest and dividends. In clause 69(3) the Bill exempts such income from the tax varying powers, on the basis, as the Scottish Secretary explained in the debate on the White Paper, that

> the exemption of savings income is almost de minimis. It does not raise very much, but an alternative arrangement would greatly complicate the system and cause difficulties in relation to the financial services industry (House of Commons Debates, 31 July 1997, c.465).

At a late stage in the debate, a further scare was provided by the wording of the referendum question related to tax varying powers, in which the word "income" was omitted. This was taken by some prominent members of the Scottish business community to imply that the current proposals were indeed the thin edge of the wedge of fiscal federalism. However, examination of the relevant clauses in the Bill leave little doubt that the current proposals are restricted firmly to the very limited tax varying powers provided by a maximum variation of 3p on the basic rate of income tax, or a sum equivalent in real terms to this. Only the UK Treasury may make amendments to this arrangement, and only for the purposes of retaining the capacity of the Scottish Parliament to realise an equivalent sum following any change in the UK tax system which might undermine this. Far from being the thin end of a rapidly thickening wedge, on closer inspection these proposals appear to offer a Scottish Parliament a permanently rigid sliver.

5.4.4 *Adverse impacts on Scottish business*

The other remaining element of investment uncertainty in the face of tax varying powers relates to that undertaken by Scottish business itself. Scotland has been characterised as having a low business birth rate. Research associated with the Scottish Enterprise Business Birth Rate Strategy (Talbot and Reeves, 1997) emphasises the importance of selectivity and targeting of assistance in boosting indigenous enterprise. Nothing in the research commissioned for this strategy or associated with it has indicated that basic rates of income tax are a significant factor in deterring Scottish start-ups.

For existing Scottish businesses, the impact of limited powers to vary income tax can be compared with the much greater powers local authorities still retain to vary business rates through periodic re-evaluations. A number of attempts to test the possibility that spatial variations in business rates, which have traditionally been significantly higher in Scotland than in England and Wales, account for some of the variations in business growth in different parts of the country have failed to identify any evidence to this effect. However, the rates burden is relatively small compared with payroll costs. Higher basic rates of income tax may exert pressure on the profits of Scottish businesses relative to the rest of the country, if Scottish workers seek compensation from employers for lower take-home pay.

The CBI in Scotland has advanced the argument that, in addition to the costs borne by employers through the additional PAYE schedules required, Scottish workers would demand higher pay to compensate them for the increased tax take and that, to the extent such claims succeeded, this would push up Scottish business costs relative to the rest of the UK and reduce both competitiveness and profitability. Based on average male earnings of around £19,000 per annum, a full increase in the basic rate by 3p would amount to approximately £300, or 1.6 per cent of the wage bill. Gibson, Riddington, Whigham and Whyte (1997) indicate that wage costs in Scotland are currently running at a multiple of just over four times gross trading profits of Scottish establishments (p.26). This suggests that if workers succeeded in passing on to employers the full costs of tax varying powers, Scottish businesses might face a squeeze in excess of 6 per cent of trading profits relative to the rest of the UK, assuming price-taking behaviour.

Much hangs on the extent to which any rise in the basic rate of income tax is absorbed by Scottish workers or passed on to Scottish employers. In turn, this rests on analysis of the manner in which Scottish labour markets work to equalise real rather than nominal wages relative to the rest of the UK. The evidence on this (Martin and Tyler, 1994; Lythe and Gilbert, 1996) remains ambiguous. In a review of the impact of the proposed tax varying powers, McGregor, Stevens, Swales and Yin (1997) identify this as one of the key factors in assessing the net aggregate effect of such proposals on the Scottish economy.

Assuming no wage-hike, their model postulates a moderate but positive boost to Scottish aggregate demand through extra spending fully funded from tax-varying powers. This is due to balanced budget multiplier effects. The extent to which this feeds through into Scottish output and employment and reduces out-migration depends on the capacity of the Scottish economy to respond to incremental increases in aggregate demand. McGregor, Stevens, Swales and Yin (1997) argue that, provided Scottish labour markets stick to national bargaining, the supply of both labour and capital will rise through an increase in investment and reduction in out-migration since

> If the Scottish people genuinely wish increased government expenditure in Scotland and, importantly, if they are prepared to pay for this in the form of higher income taxes without seeking compensating changes in their gross wage, then the fiscal innovation of the "tartan tax" may have significant beneficial effects (p.82).

Their model suggests that, in the absence of compensating wage increases, full use of tax raising powers could produce long run gains of 0.45 per cent in Gross Domestic Product and 0.42 per cent in employment, with the unemployment rate falling by 0.72 per cent. On the other hand, including an allowance for rising wage costs changes the picture, as McGregor, Stevens, Swales and Yin (1997) concede

> Overall...the net effect of the "tartan tax" on output and employment is ambiguous...and depends on whether the expansionary demand effect outweighs the contractionary supply effect...Our policy simulations...suggest that if Scottish workers were all to succeed in fully compensating themselves for the loss of take-home pay...then the adverse supply side effect would in fact predominate, and output and employment would contract (p.80).

Under these conditions, the model indicates that Gross Domestic Product would fall by 1.2 per cent in the long run, after all migration and employment effects are complete. Total employment would fall by 1.33 per cent. This would show up as an increase in out-migration, leaving the unemployment rate unaffected.

These results suggest that the net macroeconomic impact on the Scottish economy from the use of these tax varying powers is likely to be negligible, as compared with the impact of changes in the Barnett formula governing the share of public expenditure allocated to a Scottish Parliament. Despite this, any variations in basic tax rates will remain much more visible evidence of the exercise of devolution, than intra-departmental and Cabinet committee debates about block grant formulae.

5.5   Conclusion: accountability or tokenism?

Given the impact initially produced on Scottish public opinion by the use of the label "tartan tax" to describe the tax varying powers of a Scottish Parliament, it might be supposed this would become one of the key elements in the operation of Scottish devolution. The above analysis suggests that such a belief is misplaced, largely because both advocates for this power and critics of it have grossly over-estimated the capacity of this fiscal instrument to permit an elected Scottish executive any exercise of true fiscal autonomy. Current proposals confine the exercise of this power to a 3 per cent variation in the annual settlement of the public expenditure round, offering a Scottish Parliament a degree of manoeuvre well below what is currently available to Scottish local authorities. As commentators on Scottish local government have recently observed:

> The Scottish Parliament is proposed as a means of enhancing democratic accountability, but its fiscal dependence on Westminster and the inevitability of continuing arguments over spending needs will confuse accountability - as shown by the experience of local government in the 1980s (Midwinter and McVicar, 1996, p.19).

The real debate over Scotland's economic future and the real decisions about resource allocation which will determine this will not be fought out through the public exercise of this power, but in the administrative and political corridors used for determining Scotland's share of UK national expenditure. Under these circumstances, tax varying powers, far from being a watch dog the Scottish public can use to gauge the competence and accountability of its elected administration are more than likely to become the lap dog of a political compromise reached in the corridors of Westminster, Whitehall, Leith and Holyrood.

Part III

Economic development

6 Economic development: the Scottish Parliament and the development agencies

MIKE DANSON

6.1 Introduction

Promoting the opportunity to develop the economy more effectively has always been a significant element in the debate over the future governance of Scotland. More specifically, high unemployment, long term net migration, the collapse of the traditional basic industries, and domination by foreign direct investment have all been cited as reasons for seeking increased control within Scotland over the key drivers and levers of the Scottish economy. However, as argued in chapter 2 and elsewhere (McGregor et al, 1997), with an open economy dependent on British, European and world economies, Scotland faces a constrained policy environment. This inevitably limits the ability of the devolved Scottish Parliament to achieve macroeconomic objectives by following traditional policies and mechanisms for delivering such policies.

Moreover, in addition to these strictures, it is clear from the Scotland Bill that the devolved Parliament will be allowed but a limited range of economic powers. Control over fiscal, economic and monetary policy will be reserved at Westminster, as will the regulation of competition, intellectual property, research councils, and many areas of transport, energy, the welfare state, trade and assistance to industry.

Nevertheless, Dow (1997) inter alia has argued that a devolved government will have greater flexibility to intervene than this assessment may suggest. Indeed, in contrast to the balance of the debate preceding the referendum in September 1997, some have claimed that the Parliament's success in economic policy terms will not be measured by the level or financing of Scottish public expenditure but rather by its impact on the rate of economic growth and development in Scotland (Newlands, 1997).

Over the last two decades, the importance of what Doeringer et al (1987) called the "invisible factors in...economic development" has been recognised as the crucial areas for intervention. In this vein, Porter (1990) has argued for the significance of investment and innovation in explaining the promotion of competitiveness and productivity, highlighting "R&D, learning, modern facilities and sophisticated training" as key factors. More generally, "new growth" and "endogenous growth" theories follow the Schumpeterian tradition of stressing the role of competition in creating dynamic change in the economy. Nowadays, the alternative approach which stresses the specific comparative advantages of areas can be reconciled with these growth theories where agglomeration economies built on trust, co-operation and innovation are present.

Similarly, the significant role of an infrastructure conducive to innovation and development has been long associated with the growth pole theories of Perroux (1950). Having fallen out of fashion for policy and research in the 1970s, growth poles have been resurrected in the form of clusters and networking, which are seen as underpinning the successful regional economies of the Third Italy and Baden-Wurttemberg (Danson and Whittam, 1998). Indeed these comparators have been cited by the Secretary of State as the way forward for Scotland (Scottish Office Press Release, February 1998).

Within these competing theories of regional growth, a rationale can be identified for a Scottish Parliament intervening in the economy to establish conditions and institutions to promote economic development. The decline of Keynesian demand management policies and the re-emergence of supply-side concerns has led to an emphasis on the factors which affect costs of production, competitiveness, and the creation and adoption of technologically advanced methods of production (Newlands, 1997). In this context, the Scottish Parliament could have a significant impact on industrial and economic development by introducing and customising policies in such areas as training, technology, venture capital, new firm formation and the ownership of industry. However, as McGregor et al (1997) and Newlands (1997) argue, intervention will not lead to automatic improvements; rather, the need for a policy regime appropriate to the needs of the Scottish economy will be as critical as in the present state.

Any commentaries on the Scottish economy have stressed how, for many years, economic development policy has been determined within Scotland by Scottish institutions (McCrone, 1992, Danson et al, 1990), and a distinctive element in this evolving picture has been the role of the regional development agencies. Within the devolved Scotland of early next century, it will be to these established institutions that the Parliament will look to deliver many of the policy options and strategies outlined above. This chapter is structured as follows. Section 6.2 briefly considers the structure and problems of the Scottish economy that the Parliament will inherit. In sections 6.3 and 6.4, the rationale for development agencies, followed by their functions and performance, are discussed. It is argued that four key principles should guide the deliberations over what institutional forms and configurations could be adopted, namely accountability, subsidiarity, sustainability, and integration/inclusion. Applying these principles, section 6.5 considers how the Scottish regional development agencies might be evaluated. In conclusion, section 6.6 proposes how the development agencies should be reformed to operate more effectively to meet the aspirations of the Scottish people.

6.2   Scotland: on the periphery of Europe

According to the European Commission (Commission of the European Communities, 1991), the Scottish economy is characterised by a low population density, geographical peripherality, underdevelopment of much of the rural economy and the fragility of the few industrial complexes. Furthermore, the consequences of the UK joining the European Community in 1973 are seen as having been deleterious for Scotland, since the country was "weakened by an increasingly ageing industrial base and by the redirection of commercial activities towards Europe at the expense of the Commonwealth" (Commission of the European Communities, 1994, p.42).

An extensive literature demonstrates that, in this restructuring, Scotland has become progressively more dependent on external capital, agencies and forces, and on multinational capital and the EU especially. Compared to some equally peripheral neighbours, the Nordic countries for instance, the relatively subordinated economic and political position of Scotland has been significant in determining the continuing problems of the "development of economic underdevelopment" (Danson, 1991). If an environment of strong inherent growth had been established within the economy, based on successful indigenous capital, then discussions of non-Scottish contexts, limitations and assistance would have been largely redundant. It can be argued that the promise of devolution can be viewed as being as much about redressing this truncation of the potential of local Scottish enterprise as about the better governance of the administrative functions of the Scottish Office; certainly, the former has been an objective and priority of Scottish Enterprise in the 1990s.

Over most of the twentieth century, Scotland has lagged behind the UK as a whole in economic terms. Unemployment has remained higher and incomes and expenditure improved more slowly than in the South. Behind such headlines, the degree of external control and ownership of the industries of Scotland has continued to increase, sometimes through merger and takeover or through nationalisation and privatisation, sometimes through differential rates of decline and growth of native and foreign companies. Research suggests that such changes, in complex ways, put a relative brake on the rates of new firm formation and indigenous development (Ashcroft, Love and Schouller, 1987). Concomitantly, output, trade and investment have become more narrowly dependent on a few key sectors in both countries. In Scotland, electronics (and computers especially) and whisky have accounted for over half of non-oil manufacturing exports, and about 50 per cent of all manufacturing investment in recent years. Both these sectors are dominated by overseas companies, with over 90 per cent of output by non-Scottish firms, and consequently over a quarter of manufacturing employment in Scotland is in overseas owned plants, with much of the rest controlled by UK corporations with their headquarters in the South East.

After the massive restructuring of the 1970s and 1980s, with 40 per cent of all Scottish manufacturing jobs lost since 1980, Scotland could be said to be an export-oriented economy, now relatively protected from UK business cycles, although open to new sensitivities, not least the financial crisis of the Far East, since it is locked into the supply needs of multinational oligopolies in the electronics sector. More specifically, it is clear that Scotland's future depends on European markets - two thirds of Scottish exports go to western Europe (Scottish Council Development and Industry, 1995) - and the attraction of foreign direct investment from North America' and the Pacific Rim as locations for entry into the EU. Globalisation of production in essence means multinational enterprises arranging a configuration of plants across the world which meets their needs to supply in and into a number of trading blocs. The deepening reliance of Scotland on the attraction of such titans means competing for highly mobile investment, with this very competition between regions and states threatening to heighten the propensity of such capital to be mobile. Without the counteracting effect of long term, sustainable development of indigenous companies, peripheral economies such as Scotland will progressively lose further control over their own destinies; hence "the development of underdevelopment".

These apparently contradictory pictures, of a past-dependent economy attracting non-EU mobile capital anxious to surmount customs barriers, present a rationale for the new Parliament intervening to overcome continuing market failures and historical obstacles to redevelopment, as the UK and European Union have also intervened. This strategy more or less explicitly attempts to (re)create the conditions identified by Porter, Perroux, and others, for the industrial clusters and networks of successful regions and small states. While the 1970s and 1980s were dominated by regional development measures aimed at improving physical infrastructures, the future is being reoriented to favour investments in human capital, business development activities and other forms of strategic renewal. However, compared to former times, the authorities are different under (European) Community Support Frameworks, now including the European Commission and Local Enterprise Companies (LECs). In addition, powers are more restricted, and many of the key employers are outwith the public sector, with privatised utilities and former state corporations following new and different agendas.

New firm formation and small and medium enterprises have become the panaceas in the mission statements of many agencies across the developed world (Storey, 1984), and of the EU in particular. The business birth rate has undoubtedly increased since 1980 but questions may be raised over the ability of companies dependent on the local market to reverse decline. Limited success in replacing traditional major manufacturing employers has been achieved, with prosperous areas having higher rates of new firm formation (and closure), suggesting that greater levels of incomes and wealth create the conditions for enterprise development rather than the converse. Moreover, there is some evidence that a reliance on economic management through new firm birth and growth - nurtured by tax cuts, privatisation giveaways and other monetary and fiscal policies - may have promoted instability in the local economy with surplus resources flowing into new ventures during the upturn and out as readily in the recession (Danson, 1995 and 1996).

Furthermore, the supply side policies of the last twenty years have also created a more divided Scotland than before: geographically, socially, and economically. The evidence from elsewhere in Europe suggests that a lack of social integration and cohesion does not foster economic development, rather the opposite.

Building a new industrial structure based on the existing Scottish policy regimes - small service sector companies and niche suppliers to multinational branch plants - may therefore not lead to instant turnaround. Indeed new problems may be generated. Research from across the developed world seems to confirm that the common theme in the economic programmes of the Greater London Council, many US states,

Germany and the Alternative Economic Strategy could be critical: supporting indigenous, medium sized enterprises arguably presents the best opportunity for long term stable and sustainable development. Moreover, there is a clear suspicion in the work by Ramsden (1995) for the European Commission, and by Morgan (1995), inter alia, that attempts "to bridge the technology gap between European regions" will be as unsuccessful as strategies within the UK in reducing regional technology disparities (Danson, Lloyd and Newlands, 1991).

The other major planks of national and European regional development regeneration programmes - new firm formation and small and medium enterprises (SMEs) - seem equally open to scrutiny. Malecki and Nijkamp (1988) suggest that uneven development is endemic, with no possibilities of overcoming metropolitan core bias by compensating the periphery, although Vaessen and Keeble (1995) appear to see enough examples of the counterfactual - successful SME in the periphery - to argue that divergence need not be inevitable. Moreover, official evaluations for the Scottish Office (Turok et al, 1994), the Strathclyde Integrated Development Operation (PIEDA, 1993) and the European Commission raise doubts over the sustainability of many regeneration efforts and over the effectiveness of the favoured market-oriented approach. While thousands of jobs have been credited to business development activities under such programmes in Strathclyde and Eastern Scotland for over a decade, critically for the future there is no evidence of a real relative shift in these regions' economic position, with no expansion of growth industries and no consistent pattern of change.

The message that comes through from these disparate studies is that relative regional economic performances are intrinsically stable over fairly long periods of time. The European Commission's study of the future prospects for Scotland (Commission of the European Communities, 1994) suggests major interventions, that is *beyond* current planned single programme documents and other EU co-ordinated initiatives, would at best "give more stability to Scotland and facilitate the process of industrial redeployment while maintaining minimum subsistence in rural zones". This would require overcoming most of the entrenched and traditional tendencies described above, and would demand a more interventionist strategy than has been adopted hitherto by the Scottish Office and in particular by the development agencies.

6.3 The rationale for regional development agencies

Faced with the endemic problems of the Scottish economy described above, the need to intervene to address market failure has led to a reliance on the development agency approach to the promotion of regional restructuring. The establishment of the Highlands and Islands Development Board and the Scottish Development Agency, and their survival through the Conservative governments of eighteen years, have much to do with the corporatist tradition in Scotland (Fairley and Lloyd, 1995a), the divergence of politics north and south of the border over this period (Brown, McCrone and Paterson, 1996), and the consensus for intervention in Scotland (McCrone, 1992). Whether the Scottish Parliament decides to empower local authorities (as proposed by the McFadden Committee), to reabsorb the responsibilities back into the Scottish

Office departmental structure, or to continue with the regional development agencies, will depend as much on political perceptions of their potential as on objective study of their performance. It is to the rationale, structure and roles for the development agencies that we now turn.

The increased interest in economic development initiatives has been argued to be part of an attempt to stimulate greater "bottom up" development, or to develop indigenous potential, compared to many former policies that tended to be more dominated by "top down" concerns (see for example, Stohr, 1989). An important part in this process has been played by semi-autonomous institutions: regional development agencies (RDAs). An RDA can be defined as "a regionally based, publicly financed institution outside the mainstream of central and local government administration designed to promote economic development". In their studies of such bodies across the European continent, a model RDA is defined by Halkier and Danson (1997, p.245) as a body which organisationally is in a semi-autonomous position vis-à-vis its sponsoring political authority, supports mainly indigenous firms by means of "soft" policy instruments, and is a multifunctional and integrated agency, the level of which may be determined by the range of policy instruments it uses.

In the UK context, RDAs have been seen as a means of reducing the level of localised market failure in accordance with and in support of the government's macroeconomic regional policy instruments and objectives. Calling on the literature in this field (Haughton and Peck 1991; Pearce 1977), Fairley and Lloyd (1998) explore the principle of market failure as it applies to development agencies, and again record how the Scottish agencies tended to widen the definition to allow a broader degree of policy intervention than the government envisaged. They also incorporate the evolving concept of "government failure" as a reason posited for restricting intervention; by extension, this would also support devolving powers to a quasi non-governmental body more oriented to the needs of the market.

The economic argument in support of development agencies rests on several advantages over other methods of policy implementation such as local authorities, central government departments, and private sector-led bodies such as the Urban Development Corporations in England and Wales. More specifically, development agencies have been seen as the most effective tool for addressing such local market failures as risk aversion in the financial sector, poor market information, externalities in the provision of infrastructure and training, and problems associated with rapid growth and technological change (Danson, Lloyd and Newlands, 1990).

In that they are able to intervene and interact with the economy at the most appropriate jurisdictional level (Armstrong, 1997), regional agencies can bring substantial resources to bear on problems of local economic development, for instance combining regional, industrial and training policies and resources on specific projects. They represent a manageable "bottom-up" alternative, avoiding the bewildering maze of local initiatives now present in many areas, but they are also flexible and receptive to the specific needs of the industry within a region. However, a significant problem in the proposals for the RDAs in the English regions (Department of Transport, Environment and the Regions, 1998) is their failure to recognise the difficulties caused by the continued existence of the plethora of bodies and programmes in each region. In the Scottish cases, such additions to the institutional infrastructure were introduced after the Highlands and Islands Development Board and the Scottish Development Agency were established. Costs can be reduced and synergies realised by locating within a single organisation a number of responsibilities that otherwise may currently or in the future be split between different departments or quasi-government agencies (such as the provision of sites, attraction of industry, environmental improvement, sector strategy, and urban development) (Moore and Booth, 1986, p.118). In the words of the Trade and Industry Committee, LECs (the network of Local Enterprise Companies in Scotland) are "able to deliver national schemes and programmes flexibly, in response to local needs and circumstances" (Trade and Industry Committee, 1995).

Operationally, RDAs frequently combine area and sectoral strategies as opportunities arise, and offer comprehensive business services, both functions that could be more difficult to deliver if these were spread across departments and agencies. More crucial perhaps, since they are at arms' length from government, RDAs can develop a degree of operational freedom and credibility which regional departments of government may lack. They may therefore be able to have potential leverage over significant private funds, representing a strong advantage that an agency will have over the Scottish Parliament itself. In times of high mobility of multinational capital, such compromises may be necessary to attract and retain jobs, incomes and technologies. Moreover, their position outside the mainstream government apparatus may allow public policies to be pursued without invoking the ghosts of interventionism or state dirigisme. This can make the development agency approach to regional economic development more acceptable to the full range of social partners, without necessarily undermining accountability.

Although RDAs can focus on the particular needs of the enterprises and labour force of their area, they can also adopt a long term perspective. Taking a strategic view can allow policies to be followed which are to the long run benefit of the region, but which may be unpopular in the immediate period. Consequently, since RDAs are relatively isolated from short term political intervention and manoeuvrings, they should offer the potential to restructure the economy in a planned way, thus lifting the development path of indigenous industry on to a higher level and achieving greater endogenous growth. Indeed, it can be argued that distance from central government could well be fundamental to the success of such a strategy. Although the operating environment may be more closely attuned to the needs of local enterprise, a Scottish development agency could also instil a sense of regional ownership of economic development strategies while demonstrating a political commitment to the long term growth of the economy as a whole. The potential to promote and encourage trust and co-operation through such an institutional approach could engender further virtuous circles of growth and development, as described below, in ways that the Scottish Parliament and local authorities could not.

6.4   The structure and roles of the development agencies

In many ways the specific roles and functions of the Scottish development agencies are less important than the balance between their objectives and their priorities. There is a broad consensus over the macroeconomic role of government and over the detailed needs of the Scottish economy; debate is more significant over how and on what sectors expenditure should be targeted. Yet much of the discussion threatens to be concerned with who should have the powers of intervention. In assessing the present structure and performance of the RDAs, we hope to illuminate this debate.

The regional development agencies for Scotland, Scottish Enterprise (SE) and Highlands and Islands Enterprise (HIE) have responsibility for the integrated delivery of economic and business development initiatives, the provision of training and the implementation of measures to secure the improvement of the environment in Scotland. According to a concept long championed by the STUC, SE and HIE represent a radical initiative within the Scottish tradition of regional planning for economic development by bringing together the key factors of capital, labour and land.

SE and HIE aim to stimulate self-sustaining economic development and the growth of enterprise, secure improvement of the environment, encourage the creation of viable jobs, reduce unemployment, and improve the skills of the Scottish workforce. The delivery of the integrated enterprise and training services is sub-contracted by SE and HIE to a network of Local Enterprise Companies (LECs) (Fairley and Lloyd, 1998). The function of LECs is to co-ordinate the provision of the supply side of the economic infrastructure in their area, thus addressing market failure, and to provide the delivery framework for the specific services associated with training, enterprise and business development and environmental improvement. At a higher level, SE and HIE:

> provide strategic policy guidance and expert advice to the LECs on individual economic sectors; undertake major projects or research activities which extend beyond the areas of individual LECs; provide individual LECs with a range of central support services which included administrative, accounting and property services; undertake marketing and inward investment programmes for the areas in question; undertake major environmental improvement and land renewal programmes, in consultation with the LECs involved; and monitor the progress of the LECs in implementing their plans and achieving their objectives (Fairley and Lloyd, 1998, p.202).

It should also be noted that HIE has been given a social aspect to its developmental responsibilities, raising questions over the potential imposition of an all-Scottish departmental approach to economic development. This is supported by an area framework which categorises the Highlands and Islands into different priority areas: "fragile remote areas", "areas of employment deficit", "intermediate areas", and "Inverness and its hinterland".

Following the tendency for corporatist policy institutions and consensus politics to be more acceptable in Scotland, as argued earlier, these arrangements are clearly and distinctly Scottish and offer the potential for securing an integrated development framework in each area. Before discussing whether any of the functions of the RDAs should be centralised to the new Parliament (in particular the headquarters of SE and HIE), or brought under the control of the local authorities, two key dimensions need to be explored: partnership and principle.

A key element to the operations of the LECs and the RDAs is that they work in partnership. This is especially relevant in discussions over the future of the development agencies under a devolved Parliament. They are not the "all singing, all dancing" monolithic multi-functional agencies envisaged in the early 1970s. SE and HIE must work with other organisations, including local authorities, government departments, academia and training bodies, the community and voluntary sectors, as well as the private sector, to develop and deliver skills training, business development, inward investment, and so forth. It is also important that other organisations in turn recognise that the RDAs themselves bring a good deal of experience and expertise to local and regional development strategies and programmes. Whatever configuration of powers and institutions are proposed, partnership will be an essential feature not only because it is rational to share best practice and to realise synergies, but also because the European Commission insists that across the EU Structural Funds are delivered through the Scottish European Partnership model (Danson et al, 1997).

6.4.1 *Principles*

In the assessments of the roles and performances of the RDAs in Scotland, a number of more or less ad hoc areas of criticism have been raised over the years. More widely, it has been difficult to discern any scientific approach to an evaluation of development agencies, though much has been written about their programmes and strategies (see Danson, Halkier and Damborg, 1998, for a discussion of this neglect). To make proposals on the future governance and functions of Scottish Enterprise and Highlands and Islands Enterprise in this critical vacuum suggests a return to first principles, and an appreciation of the critical criteria against which the mode of delivery of economic development policies should be measured. In proposing these we are calling upon a evolving field of literature which the Regional Studies Association amongst others has debated and addressed in recent years. The four principles, which are inevitably interrelated, are: accountability, sustainability, subsidiarity, and integration/inclusion.

That RDAs should be *accountable* is self evident. Indeed, this theme exercised the Scottish Affairs Committee when it examined SE and HIE in 1995/96 and, despite the heat generated around this issue, there were but few recommendations on improving democratic accountability. Others have thought otherwise; the Macfadden Committee for instance argued for the powers of the LECs to be transferred to local authorities, though the promised "bonfire of the quangos" has not been as great an issue in Scotland as in Wales. What seems clear from the experiences of the Scottish RDAs and others elsewhere (Hughes, 1998) is that control over the strategic, long term objectives and priorities of SE and HIE is necessary, but crucially there should not be day-to-day interference in delivery mechanisms and projects. The latter should be assessed through appropriate techniques and forms, for example annual reports, monitoring frameworks, targets, and performance criteria.

For development to be *sustainable*, it must involve the whole community and be accepted across all the social partners, including trade unions, small and medium enterprises, community and voluntary sectors. Operationally, there are questions over the strategy which has promoted a branch plant economy through inward investment at the expense of long term indigenous development (Ashcroft, Love and Schouller, 1987). There is a degree to which the new dependencies created in the Scottish economy identified earlier are unsustainable and so unsuitable in the Scottish context. On this criterion, the role of Locate in Scotland, the inward investment body for Scotland, would be called into question, with the implication of the need for a greater emphasis on clustering and networking in its remit.

A further common term in the 1990s, *subsidiarity*, has been introduced into the evaluation of many policy areas. Following Armstrong's approach (1997), this is taken to mean taking decisions and delivering policies at the most appropriate jurisdictional level. In other words, at times for certain functions the "local" will be the most efficient level of developing for instance training policies, while in other circumstances the regional or Scottish levels will be more appropriate. Consequently, training of software engineers would be more appropriately organised across the nation's universities rather than in the locality, and there are important economies of scale and scope to be realised at all levels. The benefits of a flexible yet strategic and objective approach can be considerable, and will undoubtedly occupy the boards of the development agencies and the committees of the Parliament - but these deliberations could be at the expense of efficient operations on the ground.

Finally, *integration and inclusion* have become important themes for policies at the end of the millenium. The need to maximise the value added by the Scottish economy and to capture the benefits of the higher functions of national and global corporations operating here suggests that greater attention has to be paid to the linkages between plants, offices and services. The fixation of Scottish Enterprise and other commentators on the leading high tech industries of today is in many ways as destructive as the focus of debate in the past on steel, shipbuilding and coal. Thus, traditional sectors such as textiles have suffered relative neglect because of their image as a declining industry, compounding their inherent conservatism and under-capitalisation (Danson and Whittam, 1998).

The potential of such key areas of the Scottish economy is being dismissed in current SE plans for clustering, despite successes abroad in "turning around" older staple sectors. Locate in Scotland has tended to follow an implicit policy of promoting certain locations in Scotland (especially New Towns, suburban and green field sites, latterly in enterprise zones in Lanarkshire) to maximise the opportunities of attracting inward investment, regardless of the impacts on other markets - labour, training, and property for instance - and to the damage to the remainder of the country. Consequently, old industrial and rural areas, inner cities and peripheral estates have seen precious few manufacturing or service jobs directed their way in the past twenty years, with minimal consideration of their access to the new industrial sites. This raises questions over the potential enhanced role of structure plans in the economic development process, but also over the limitations on such powers threatened by the multinational agreement being negotiated through the World Trade Organisation. This could restrict the ability of the Scottish Parliament to impose greater controls over the supply and sourcing policies of inward investors.

The inclusion of small and medium enterprises in the development and the administration of economic policies has been a perennial problem in the UK. With a weak Chambers of Commerce system and with a dual economy which excludes most indigenous entrepreneurs from decision making fora within trade and employer associations, there is a real need to ensure that the interests of the mass of locally owned concerns are heard in the LECs industry networks. Without a strong Scottish presence among the commanding heights of the economy, especially in the leading sectors, there is a danger that plans for improved networking and clustering will fail (Danson and Whittam, 1998).

Much of the debate over integration has inevitably centred on the need to reduce social exclusion of the long term unemployed, women, the young and ethnic and peripheral communities. While initiatives, programmes and partnerships over the years have been established to address some dimensions of the lack of inclusion of many in society, that the scale and depth of inequality has continued to increase is without doubt. Broadening the remit of SE to encompass the social aspect of its developmental responsibilities, as HIE is charged to undertake, would go some way to meeting this division. However, a multi-agency, multi-annual, and multi-functional approach will be necessary to overcome the obstacles to improved living standards for all in Scotland. Partnerships between local authorities, LECs, Scottish Homes, employers, trades unions and local communities are showing some promise of advancing the position of the excluded. Critically LECs cannot have an implicit slogan and mission statement of "our business is business" if such progression is to become fundamental and irreversible.

These principles suggest a need for the objectives, programmes and actions of LECs and others involved in economic development to be transparent, as indeed the production and criticism of structure plans must be transparent. Further, linkages between sectors, enterprises, markets, locations and organisations can be key to improvement in the economy as a whole and of its parts. The Scottish Affairs Committee noted how crucial mandatory consultation by LECs of local authorities could be, not least to secure greater legitimacy within Scottish local governance for the enterprise networks (Fairley and Lloyd, 1998).

6.5   Evaluation and performance

As described in the introduction to this chapter, the competing explanations of economic growth and performance have certain common features. They consider the creation and encouragement of specialised skills and services, and the exploitation of research, technologies and innovation, to be the critical drivers of a successful strategy for regeneration. Mechanisms to ensure the commercialisation of science and technology from higher education and other institutions, the growth of new firms, the development of existing indigenous enterprises, and the transfer of technologies and processes into the wider economy, are all recognised as areas where market failure may demand significant intervention to secure advantages for the nation as a whole.

There has been relatively little analysis of the performance of the development agencies since the merger of the former agencies and the training agency in Scotland. Much of the attention given to them has focused on their individual programmes and policies, and on issues of accountability. There have been calls for the boundaries of the LECs in the SE network to be coterminous with those of local authorities or sub-regional groups of authorities, all the more necessary given the abolition of the regional councils in 1996. Minor changes have been made towards reducing some of the anomalies caused by the lack of congruence, but further modifications could usefully be made to make the LECs' jurisdictions closer to the networks of both local administrations and local labour, industrial, and property markets. Addressing the need for efficiency and legitimacy, SE has recently been involving a broad range of organisations and partners in a wide-ranging and comprehensive review of its skills strategy. The full range of social partners has been consulted in this ongoing process and this perhaps illustrates the potential for local, regional and Scottish consensus under the Parliament.

When the Scottish Affairs Committee proposed that this comprehensive skills strategy could be linked to sectoral targets in partnership with industries (Fairley and Lloyd, 1998), they were perhaps pointing up the continuing need for such integration. Moreover, they were using one of the characteristics of RDAs given above, namely that they allow public policies to be pursued without invoking the ghosts of interventionism or state dirigisme. Balancing this need to be acceptable to private enterprises with the need to be accountable has been recognised as crucial more generally in Scotland, according to a report on the views of selected members of the Scottish Council Development and Industry (Scottish Council Development and Industry, 1997). Undoubtedly, the desire to control the quangos and to reduce the democratic deficit are strong factors in support of the Parliament concerning itself more closely with the regional development agencies in Scotland, but without losing the advantages of this form of intervention.

The efforts to be more inclusive with regard to the development of skills reflects concerns over the lack of a central strategic overview of the problems of the Scottish economy, and the problems of co-ordination, as described above. In other markets, such as land, continuing and expanding calls for reform are indicative of the criticism that the RDAs have failed to change the culture of business and economic players. This stands alongside concerns that their existing policies have been inappropriate with regard to employment creation, business starts, and so on.

With employers in Scotland continuing to be reluctant to meet the cost of training in modern times (Danson et al, 1990), there remains a strong economic argument in favour of employers being obliged to invest in training. Reconfirming a long held commitment, the STUC has argued that businesses should be required to fund a training programme equivalent to 0.5 per cent of payroll costs (Scottish Trades Union Congress, 1992). Meeting the training needs of a competitive economy implies the need for intervention in the market far beyond the proposed minimum wage and the maintenance of a flexible labour force. Reincorporating the trades unions and invigorating the employers' involvement will be two of the principal priorities facing the Scottish Parliament. Given their restricted powers, the RDAs may prove the most efficient mode of intervention in the labour market.

In the literature on industrial clusters, networking and learning communities, the issues of technology policy, innovation, new firm formation and the ownership of industry are all closely connected and provide one of the prime examples of the way in which the Scottish Parliament could in the long term increase the dynamic efficiency of the Scottish economy (Danson, Lloyd and Newlands, 1990; Newlands, 1997). Yet there has been an undercurrent of concern over many of these issues and in particular over the implications of a reliance on foreign direct investment for the promotion of indigenous growth. Consequently, much evaluation and analysis of the operations of the Scottish development agencies has focused on the attraction of inward investment to Scotland, which has been such a major concern of the Scottish Office and Scottish Enterprise (and their joint agency Locate in Scotland). It has been noted above that Scotland has become dependent for much of its dynamism on the overseas-owned electronics industry, with all that entails for control over the economy and the potential for indigenous development. Recent indications are that these restraints should be addressed by seeking to locate major research and development plants here in order to embed these leading sectors into the Scottish industrial environment. This would certainly build on the comparative advantages of the economy, not least the high level of skills and the research facilities and traditions of the educational system.

However, whether a real Scottish presence in the new technologies - and beyond just the electronics sector - can be established without significant venture capital investment is doubtful, and the well-established arguments for a Scottish industrial investment bank are returning to the debate. While the financial sector in Scotland is significant in global terms, it remains less than effective in the provision of funds for indigenous enterprises. Dow (1997) especially has argued for the closer involvement of the Scottish banking sector in the Scottish economy, to address some of the limitations of the underdeveloped industrial structure and to redress past neglects. Without the industrial banks of such competitors as the German Länder, the Scottish Parliament will need to be innovative in its use of indigenous resources; however, the land that invented investment and unit trusts should be able to mobilise such funds more effectively than at present. It is apposite in this context that many believed that the establishment of the Scottish Development Agency in 1975 would create such a financial vehicle, and it took many several years to conclude that its operations were focused elsewhere - primarily as Europe's largest industrial landlord.

Despite the benefits of introducing new technologies, investments and management skills to Scotland, concerns over the role of Locate in Scotland and of inward investment have focused on the deepening of the branch plant syndrome (Standing

Commission on the Scottish Economy, 1989, p.47). Few product and process innovations are not developed in the plant in which they are first designed, and there is little inter-regional transfer of such innovations; these factors help explain Scotland's low rates of new firm formation and innovation as well as the under-representation in high technology growth sectors. Moreover, staff at branch plants do not acquire the skills, business contacts or ideas to enable them to set up their own firms or mount a management buy out.

As Newlands (1997) argues, the Parliament could promote "a shift in the priority given to the attraction of inward investment and in the issues raised in Locate in Scotland's discussions with potential inward investors" (p.125). Reflecting Dow's arguments, he proposes that stronger commitments could and should be sought on such issues as the location of higher corporate and research functions, technology transfer, and corporate recruitment, sales and purchasing policies. The Scottish Parliament might also pursue the suggestion that the Scottish public sector and financial insitutions should combine to establish a "White Knight" fund in order to strengthen existing Scottish businesses and to enable those that wish to maintain their independence to resist external takeover (Standing Commission on the Scottish Economy, 1989).

Without necessarily raising public expenditure, and within the powers granted to the devolved Parliament, efforts could be made to strengthen co-operative networks further. This would reflect both the economic underpinnings of clustering and also the role political institutions can play in shaping economic performance more effectively by influencing the rules and norms of behaviour (Hodgson, 1989; North, 1994).

Returning to the rationale for the establishment of regional development agencies as argued by such as Danson, Lloyd and Newlands (1990), and Halkier and Danson (1995), RDAs are not only

> the "manageable" bottom up alternative, avoiding the bewildering maze of local initiatives', but they also allow for flexibility and receptiveness to the specific problems of indigenous industry within the region. At the same time, a position outside the mainstream government *apparatus* appears to make it possible to pursue public policies without evoking the ghosts of *interventionism or state dirigisme*, and so to make it easier to adopt a *long-term perspective*, while the *distance from government* frequently generates an operating environment more closely attuned to the needs of enterprise (Halkier and Danson, 1995, p.1, emphasis added).

In other words, the perceived advantages of RDAs as a form of regional policy delivery institution could well be compromised by any moves to have control of their day-to-day operations by the Scottish Parliament. Similarly, whether the costs of closer involvement of the RDAs in partnerships and formal networks under both national and EU programmes would be worth bearing will depend on the benefits realised and the synergies released by these alternative models of economic development.

6.6   Conclusions

With restricted powers and a hostile and limiting European and global economic environment, the Scottish Parliament will face a need to balance aspirations against its capabilities. It will need and have a powerful desire "to do something" in economic development and to do so more directly than institutions do at present, although Newlands (1997) has maintained that the growth function and the efficiency of intervention is significant already. There will be a strong temptation to reabsorb Scottish Enterprise especially, and perhaps Highlands and Islands Enterprise also, back into government, with some pressure to transfer the powers of the LECs to local authorities.

Given the rationale for RDAs, and on the basis of the principles adopted here as applied to this form of intervention, we would argue that this pressure should be resisted. Nevertheless, there is a need for improved democratic control at all levels, and of better accountability of the strategic functions of the agencies particularly. It is worrying, therefore, that the Labour government has failed to legislate for the statutory inclusion of local authorities, trade unions and the community on the boards of LECs, European partnerships and other such institutions.

We would also oppose the transfer of the powers of the LECs to local authorities. Since reorganisation, many of these are now too small to deliver business and training services effectively and efficiently, while consortia or joint boards appear to be a second best solution. Experiments in partnership, such as the Ayrshire Economic Forum, the Ayrshire Engineering Group and the networking of the HIE Community Land Unit, illustrate the advantages of improvements to co-operation and trust across the economic landscape of Scotland. In many fields, especially business services and certain manufacturing specialisms, the agglomeration economies enjoyed by the metropolitan regions of Barcelona, Frankfurt, Milan, and their equivalents across the developed world, point to the need for a higher rank of development agency operating at least at the Scottish level.

Calls for more revolutionary reforms threaten to be a distraction in the short term, where continuity and confidence will be fundamental to fulfilling longer term objectives. This is especially critical at a time of change with the introduction of the new Parliament, compensatory changes in England, EU enlargement and reductions in Structural Fund support. Indeed, the experience of successful regions elsewhere in Europe suggests an evolution of the Scottish model of partnership as desirable, if the advantages of this tested approach are applied to economic links as well as to institutional relationships. This will involve the Scottish Parliament in radical intervention in the Scottish economy, especially if it incorporates the principles of accountability, sustainability, subsidiarity and inclusion into its activities. Anything less will appear as mere posturing.

7 Economic development: the Scottish Parliament and local government

JOHN FAIRLEY

7.1 Introduction

Scotland's local authorities have a long history of involvement in economic development. This role has continued through the radical restructurings of the local government system in 1929, 1975 and 1996, though it was only the last of these that provided a clear statutory locus for councils in economic activities. Local authorities have also had to develop their roles in the context of changing central-local relations, and more recently in the context of complex institutional relationships as economic development became a "multi-level" activity. This multi-level system is likely to develop in new ways to take account of the opportunities presented by the creation of the Scottish Parliament, and this may affect the roles played by local government (Fairley, 1997).

Most of the local authorities supported the creation of the Scottish Parliament and the work of the Scottish Constitutional Convention. However, it is not clear whether the Parliament will bring centralisation, decentralisation, subsidiarity or new forms of partnership for economic development. Indeed, this is not entirely for the Parliament to decide.

This chapter first surveys the modern development of local government. Sections 7.3 and 7.4 then consider the changing local government framework and context for local economic development. Section 7.5 is concerned with the practice of local government economic development. Finally, there is an extended discussion and assessment of the possible impact of the new Parliament on these areas of activity.

7.2 The evolution of the local government system

The three major reforms to the structure of local government this century took effect in 1929, 1975 and 1996. The concerns of these reforms varied, but concepts of efficiency were always central and they took precedence over the need to improve democracy at the local level. Each reform reduced the number of elected authorities and the number of locally elected politicians, and by 1996, with only 32 councils and 1161 politicians (SLGIU, 1995), Scotland had fewer elected representatives and institutions relative to population than most other countries in Europe.

The 1929 Act represented the second attempt to rationalise the local government system. It put in place a complex network of over 400 councils of five types, namely

103

small burghs, districts, counties, large burghs and counties of cities (Wheatley, 1969, para.48), and this system lasted until the 1960s. When it conducted its detailed examination of this system, the Wheatley Commission found that it had "failed to stand the pace...[of]...the greatest changes that have ever taken place in society" (Wheatley, 1969, para.106). The 1973 Act, implemented in 1975, represented a heavily modified version of Wheatley's radical recommendations. It put in place a simpler system of three all-purpose island councils, nine "strategic" Regional Councils and 53 District Councils. The small island councils and the large regions controlled the "strategic" services with the largest budgets, namely education, roads and social work, though all three types of council had a role in economic development.

The regional services were "strategic" in the sense which was fashionable at the time, in the sense that they were deemed to be most effective when they were planned and provided for a large population. The large regional councils were very large and operated on a scale which would not be regarded as "local" in most of Europe. Strathclyde Region, for instance, covered about half of Scotland's population. Whatever levels of operational efficiency and professional quality they achieved, the large regions became complex bureaucracies that were riven with departmentalism, and they were often felt to be remote from their communities. Moreover, relations between regions and districts were often difficult and sometimes oppositional, and these problems were clearest in some of the main "city regions" (Davidson and Fairley, 1998).

The Conservatives had a number of objectives in reforming local government (Fairley, 1995). In particular, they wished to encourage an "enabling" approach within which councils would retain responsibility for public services without necessarily delivering them directly. Moreover, they wished to end the confusions of the two-tier system by introducing a system of one council per area. However, the reforms implemented in 1996 were controversial largely because they stemmed from the Conservative Party's manifesto commitment (Lang, 1994) rather than from a process of objective research. Consequently, critics accused the government of seeking partisan advantage, of creating local government units which were financially unstable and technically unviable (Midwinter, 1993, 1995), and of pre-empting what should be the proper business of the Scottish Parliament. However, the move towards a single tier system of unitary councils was accepted in principle across the political spectrum, partly because of the growing criticisms of the Wheatley system, partly because of the re-emergence of interest in revitalising local democracy, partly because some felt that the all-purpose island councils offered a model for the rest of Scotland (Kennedy, 1989) and partly because the large regions presented an obstacle to the creation of the Scottish Parliament.

The reforms of 1996 were rather complex in that they introduced a number of types of change to Scotland's local government system (Fairley, 1995), and this makes it very difficult to generalise about their impact on economic development. Throughout mainland Scotland, the Regional and District Councils were abolished and replaced by 29 new unitary councils. In some parts of Scotland, such as Strathclyde, Lothian, Central, Tayside and Grampian, the most visible aspect of this change was the ending of the large Regions and the loss of their strategic capacities. However, in other areas such as Highland, Borders, Fife and Dumfries and Galloway, the geography of the unitary councils was identical or very similar to the former Regional Councils, and in these areas it was clear that the reforms would bring some consolidation of District and Regional activities in a context of relative stability and strengthened institutional capacity. In the four main cities, the unitary boundaries were similar to those of the former District Councils. In a few areas, entirely new local government areas were created, and some of these new unitary councils were large, such as Aberdeenshire and the Lanarkshire authorities, and in these areas the reforms brought a new strategic capacity and focus.

7.3   The changing local government framework for economic development

The "Wheatley reform" of 1975 had acknowledged that both tiers of local government then being established had a role to play in industrial development. In s.83, the legislation provided a wide-ranging economic development power, though this was financially limited to the product of a 2 pence rate, and this was eventually "frozen" at its current value when the "poll tax" was introduced in 1989. Like the previous power, s.339 of the Local Government (Scotland) Act 1947, s.83 represented a form of "general competence" for local government, although Wheatley (1969, para.640) commented that the 2p cash limit "virtually empties the provision of real significance".

In 1996, the new unitary councils were strengthened by gaining for the first time a clear statutory power for economic development. While this remained discretionary, it was not cash-limited (Hayton, 1994a; Fairley, 1996a). On 23 March 1988, Tony Benn and other MPs of the Labour Left introduced their Local Authorities (General Powers) Bill to Westminster. This Bill was heavily influenced by the Greater London Council's radical economic experiments and, had it succeeded, it would have given local authorities throughout Britain a wide range of economic powers and responsibilities. In the following year, the Conservative Government gave councils in England and Wales a clearer but restricted economic development power which was not cash-limited, and the 1994 Act extended a similar provision to Scottish councils (Hayton, 1994a).

The 1996 reform gave councils a stronger legal power to engage in economic development if they so wished, and this was very important in a system based on the concept of *vires*. There was no record of a Scottish council having faced legal challenge for its economic activities, but the absence of an adequate power may have encouraged caution or even a degree of "self censorship" in some councils. However, the provision of the power was not the same as full encouragement to use it. Nevertheless, the new councils were also strengthened in that, by having responsibility for all local government services, they could plan them all together. This greatly enhanced the possibility of more "corporate" and strategic local government, and some councils, for example Aberdeenshire and Aberdeen City, began to look at the economic impact of all their service roles.

The 1996 reform was widely regarded as having been badly costed and inadequately funded. After the 1997 General Election, the new Labour Government chose to follow its predecessor's spending plans and continued to impose real cuts on local government. By the end of 1997, the unprecedented squeeze on local authorities was leading some to question their ability to continue to fund any activity that did not help to meet a statutory obligation. Consequently, some local politicians were beginning to wonder whether it would not be better to transfer economic development to the Local Enterprise Companies (LECs). The distribution of economic development powers between local government and the LECs was discussed in chapter 6 and is considered further in the final section of this chapter.

7.4   The changing context for local economic development

In the 1920s, economic development was not yet viewed as a proper sphere of state activity, and economic policy was still largely laisser faire in its intent, with the Treasury dominant. As a consequence, there was little active involvement by government and its agents, and, as the only active local agencies, councils may have had more discretion and freedom of choice in policy in the 1930s than they were to enjoy later. Where councils had the policy and entrepreneurial capacity, and the necessary resources, they seemed to face few restrictions on what they could do.

In the 1930s, local authorities became active in the process of creating new economic development agencies for Scotland outside local government. With the support of the Scottish Office, the Convention of Royal Burghs set up the Scottish National Development Council (Paterson, 1994, p.118). In addition, Secretary of State Tom Johnston set up the Scottish Council on Industry in 1942, with the support of the local authorities, chambers of commerce, trades unions and others. Between 1942 and 1945 it secured the authorisation of some 700 new enterprises and substantial extensions, and it "rapidly became the most effective pressure group in Great Britain", and the envy of the English regions (Pottinger, 1979, p.94). In 1946, Johnston merged these bodies into the Scottish Council for Development and Industry (SCDI).

The SCDI established a Committee (Levitt, 1996) under the chairmanship of the (then) managing director of Ferranti in Edinburgh, J. N. Toothill, to examine the position and prospects for the Scottish economy, and this was welcomed in the House of Commons in November 1959. The Scottish Office seconded senior staff to the enquiry, and the Toothill (1961) Report became the basis for a national plan prepared by the Scottish Office (Paterson, 1994, p.120).

In 1965, the Highland and Island Development Board (HIDB) was established with its headquarters in Inverness. The continued strengthening of Scottish institutions, coupled with some limited forms of devolution, meant that by the mid 1970s, with the establishment of the Scottish Development Agency (SDA), Secretary of State William Ross "could say with manifest justification that he was Scotland's industrial Minister" (Pottinger, 1979, p.187). In the 1980s and early 1990s, similar processes led to the almost complete devolution of responsibility for training policy to the Scottish Office (Fairley 1996b).

These institutional developments were pursued primarily to improve public policy and, at times, to extend Scotland's area of policy autonomy. Generally, they were shaped by perceptions in London of the evolution of the "national question" in Scotland (Paterson, 1994; Levitt, 1996; Levitt, 1998). While they were not pursued with local government in mind, they certainly affected the scope for, and the style of, local authority economic development.

In some ways, local authority roles were enhanced, since councils could work as partners or agents of national and UK agencies. In 1985, councils provided over 70 per cent of the places on the Manpower Services Commission's (MSC) Community Programme for the adult unemployed, a much higher proportion than their counterparts provided in England and Wales (Maxwell, 1989, p.150). However, while Councils could work in "partnership" with the SDA and so attract new resources for development, for many councils the relationship was uneven and council aspirations had to be trimmed to fit the SDA template, though in the Highlands and Islands the rather weak pre-1975 councils were able to exert some influence on the HIDB to secure developments which could not have happened without the Board.

In the 1980s and 1990s, the European Union's Structural Funds became important to most of Scotland's councils (Danson et al, 1997), and by the late 1980s, economic development, like local government itself (Fairley, 1997) had to be viewed within the framework of a complex and dynamic multi-level system. For instance, the effective local authority had to engage with Brussels and assist in the implementation of European policies (Danson et al, 1997). It would also be a contractor to the Scottish arm of the Sheffield-based MSC in its efforts to alleviate unemployment. Central belt councils might work with Locate in Scotland to provide the key infrastructure for inward investors, and with the Scottish Office to tackle deprivation through the Urban Programme. Grampian Regional Council would work with the Departments of Energy and Trade and Industry to meet the development needs of the oil industry and its supporting sectors. Councils would be development partners of Scottish quangos, notably the SDA. They would work in vocational education through the further education colleges, and later in partnership with them when the colleges were "incorporated" and placed under Scottish Office control by legislation in 1992. In rural Scotland, councils would work with the EU, as well as government departments and quangos responsible for agriculture, fisheries, forestry and tourism (Scottish Office, 1997c). Furthermore, councils retained the legal power to devise their own policies to meet local needs.

The changing institutional framework therefore provided councils with more opportunities to work with other organisations for economic development purposes. This allowed them to attract additional resources, though this was sometimes at the cost of some diminution of their capacity to innovate and act independently. A new ideology arose within Scottish local government which sought to define economic development as a "partnership activity" (McCaffer 1995). In England, however, a more independent and radical local economic development tradition survived for longer within a simpler institutional framework, although it received a major setback with the abolition of the Greater London Council and the metropolitan councils in 1986. Until the end of the 1980s, the "partners" of Scottish councils were regional, national, UK or international in nature. Local authorities experienced no locally-based competition in their economic development role, though that changed when legislation in 1990 set up Scottish Enterprise (SE) and Highlands and Islands Enterprise (HIE), and required them to decentralise their operations (Fairley and Lloyd, 1995b; Harding et al, 1997). The Scottish Office ensured that SE and HIE operations were decentralised to two policy and programme networks made up of 22 employer-led LECs, and the 1990 Act required HIE to consult the local authorities in its area. Following the 1996 changes, the LEC boundaries were adjusted to be closer to those of the local councils.

The LEC networks are discussed in detail in chapter 6. The important point here is that they brought significant changes to the context for local authority economic development, partly by providing councils with a degree of locally-based competition. The impact on councils and their responses were complex matters which varied across Scotland. In some areas, councils welcomed the new developments, and were actively involved in helping to form, resource and support the embryonic LECs, though in a few areas there was friction and conflict (Fairley, 1992a, 1992b). Elsewhere, many astute councils realised that the LECs had budgets to spend but lacked the experience and the human resources needed to secure their "performance" targets, and many projects which local authorities wished to fund but could not were rapidly brought "on stream" (Fairley, 1997) through the deployment of the traditional local authority skills of persuasion and influence. Councils quickly came to realise that they were the equals of the LECs, and they preferred this to being the local agents and subordinate "partners" of national quangos. Nevertheless, councillors continued to be concerned that the LECs were run by local elites and that they could decide and fund their priorities without discussion with the local authority and therefore without accountability to the local community.

By the late 1990s, councillors were also expressing concern about the range and diversity of the quangos whose decisions affected the local economy, but which were not locally accountable. For instance, Scottish Homes had become the main government agency for directing investment in public sector housing, a service which Wheatley had recognised as one of the important supports for economic development. The Scottish Environmental Protection Agency took some powers away from the District Councils and became one of the key players in the strategically important debate over "sustainable" economic development. Tourism, which supported about 13 per cent of the workforce in the Highlands and Islands (HIE, 1997), had been "regionalised" within a framework of institutionally divided responsibility for funding the boards and planning the industry. In addition, Scottish National Heritage faced criticism for counterposing environmental protection with economic development and often blocking the latter.

Consequently, the new unitary councils, striving to be more "corporate" and to take a "holistic" overview of local development needs, were faced with three problems. The first was partnership "confusion and fatigue", resulting from the need to be involved in a bewildering range of bilateral partnerships with agencies from outside the local area. The second was a growing feeling that public policy itself was fragmenting their communities, and that "partnership" was the inadequate remedy being offered by the

Scottish Office. The third was the problem posed by the gathering budgetary crisis, particularly for discretionary services like economic development.

7.5 The practice of local government economic development

Local authorities became involved in economic initiatives for a variety of reasons, prominent amongst which was the desire to combat poverty and unemployment. Their early involvement in such action has been little researched. However, the "big is most effective" perspective, which has dominated debates on local government since the 1960s, has produced the general impression that the pre-Wheatley systems were simply too fragmented amongst too many small councils to be effective for development. It is important now that this rather one-sided view is challenged with the evidence which is available.

In this context, Kirkintilloch, Scotland's oldest Burgh with a population of some 12,000 in the 1920s, is interesting in that many of its initiatives are recorded through the memoirs and biography of Tom Johnston (Johnston, 1952; Galbraith, 1995), the council leader who went on to become Scottish Secretary. In the conventions of modern Scottish local government, Kirkintilloch would seem a ridiculously small unit. However, Johnston's commitment to local democracy led him "to believe firmly in the importance of government at the narrowest community level" (Galbraith, 1995, p.35), and this included local government action on the local economy. The small council had recycling initiatives, a profitable municipal cinema, and took various actions to help the local unemployed, but it is best known for setting up Scotland's first and Britain's second "municipal bank". The bank opened on 22 March 1920 under the available Companies legislation, and other banks followed in Irvine, Clydebank, Motherwell, Peebles and Selkirk (Galbraith, 1995, p.32). (By contrast, Birmingham, the first to open a bank, had gone the expensive and complex route of seeking explicit Parliamentary approval.) The Kirkintilloch initiative paid off the town's debt, secured a significant reduction in local taxes, gave the citizens a direct financial stake in local government and provided a local development fund. In 1932/33, the bank had over £68,000 on deposit, though the UK Treasury was unimpressed and quickly secured legislation to prevent the further spread of the local banking movement in Scotland.

Pre-Wheatley local government also produced some examples of effective voluntary collaboration between councils for economic development purposes. These are interesting in themselves, but also because of the difficulty which contemporary local government seems to have in effecting such arrangements. We have already noted the prominence of the Royal Burghs in the establishment of the National Development Council. In addition, in the late 1960s the local authorities in the Grampian area, responding to an influential economic report, came together in a voluntary partnership intended to develop the local economy. The North East of Scotland Development Agency (NESDA) quickly focused on the development implications of the emerging oil industry. NESDA was regarded as very effective and it influenced the design of the SDA and for some years after 1975 it worked in part as the SDA's agent for the North East. However, the Wheatley reform undermined its effectiveness as a local government collaboration, and once NESDA became an arm of the new Grampian Regional Council, the District Councils' motivation to participate was reduced.

However, it was really after the Wheatley reforms that economic development began generally to be recognised as a distinct and legitimate sphere of local government activity. The need to respond to local issues outweighed the inadequacy of the available statutory power and these issues varied widely according to the structures and development trends of local economies. For instance, in Glasgow the dominant concerns were urban regeneration (Keating, 1988) and the unemployment which resulted from the decline and collapse of the old industries. Strathclyde Regional Council shared this concern for regeneration; moreover, it recognised economic development as one of its corporate priorities in 1975 (McCaffer, 1995), adopted a radical, area-based deprivation strategy in 1976 (Young, 1983), and also acted to support its rural and island communities. Grampian Regional Council's concerns were dominated by the pressures of the oil sector, and Shetland secured its own legislation to help it deal with its oil pressures. While Aberdeen District Council shared the concern with oil, it also tried to slow the decline of its traditional industrial base. By the mid-1980s, 2p rate expenditure for economic development by all Scottish councils was estimated at some £5.8 million (Ramsdale and Capon, 1986, pp.16-18).

The variety of issues which they faced, together with the high degree of discretion which they had in a non-statutory service, led to councils adopting a range of arrangements for the organisation and management of their economic development activities. The most common arrangement was to locate the service in the Planning Department, though critics argued that the essentially regulatory function and culture of land use planning tended to impose a conservatism on economic development. A similar point was made of those councils, like Edinburgh District Council, that located economic development in their Estates Department. The dominance of these two models, and the emerging hegemony of the SDA, produced an approach to economic development which was often "property-led", namely over-concerned with "hard" infrastructure and insufficiently concerned with education and training. However, a small number of councils experimented with free-standing departments for economic development, or located the service within the Chief Executive's department.

Strathclyde Region was by far the largest council and the largest actor in economic development, and its attempt at a corporate approach required each service department to produce an Action Plan detailing its contribution to the overall strategy. The Council innovated in a range of economic activities, including the early access of European funding, the use of these funds in employment and training subsidies, the creation along with the (then) Paisley College of a network of community enterprises (Young, 1983), the development of anti-poverty and deprivation strategies, the development of a co-ordinated approach to large plant closures, and support for business which cost some £12 million per year in the 1990s (McCaffer, 1995). Strathclyde Region also did many other things which were vital to rural and island economies, but many of its actions would not show in the accounts as economic development expenditures. Scottish Office (1997d) data show that the net revenue expenditure by all councils within the Strathclyde area on planning and economic development was £59.4 million in 1994/95, while the gross capital spend was a little over £25 million in the same year; these figures were respectively 51 per cent and 25 per cent of the Scottish totals.

It is interesting to compare the ideologies of the very large Strathclyde Regional Council (SRC) with the Greater London Council (GLC) of the early 1980s. While both attempted the very difficult task of implementing a corporate approach, the GLC based its strategy on a comprehensive analysis and critique of the ways in which contemporary capitalism was thought to be destabilising the London economy (GLC, 1985a, 1985b). The GLC considered that the corporate direction of its budget and the targeting of its economic development expenditures could have a significant impact on the capital, and it aimed to spend as much as it could while remaining within the 2 pence cash limit. It also strongly promoted equal opportunities and its Women's and Ethnic Minority Committees had a strong voice in economic development. The political leadership was strongly socialist, seeing itself as the heir to a long English tradition of protest and dissent, and the GLC therefore aimed to both influence the UK policies of the Labour Party and to contest those of the Conservative Government.

The SRC strategy, however, was based not only on a strong identification with and commitment to the poor and the unemployed, but also on a radical critique of local government's failure to assist these groups. Addressing the issue of concentrations of deprivation in west central Scotland, Young (1983, p.225) observes that it "is surely not a coincidence that such 'apartheid' was most evident in that part of Britain in which 'the local state' was so dominant". He continues: "The reality was administrative, political and professional neglect creating a group of second class citizens" (p.229).

More specifically, the SRC corporate strategy was equally concerned with improving economic and social opportunity, and with improving the performance of local government. Since it was partly based in the belief that local government could not make any rapid impact on "basic economic problems" (Young, 1983, p.242), it was implemented within a partnership approach wherever possible, and the SRC became very good at levering resources from Europe and from the SDA (Keating, 1988, p.192). However, while the SRC was committed to equality of opportunity, it did not seek to emulate the empowering strategies of the GLC. The political leadership in the council was "labourist" rather than socialist, reflecting the ideology of the right of the Labour Party. Nevertheless, this difference between the two is not a simple matter of "left" versus "right", and the SRC could lay claim to a long tradition which sought to downplay or eliminate the "politics of economic development". This tradition goes back at least to the pragmatism which Tom Johnston displayed both in Kirkintilloch and as Scottish Secretary.

If the SRC was the dominant organisation in local government, it probably also dominated local economic development as far as the Scottish Office was concerned. However, this dominance threatens to conceal two very important points. The first is that all 65 councils in the Wheatley system were involved in economic development. The arrival of "Objective One" funding from Europe (Danson et al, 1997) made it a priority for the councils in the Highlands and Islands area, and Ross and Cromarty District for instance had already established a reputation as a creative force in economic development. Amongst its activities, this council promoted music and cultural festivals both for their own community importance and for their potential to generate tourism income, and by the mid-1990s the *Feisean* movement embraced some 27 local festivals (Scottish Office, 1997c, p.10). Moreover, the arrival of HIE provided both the mechanism and the legal competence to take forward the long-held dream of the local authorities for the creation of a University of the Highlands and Islands (Newlands and Parker, 1997) and the UHI was promoted and developed as both an educational and an economic development project. In addition, a number of District Councils, led by Edinburgh and Stirling, accessed the European Social Fund in order to establish women-only technology training centres. Furthermore, across Scotland, from Glasgow to Grampian, councils were working to generate economic benefits from their international links; these efforts ranged from support for trade missions and marketing to the Memoranda of Understanding on economic development which were held by Grampian Regional Council and the Atlantic Provinces of Canada.

The second point is that, within a small community, modest economic initiatives may be of strategic value, and the size of local government unit is not necessarily a good guide as to whether it is economically strategic or effective.

If all Scottish councils were active in economic policy, there is some evidence that suggests that they may have been less enthusiastic than some of their English counterparts. It was GLC policy to spend up to the 2 pence limit and to keep very detailed accounts in case of legal challenge. For instance, research done for the Widdicombe Committee (Ramsdale and Capon, 1986, pp.14-15) showed that, in 1984/85, the Regional and Island Councils spent only 38.3 per cent and the Districts a mere 12.6 per cent of the cash-limited funds available to them under s.83. By contrast, the GLC and the Metropolitan Counties spent 82.7 per cent of their total available funds.

However, it could be argued that this difference was largely the result of the "new left" ideology of the GLC and "the Mets". Elsewhere in England, and even in the inner London Boroughs, the spending performance was below that of the Scottish Regions and Islands, the latter having increased their "2p rate" expenditure by 180 per cent in real terms during the 1981-85 period. Moreover, it must be remembered that English councils could not access the funds of bodies like the SDA and the HIDB, and they may therefore have been forced into a greater reliance on funding solely through the rates. In addition, the local partners available to English councils, namely the Training and Enterprise Councils (TECs), were considerably weaker than the Scottish LECs (Fairley and Lloyd, 1995b).

The Convention of Scottish Local Authorities surveyed the economic development efforts of the Wheatley councils in 1980/81, and subsequently commissioned two academic studies. Lloyd and Rowan-Robinson (1988) noted that by the mid-1980s councils generally had some involvement in economic development, and that there was a widening range of initiatives, including new efforts to involve education and the schools. McQuaid (1992) employed a narrow definition of "local economic development" and found that councils spent some £90 million in 1990/91, about 60 per cent of which was accounted for by the Regions and Islands councils. While this is significant, it understates the real importance of local government to the economy, and the Scottish Office (1997d) showed that all councils' net revenue spend on planning and economic development stood at £117 million in 1994/95, while their gross capital expenditure was £102 million. Again, it could be argued that other items of local government expenditure are just as important for the economy as those caught by this definition.

By 1996, therefore, most of Scotland's local authorities were active in economic development. Their experiences in the Wheatley era, and their abilities in accessing funding from and implementing the policies of the EU, gave them a new confidence which they took into the new local government system. In addition, unitary status provided a new capacity for considering and planning the overall impact of a local authority on its economy. However, the institutional framework for economic development had become very complex and somewhat fragmented, and by the time of the referendum in September 1997 there was a growing suspicion that the new Parliament might be unlikely to leave local economic development untouched.

7.6   The potential impact of the Scottish Parliament

The key to the attitude of the Parliament to local economic development lies in the 1999 elections since the politics and party loyalties of the 129 MSPs, and to some extent their personalities and individual aspirations, will determine the Parliament's stance. At the time of writing there is a general expectation that the Labour Party will have the largest group of MSPs, but that it will be required to govern in coalition. This suggests that the evolution of Labour's currently unclear policies, and the choice of coalition partner(s), will also be important factors.

The Parliament will not control monetary policy, interest rate and fiscal policies or general macroeconomic policy since these matters are "reserved" to Westminster, and some of them may pass to Europe. However, the White Paper specifies a wide range of economic policy areas for which the Parliament will have responsibility, primarily comprising the existing functions which the Scottish Office has acquired. This suggests that the Parliament will have an economic policy, and that it will be able to shape this (Bell and Dow, 1995). In other words, it will become a significant player within the existing multi-level system, and therefore yet another agency in an area which is already institutionally congested.

Indeed, the wide support for a Scottish Parliament was partly based on the belief that a democratic Scotland needs an economic policy more in tune with its needs and aspirations than the policies offered by Conservative Government in the 1980s and 1990s. It was further expected that a greater degree of economic policy autonomy would bring benefits to Scotland:

The advent of a Scottish Parliament by the year 2000 will bring unprecedented opportunities for a more integrated approach to achieve sustainable development for rural Scotland, as for other parts of Scotland (Scottish Office, 1997c, para.17).

The local authority role in economic development may therefore be reshaped in two principal ways by the developing Parliament. First, it may be recast as a result of the emerging economic policy stance of the Parliament; this important area has so far been little discussed. Second, it may be recast as a result of the Parliament's attitude to local government; this has been rather more discussed and is the focus of an enquiry by an independent Commission. There is an expectation in local government, particularly in the light of the decentralising aspirations of the Scottish Constitutional Convention (SCC, 1995), that this recasting may be to the benefit of councils, but there is also a fear that the newly-elected MSPs may take a different and centralising view. In general terms, the recasting could take a limited number of forms, as discussed below.

7.6.1 An "added value" approach?

The MSPs may decide to build on what exists and to seek to add value through the Parliament. Four areas for action are suggested, as follows. First, the Scottish Parliament could seek to encourage more coherence in the currently fragmented system. In the late 1990s, fragmentation is evident in many aspects of local economic development and particularly in vocational education and training (Fairley, 1996b). However, greater coherence could be introduced by establishing a national framework for development, either sectorally, for instance for the tourism sector, or on an area basis by encouraging localities to adopt the institutional mix which best suits their situation (Fairley, 1997). In addition, the Scottish Parliament could encourage closer relationships between the LECs and local councils where this is appropriate (Peacock, 1997), and this could involve the Parliament supporting particular kinds of local initiative, for example the formation of a strategic partnership by the local authorities and the LEC (Grampian Enterprise) in North East Scotland.

Second, the Parliament could represent the Scottish interest in UK and European forums in ways not previously possible. Third, the Parliament could bring economic development within the frame of democratic scrutiny. While local authorities already provide this for their own actions, albeit in a weak form, they could be given more influence over the LECs and other agencies such as the colleges, particularly perhaps where councils are most active in trying to tackle the agenda of "democratic renewal". And fourth, the Parliament could become an advocate of better managerial and democratic practice by encouraging and supporting forms of monitoring and evaluation that involve the local community.

7.6.2   *A centralising force?*

The Scottish Parliament could seek to centralise economic development, and this could happen in a number of ways. New MSPs seeking a role could ask the question which Keating (1988) posed for Glasgow: "Who controls economic development?", and they could decide that such prestigious activity belongs to the centre. Clearly, the political aspirations and the personalities of the MSPs will be critical factors. They could seek, in the simplistic manner of the popular management writers, Osborne and Gaebler (1993), to retain for the centre the strategic role of "steering", while allowing local authorities to do the "rowing". This would be unfortunate because, in a multi-level system, strategy and policy-making are necessarily shared activities. The third and most likely possibility is that centralisation is allowed to happen by default. In this scenario, cash-starved local authorities are allowed or encouraged to cease providing those services that they are not required by law to deliver, in a process of "statutory entrenchment". Local economic development would then be handed over to the LEC networks, and it would appear that local authorities themselves had chosen this option.

However, it is important to recall that the expenditure on local authority economic development is very small compared with total council spending. In the mid-1980s, the discretionary "2p rate" spend by Scotland's councils (Ramsdale and Capon, 1986, p.14) amounted to only 0.34 per cent of total rate and grant borne expenditure. This factor, together with the discretionary nature of the service, probably explains why the Scottish Office has not tried to impose the kind of central controls which exist for the main local services, namely schools, roads and social work. Small may therefore prove to be beautiful for those who want economic development to remain with local government, since local authority economic development may simply be too small an item to interest the new Parliament, particularly during its early, very busy years.

On the other hand, if, as is widely expected, the Labour Party forms the largest political grouping in the new Parliament, some degree of centralisation seems likely. Prior to the 1997 General Election, Labour promised some degree of democratisation and community accountability for the LECs, and it also promised a degree of policy centralisation by the ending of the LECs' status as private companies by turning them into "subsidiaries" of SE and HIE (Fairley, 1997). Since the General Election Labour has opted for a strong degree of policy continuity raising concerns in local government that SE, HIE and the LECs are the preferred institutions.

7.6.3   *A force for decentralisation?*

Any major policy centralisation would be a betrayal of the Convention (SCC, 1995) as well as a clear departure from the intentions of the White Paper (Scottish Office, 1997a). The latter is quite clear (para 6.2) that:

> In establishing a Scottish Parliament to extend democratic accountability, the
> government do not expect the Scottish Parliament and its Executive to

accumulate a range of new functions at the centre which would be more appropriately and efficiently delivered by other bodies within Scotland.

This could of course be interpreted in favour of local authorities, the LECs or both, though it is clear that both councils and LECs could be vulnerable and have much to play for. We have noted many of the issues before local government. Less discussed, however, is the fact that LECs are not specified in or required by the 1990 Act (Fairley and Lloyd, 1995b), and the LECs were the choice of the Scottish Office under the control of a Conservative administration which wished to give the private sector a bigger role in public policy. Moreover, the Act also allows for devolution by SE and HIE to "local partnerships", and the creative use of the legislation could encourage a genuine institutional diversity based upon the emergence of the real, local "drivers" of economic development.

Futhermore, it is a belief of both the SCC and the White Paper that Scotland needs democratic renewal at both local and national levels. The former is unlikely if local government continues to lose areas of responsibility, and it is a belief of both that public policy is greatly over-centralised in the Scottish Office. The second belief suggests that the Parliament will seek out appropriate areas of current Scottish Office control and decentralise them to local agencies, and in some areas there are signs that this process may have begun. The Scottish Office approach to structural fund governance is interesting in this context since the activities of choosing priorities and implementing programmes have been ceded to regional partnerships (Danson et al, 1997), and as a result of this process the expertise and experience needed for policy making is likely to quickly become decentralised.

7.6.4   New forms of partnership?

The Wheatley Report wanted to see a new form of partnership between local authorities and the Scottish Office, though this did not develop. The relationship which did develop was, in management terms, generally a "low trust" relationship in which the centre specifies and controls, and the local authorities implement and comply. Wheatley argued (1969, para.1050) that:

> We view the proper relationship between central and local government as one of partnership. Each must respect the other's individuality as a separate piece of the constitutional machinery of the country, rather than as a mere means of getting work done or as a source of revenue.

The Scottish Parliament may choose to pursue this dream, but the implications of such a course would be profound. The prevailing culture and attitudes in the Scottish Office would need to change, and the preference for centralised and uniform policy approaches would need to be reversed. Local government would need to become accepted as a genuine and equal partner in government rather than simply the local manager of national policies, and the Scottish Office itself would need to internally co-ordinate its currently fragmented dealings with local government, as Wheatley recommended. Local authorities, for their part, would need to adopt a more positive view of the Scottish Office, and to develop their own policy capacity so that they were equipped to play a more equal role at this level.

As far as local economic development is concerned, the Scottish Parliament could do a number of things to promote a more modern form of partnership. For instance, it could enhance councils' roles at the expense of the various quangos active in the field, and there have been calls for the LECs' activities to be transferred to local authorities (Fairley, 1997). The Parliament could also ensure that local authorities are adequately funded so that they are not reluctantly squeezed out of or tempted to withdraw from economic development. Moreover, the Parliament could offer councils a "power of general competence" (McFadden 1997). Such a power would not in itself be very important for local economic development. We have noted that Scottish councils did not use most of their capacity under the "2p rate" system in the 1980s, and since the 1994 Act there has been no real statutory constraint on local authority economic development. However, such a power would be of more than symbolic importance since it would permit more rapid development of projects where competence was in doubt or where legal challenge could be posed, for example the University of the Highlands and Islands. Furthermore, it would indicate that a basis of trust existed between the two layers of elected government, which in turn would create the basis for more effective forms of partnership.

Acknowledgements

Helpful comments on an earlier draft were made by Stuart Borrowman, Dr Howard Fisher, Gordon McIntosh, Professor Lindsay Paterson, Peter Suttie, Paolo Vestri and the authors. The views expressed in the chapter are those of the author.

Part IV

Spatial impacts

8 The Scottish Parliament and the planning system: addressing the strategic deficit through spatial planning

GREG LLOYD

8.1 Introduction

The constitutional reform associated with the creation of the Scottish Parliament will undoubtedly have the effect of facilitating a strong democratic expression of interest in the future of the Scottish economy, society and environment. It will inevitably be accompanied by a raising of a series of expectations concerning the future management of the economy, the delivery of services and the quality of the environment. In this respect, the vested interests may be territorial or sectoral in character; such interests may have been building up for some time, but they are now being given added impetus as a result of the perceived potential of constitutional reform. Any special pleading, however, will create difficulties for the Scottish Parliament in mediating between them, particularly in the immediate term, and in attempting to set appropriate agendas for action. There is also the concomitant danger of failed expectations on the part of the electorate, which could be damaging to the new institution (Nye, 1997). In this context, assertive processes of governance, planning and public administration could prove essential to addressing these matters by setting agendas for action and establishing a basis for consensus and a framework for consistent policy implementation. For example, in the debates leading up to the referendum on the Scottish Parliament, it was suggested that while

> devolution undoubtedly does provide opportunities for influencing the Scottish economy, possibly significantly, the scale and even direction of effects depends on the particular contribution of policies pursued by the Scottish Parliament and the reactions of the Scottish people to them (McGregor et al, 1997, p.208).

This suggests that attention needs to be paid to the alternative management approaches that are available to the Scottish Parliament in devising strategies and policies for labour, capital and land in order to secure an efficient economy whilst taking account of likely resource restrictions as well as the high expectations of the Scottish people.

This chapter considers the role of the land use planning system in providing a framework for accommodating the interests associated with planning and development at national, regional and local levels of decision making. Land use planning is an accepted and legitimate activity of government which is intended to address the wider social and community conflicts associated with the use and development of land and property (Cullingworth and Nadin, 1994). The economic rationale for establishing a regulatory framework for land use planning with controls over the development of land within approved plans for its future allocation was to facilitate a more efficient, profitable and socially responsible land market. It has evolved over time as a facilitating process of conflict mediation associated with the development of land and property, economic development opportunities and the provision of infrastructure to support that development (Healey et al, 1988). Yet, the contribution of land use planning is much wider than this. As a process, it brings together in a co-ordinated manner land use, property development and infrastructure provision so as to provide the foundations for local and regional economic development, job creation and inward investment.

At the present time, however, there is a strategic deficit within the institutional and policy arrangements for Scottish land use planning practice. This is not a new problem, but it is now emerging within a different policy and institutional context, including the integration processes taking place in Europe (Henig, 1997). In 1972, for example, a Select Committee on Land Resource Use in Scotland recorded that:

> it is important to know whether there exist clear and explicit strategies for the countryside in general and rural land uses in particular; whether they are mutually consistent and by what machinery they are achieved over the whole or part of Scotland. If there seems to be a lack of such an explicit strategy, the question will arise whether policies designed for particular ends, whether primarily concerned with land use or not, are sufficiently co-ordinated in both their formation and their execution, and have sufficient regard for the resource base itself. Thirdly there is the question whether sufficient regard is paid to monitoring and evaluating existing polices and land use trends, as a basis for informed policy making in the future. Lastly, there should be borne in mind the adequacy of information on existing uses and trends, including those factors intrinsic to the land itself, such as capability to support existing uses, and man-made features such as land tenure and the size of management units (HMSO, 1972, p.3).

Notwithstanding the measures subsequently put into place to address the issues identified by the Select Committee there has been a more recent erosion of the arrangements for strategic planning in Scotland. Today, a strategic planning deficit exists which represents a fundamental challenge for the Scottish Parliament to address. A failure to do this will limit the potential of the land use planning system in making a valuable contribution in the new context of constitutional reform in Scotland.

In the next two sections, this chapter reviews the current arrangements for land use planning in Scotland and highlights the nature of the strategic deficit in the planning framework. Section 8.4 then considers the case for a robust strategic planning framework which would capture current trends in Europe and which would provide a context to the consistent devising and implementation of policy across Scotland. Section 8.5 advocates some of the national and regional arrangements that would provide such a strategic planning framework for the Scottish Parliament. Finally, section 8.6 presents the main conclusions.

8.2 Current arrangements for land use planning in Scotland

The Scottish land use planning system comprises: the preparation of development plans which set out the community interest in land use and development; development control as the means of regulating land development; central government guidance to establish planning priorities and best practice; and public participation to provide a democratic basis to planning processes. Over the last fifty years the land use planning system is viewed as having achieved a high quality of environment and the resolution of conflicts over land use and development (Cullingworth, 1994). In practice, the structure of the Scottish land use planning system is similar to that in England and Wales, although the culture of Scottish planning has differed as a consequence of its particular administrative and institutional features (Hayton, 1996; Rowan-Robinson, 1997).

In terms of structure, the land use planning system is administered at two levels - national and local. At the national level, the Scottish Office provides an overview of the management of the Scottish economy and its physical infrastructure, with a strong regional emphasis involving the integration of economic and land use matters (Paterson, 1994). This was illustrated in the regional planning studies conducted throughout Scotland in the earlier post war period, for example the Tay Valley Plan, West Central Scotland Plan and Development Plan for North East Scotland (Wannop, 1995). More recently, this assertiveness has been reflected in the Scottish Office's administrative capacity in representing Scotland in the European Union (Wright, 1995). Today the Scottish Office sets out strategic land use policy guidance through Circulars, National Policy Planning Guidelines (NPPGs) and Planning Advice Notes (PANs). Circulars provide statements of government policy and guidance on policy implementation through legislative or procedural change. NPPGs provide statements on government policy on nationally important land use issues and other planning matters, supported where appropriate by a locational framework, and they identify land resources having national significance in Scotland which should either be safeguarded from or for development. PANs provide advice on good practice and other relevant information (Lloyd, 1994).

At the local level, local authorities provide the administrative structure for structure and local plans which set out the social interest in land use and development and the development control process which regulate land and property development to conform to the development plans. The structure of Scottish local government in the 1970s is viewed as having facilitated the strategic approach to land use planning practice (Rowan-Robinson, 1997). This comprised a two tier structure of Regional and District councils. The Regional authorities were responsible for strategic functions including structure planning, the provision of infrastructure, social work and industrial development. The District councils assumed the responsibility for local planning, development control and housing. The two tiers and their associated responsibilities complemented one another, and, notwithstanding some conflicts of interest between them, the institutional arrangements provided a powerful strategic approach to planning, development and infrastructure provision.

The strategic approach to land use planning and the management of change in local areas may be illustrated by the innovative regional report measure that was introduced to facilitate the reorganisation of Scottish local government in 1975. Regional reports were intended to provide a statement of the policy agendas of the new Regional authorities and to reflect their corporate approach to prevailing and anticipated economic, social, environmental and land use issues and circumstances. More importantly, perhaps, the regional reports were intended to assess the available resources and competing priorities of the Regional authorities, and thereby to provide a strategic context to decision making and investment planning by District councils, private interests and other public sector bodies. The regional reports were to concentrate on policy decisions and were to reflect the corporate approach of the Regional council to economic, social, environmental and land use issues. More specifically, the reports were to indicate their land use implications, address the region as a whole and identify areas where positive planning action was required. Further, they were to provide a basis for assessing the land, manpower and investment requirements of the regions, considering available resources and competing priorities, incorporating consultation with other public sector bodies and with private industrial interests. The regional reports were to indicate what form of planning action was considered necessary in those areas and the extent to which this was to involve a variation in existing investment patterns. However, the regional report concept had one further and highly significant role - it established the foundations of a national perspective on strategic planning in Scotland both at a descriptive level and in terms of policy implementation. By May 1976 the required reports had been submitted to the Secretary of State for Scotland, providing a Scotland wide perspective of the strategic management of change by local government (Lloyd, 1996).

These arrangements suggest both a structure and culture of strategic planning which informed land use planning practice in a number of ways. The regional reports provided a policy context to the preparation of structure plans and local plans, with the associated allocation of infrastructure to support land development. The strategic policy guidance issued by the Scottish Office provided an ongoing overview of planning priorities for selected land use issues such as the onshore developments associated with North Sea oil and gas, skiing, agriculture and out of town retailing centres. Throughout the 1970s and 1980s, in particular, the distinctive strategic characteristic of the Scottish planning system was acknowledged. Indeed, it was noted that the structure and culture of strategic planning provided "a sounder foundation for the preparation and implementation of development plans" (Hayton, 1996, p.78). In this respect, the strategic (or co-operative) approach to planning practice and the management of urban and regional change can be linked to the broader corporatist culture which had prevailed in Scotland and which encouraged an acceptance of the need for integrated action to address Scotland's specific needs and circumstances (McCrone, 1992). This cultural environment created a consensus on the need for intervention through planning and development which included the creation of regional development agencies.

8.3   A strategic deficit in planning?

In more recent times, however, that strategic perspective has been eroded in a number of ways. In part this is due to the political and ideological moves away from the concept of regional planning. Regional planning is a specific form of intervention in the spatial and institutional economy which attempts to provide an integrated approach to the management of economic, social and physical change in defined geographical areas. In general, regional planning operates at a sub-national scale of administration, thereby providing a strategic framework for agenda setting, resource allocation and decision making at the local level by local authorities, public sector agencies and the private sector. In practice, regional planning is caught between the national policy agenda for the management of industrial restructuring and economic change and the local outcome and response to that change. Not surprisingly, perhaps, the experience of regional planning in Britain has been a relatively chequered one (Glasson, 1992). Furthermore, the rise and fall of regional planning has reflected emerging economic priorities and political pressures associated with arguments concerning the relative efficiency and effectiveness of intervention and markets. Notwithstanding these powerful influences, however, regional planning has been described as representing "an enduring but inconstant feature of public affairs" in post war Britain (Wannop and Cherry, 1994, p.52).

Local government reorganisation in the mid 1990s is perhaps the most important factor to be considered in the creation of a strategic planning deficit in Scotland. The Local Government (Scotland) Act 1994 introduced a streamlined, single tier, market oriented, enabling system of local governance (Paddison, 1997). This process of local government reorganisation replaced the established two tier structure of Regional authorities with responsibilities for the strategic functions of provision of water and sewerage infrastructure, social work, roads and transport and structure planning, and District authorities with responsibilities for local services and housing, local planning and development control. Interwoven into the two tier structure were powerful intellectual arguments for an assertive strategic planning approach which provided leadership in the management of change, a strategic overview of key issues and the co-ordination of policies by different public and private bodies (Lloyd, 1994). As a consequence, it has been argued, for example, that the Regional authorities:

> brought a vision and breadth of perception to the physical development of...[Scotland]...bringing together...economic land use and transportation needs within a coherent strategic framework...in a way which has reconciled the apparently irreconcilable and ensured a consensus amongst the wide range of public, private and voluntary interests (Midwinter, 1995, p.xii).

Local government reorganisation has served to erode that strategic element since it has involved the fragmentation of the established strategic Regional authorities into 32 unitary councils. Moreover, this process has not been even across Scotland as can be seen by comparing, for example, Fife and Tayside, and it has inevitably destabilised the strategic perspectives of metropolitan regions, the relationships with their rural hinterlands and the dynamics of local housing and labour markets. Furthermore, the strategic arrangements for regional planning will be diluted further as a result of the transfer of water and sewerage responsibilities from the councils to three new centralised Public Water Authorities. This is significant since it erodes the ability of local authorities to secure the strategic management of change and the provision of services for land and property development. Instead of the old regions being the focus for the allocation of infrastructure, the new arrangements are based on very much larger geographical areas. When combined with resource restrictions for the provision of water and sewerage, the strategic management of development becomes more difficult.

Local government reorganisation has also involved changed arrangements for structure planning in Scotland. In some instances, the established structure plan areas have been broken up and reformed into new Structure Plan Areas. This may be seen as a major disruption to the existing regional strategies for land use and development (Hayton, 1994a, 1995). Certainly, the new structure plan areas will have to be made more compatible with local housing and labour market areas. Another dimension to the loss of a strategic approach to planning and the local management of change was the failure to maintain the regional report preparation exercise. This was a "one off" matter which served its purpose in terms of a process of institutional change. A related issue arose from the changes to the planning system itself. In short, the focus of land use planning has become relatively more localised and site specific. This is a principal consequence of the effects of the liberal market ideology associated with Thatcherism on the scope, focus and operation of development planning and the development control system (Thornley, 1993). It is important to note, also, that the realignment of land use planning controls with the interests of the private property development sector has continued in the post-Thatcher period (Allmendinger and Tewdwr-Jones, 1997). The outcome of this realignment may be exemplified by the focus of recent planning legislation in relation to a plan led system which has formalised the procedures of the planning process (McGregor and Ross, 1995). Taken together, these processes suggest that the strategic elements to the Scottish land use planning system have been badly eroded. This begs the question of the future of strategic planning under a Scottish Parliament.

8.4   A cascade of strategic planning for the Scottish Parliament?

Land use planning systems, comprising development plans and development control, "claim to offer a democratically acceptable machinery for defining the collective interest in environmental issues in places, at a time when social heterogeneity and cross cutting social cleavages make reaching agreement democratically an increasing problem" (Healey, 1994, p.40). In order to achieve this, development plans and development control activities by local authorities cannot take place in a vacuum. Strategic planning offers the potential of a more robust framework to accommodate the regional and local impact of economic, corporate and industrial change, and also accords with emerging ideas about the role of planning. There are a number of advantages to be gained from a strategic perspective provided through the land use planning system, including consistent formulation and implementation of policy, consensus over public and private investment decision making, greater certainty over institutional activity and an ability to address uncertainty through a contingent approach (Diamond, 1979; Bruton and Nicholson, 1985).

Furthermore, it is important to acknowledge that strategic planning straddles the policy field between national and local levels of decision making. This strategic level of public policy and administration enables economies to address external forces of change such as those associated with the globalisation of economic activity, investment and development, ownership and control, risk taking and accountability which create circumstances of considerable uncertainty for Scotland. Globalisation and international competitiveness have resulted in a marked concentration of economic and corporate power and have created a degree of financial and industrial mobility that can bypass the regulatory frameworks based on the nation state (Group of Lisbon, 1995). These

> processes which are re-writing the rules of world order are the old masters of global space, the state formations that have historically divided territories and organised economies, ruled sovereignly over populations and corporations, disciplined subjects and consolidated identities. Absolute rulers no more, the slipping power of states threatens the advent of an unruly world, a world no longer amenable to the state-centric ruling systems and disciplining institutions of the past (O'Tuathail et al, 1998, p.1).

The outcomes of these processes can be better managed within a robust planning framework. In the context of inward investment for example, an appropriate managed approach requires more than piecemeal incrementalism as the basis of an effective inward investment strategy. A strategic approach drawing on best practice, industrial and corporate strengths, available finance and networking would be appropriate to create a new source of competitive advantage for Scotland (Botham, 1997). It has been argued that in such circumstances planning is necessary to address the uncertainty and to provide for a "balance to be struck between the pursuit of regional policies geared to the global economy and the economic competitiveness between the major blocks in the economically advanced nations and the pursuit of a more environmentally sustainable and equitable growth" (Glasson, 1992, p.204).

At the present time, the concept and process of strategic planning corresponds to emerging ideas about economic management in such uncertain circumstances. In particular, drawing on recent research in the United States, there is the argument that the "clouding veils of national jurisdictions, as seen through the nationalist paradigm, obscure [the] line of sight between local economic commons. The regional paradigm pierces these veils and clearly reflects that the critical economic relationships are between or among regional economic commons" (Barnes and Ledebur, 1998, p.122). In this context, the region may be seen as:

> a single economy, an economic commons, overlaid with multiple political jurisdictions [which] provides a radically different perspective for policy and

policy making. If interdependence is a signature economic characteristic of the region, collaboration becomes a key to success in economic governance of the commons. In other words, if economic interdependence is a fact, collaboration is a defining political challenge. A region's success in responding to this challenge may be a critical determinant of its economic future (Barnes and Ledebur, 1998, p.93).

This coincidence of ideas is mirrored in the arguments and ideas associated with European spatial planning practice. For example, it has been asserted that the traditions of spatial policy formulation and implementation in Europe offer considerable potential for a positive and innovative influence on British planning practice (Hague, 1996). The argument of the need to draw down on a wider European experience of planning is not new. In 1972, for example, the Select Committee on Land Resource Use in Scotland acknowledged that:

> the entry of the United Kingdom into Europe will mean that many aspects of land use policy and machinery will have to be reviewed. Those defects in planning which in the past could have proved detrimental to Scotland's development will now become even more crucial. Conversely the benefits likely to be achieved from a smoothly and swiftly working planning system will be greater than existed previously. Because at the European scale Scotland is one of many regions with an urgent need of economic development it will be even more important than in the past to have a clear Scottish policy on land resource use. Advanced planning of the necessary infrastructure to support the land allocation policy will be required (HMSO, 1972, p.4).

In a more contemporary fashion, the emerging European tradition of spatial planning is attracting critical attention, and it is of particular significance for the case for strategic planning under the Scottish Parliament. Spatial planning is described as:

> setting frameworks and principles to guide the location of development and physical infrastructure. It consists of a set of governance practices for developing and implementing strategies, plans, policies and projects, and for regulating the location, timing and form of development. These practices are shaped by the dynamics of economic and social change, which give rise to demands for space, location and qualities of places. These dynamics also shape expectations about how demands will be met, and the values accorded to the attributes of places and buildings. The demands are mediated through local political systems and practices and by regional and national government politics and administration. Through these interactions, general economic and social tendencies interrelate with local conditions and concerns to produce distinctive, contingent responses to the dynamics of urban region change (Healey, 1997, p.4).

In practice, this suggests an approach to the process of planning that reflects an awareness that spatial planning has shifted its focus from a concern with purely physical planning and land use matters to a wider concern for social, economic, environmental and political issues. This is interpreted as "a return of the importance of strategic thinking in planning" (Alden, 1996, p.10). The potential of this approach is important in enabling planning to address emerging pressures in environmental, social and economic change (Newman and Thornley, 1996; de Roo, 1993; Roberts, 1993).

What options are there available for the Scottish Parliament to provide a strategic planning framework? Diamond (1979) has asserted that strategic planning should be capable of assuming a variety of forms which may be deemed appropriate to prevailing circumstances. In this context, Bruton and Nicholson (1985) advocate a hierarchical system where a national-regional-local system of planning exists to enable a dialogue of national interests, regional proprieties and local circumstances to be mediated in such a manner as to allow for contingency and uncertainty in economic, social and environmental change. The prospect of constitutional reform in Scotland and Wales has prompted calls for a wider debate about the future form and scope of strategic and local planning arrangements (Hayton, 1997a; Smith, 1997). In particular, Hayton (1997b) has suggested the creation of unitary development plans at the local level as an opportunity to create a more efficient land use planning framework. It is important, however, that attention should be paid to the strategic aspects of local planning. Whilst accepting the arguments that arrangements for local planning could be the subject of critical review and possible overhaul, it is argued here that adequate provision for a local dimension to land use planning already exists and that this provides for the forward planning of land use and development in the community interest, the arrangement of development priorities and the provision of infrastructure and the regulation of development. The critical task now is the creation of an appropriate strategic planning framework.

8.5   A national-regional planning system for Scotland?

In considering the future of land use planning under the Scottish Parliament, Hayton (1997b) has argued the case for a national plan "covering the whole of Scotland, which incorporates policies, regardless of their origin, which have national implications" (Hayton, 1997b, p.22). Again, this is not a new idea. In 1972 the Select Committee on Land Resource Use in Scotland supported the case for the preparation of an indicative plan for Scotland to be conducted at a national scale. A regional dimension would be secured by demonstrating how the plan was intended to utilise the land for urban, industrial and recreational purposes. The Select Committee thereby recommended what was in effect a national structure plan which would embody a national industrial strategy together with a comprehensive and integrated regional planning system of land use zoning and land allocation policies. It stressed:

> the need to strike a balance between on the one hand, too specific guidelines which produce an over rigid system in this age of fluctuating population trends, rapidly changing technology and surprising discoveries of natural resources and on the other hand an insufficiency of national policy guidelines which result in excessively overlapping claims being embodied in development plans and an insufficiency of information being available to entrepreneurs anxious to exploit some new opportunity. Clearly this is a

difficult balance to strike to everyone's satisfaction but we are of the opinion that the weight of evidence is that insufficient guidelines have existed in the past and that more emphasis should be given to remedying this in the near future than the Government perceive at present (HMSO, 1972, p.11).

For the purposes of the Scottish Parliament, Hayton (1997b) suggests the National Plan would have two main roles: the spatial expression of the public policy agenda in Scotland and a statement of nationally important land use policies. The latter would be similar in intent to the existing compendium of NPPGs. History shows us again that these ideas have already been rehearsed and that there is a powerful case for an indicative plan for Scotland. The Select Committee on Land Resource Use in Scotland (HMSO, 1972) noted that:

> there is a need to prepare an indicative plan for Scotland on a national scale which will show how it is intended to utilise the land for urban, industrial and recreational purposes. To prepare such a policy plan it will be necessary to take into account the views of planning authorities, industrialists, trade unions and many other interested parties. The structure plans of the new regional planning authorities must conform with the national indicative plan. This is an essential step if Scotland is to compete for industry on favourable terms with other European countries. Developers must be encouraged by simplifying and shortening planning procedures, and as a first step a forward looking national plan is required, setting out what areas can be designated for future use. More detailed plans would then be drawn up by regional and district authorities. Where sites have been identified as suitable for particular industrial purposes inquiries should commence prior to planning applications being received so that prospective developers could be told for certain which sites are available and in accord with the strategy for Scotland. They could then plan a programme of development knowing that one decision did not hang upon the result of a planning inquiry yet to come. Such an arrangement would not in any way prevent the local planning authority from imposing proper planning conditions to achieve the necessary environmental and pollution standards (HMSO, 1972, p.13).

There is interest elsewhere in such an approach. In Wales, for example, in anticipation of the creation of the Assembly, there is a proposal to put into place a national economic development strategy. This would represent a new approach to regional and local economic development in Wales, based principally on a radical overhaul of existing development agencies and inward investment bodies. This proposal advocates an all-Wales strategy framework which "will define the essential priorities that need to be tackled; the key policies and mechanisms for addressing them; how funding will support them; and how progress will be evaluated and reviewed" (Welsh Office, 1997, p.2). The Consultation Paper proposes measures that will enable economic priorities within Wales to be articulated and policies put in place to address the associated economic and social differentials. To this end, forums will be established for four geographical jurisdictions to act as a focus for the integrated work of the various agencies involved. Throughout, the document stresses the need for local control and action to ensure democratic links within a partnership of different interests.

Within a national context for indicative planning, there is also a case for a process of regional planning to provide a strategic perspective on the management of change in defined geographical regions in Scotland. This could facilitate greater consistency in decision making by different interests, and could provide an agenda for the implementation of local and regional development initiatives. In short, a process of regional planning could be put into effect which could provide the foundation for the national planning framework. At the present time, there is a renaissance of interest in regional planning ideas and this may be linked to the devolution debate in Wales and Scotland (Stewart, 1997). Certainly, in England and Wales there has been a rediscovery of the merits of the structures and processes of regional planning which seeks to provide spatial coherence and detail for economic activity and to establish a strategic context within which local priorities can be identified and articulated. In particular, the adoption of regional planning guidance is viewed as an appropriate vehicle to establish a strategic framework within which local authorities could discharge their statutory responsibilities.

The process of regional planning guidance is based on both bottom-up and top-down consensus building. In England and Wales, neighbouring local authorities form conferences to debate the form of regional planning guidance required for their area, and, after taking on board representations from key players, advice is submitted to the Secretary of State. Draft guidance is then published allowing for further deliberation, negotiation and debate. Finally, the regional planning guidance is set out for implementation by the participating local authorities. While research evidence shows that the process has not been even or problem free, it does provide a relatively effective and speedy vehicle for strategic planning for regions experiencing different economic, social and environmental circumstances. The process is also an open one, and it provides for the full involvement of all key players (Roberts, 1996b).

Is there a case for regional planning guidance in Scotland? A strategic perspective of this nature allows for national priorities to be put into place; allows for an integrated approach to be devised between the key players; allows for the resolution of conflict between institutions charged with different responsibilities; and can help overcome individualistic behaviour by any key player (Roberts, 1996b). Once again, history provides a valuable insight. The Select Committee on Land Resource Use in Scotland argued in 1972 that:

> regional plans have not existed, at least in a form in which they could be readily implemented. Many plans have been produced by local authorities, but the machinery has not been capable of welding them into a regional strategy. In areas where there was a clear need to look at the whole picture the Scottish Office promoted studies, but these can only be advisory, and no local authority is obliged to implement them, although they may adopt them if they so wish, and the Scottish Office has tried to take out those parts which might be of use to local authorities and to arrange for their implementation e.g. New Towns.

But, since there are as yet no regional authorities, plans of a regional nature cannot be readily imposed (HMSO, 1972, p.7).

There is already an interest in this form of regional strategic planning. In considering the relationship between a Scottish Parliament and unitary local government, for example, Sinclair (1997) advocates a process of community planning which would provide for community leadership. This is perceived as an essential foundation for effective local governance. In particular, "councils should be given a duty of community planning which would extend the concept of the old regional reports and would require all local agencies, such as Local Enterprise Company, Health Board and the Scottish Homes office to submit their annual plans to their local council" (Sinclair, 1997, p.17). The community plans would draw together the activities and policies of the various agencies concerned with the social, environmental and economic management of cities and regions in Scotland.

The community plan proposal draws on the experience of the earlier regional reports and seeks to address the absence of a regional perspective brought about by the loss of the old Regional authorities. It would have a number of important benefits at this level and would allow for the amalgamation of priorities, resources and policies within broad geographical areas or regions of Scotland. It would also enhance the process of openness and accountability in government and facilitate the achievement of principles of subsidiarity. The process of preparing, debating and implementing regional planning guidance dovetails and builds on the community plan idea, which involves the same process at a local level (Sinclair, 1997). The advantage is that regional planning guidance would provide for a national perspective for the Scottish Parliament, draw together national level priorities, problems and policies for different areas of Scotland and integrate and facilitate local consensus building and accountability. More significantly, regional planning guidance enhances the potential of the community planning proposal and, once established, would give community plans far greater authority. This would then help to overcome anarchic interest group lobbying through a managed framework for change for regions in Scotland.

8.6   Conclusions

This chapter has argued the case for a strategic framework of national and regional planning to ensure the full potential of the participative and integrative processes involved in land use planning. It advocates exploring the historical experience of policy innovation in Scotland and the earlier deliberations on an appropriate form of planning system, as well as the insights provided by the arrangements for regional planning guidance in England and Wales. Although these initiatives may have been far from perfect in practice, they nonetheless offer ways forward to fully realise the potential of strategic planning within and by the Scottish Parliament in order to address the different social, economic and environmental characteristics across Scotland. The principal focus, however, should be on the process and not the structure of strategic planning. It is not intended to focus attention on the creation of bureaucratic levels of national, regional and local intervention under the Scottish Parliament. What is more important is to release the potential of the dialogue and participatory aspects of planning, exemplified by the regional report, regional planning guidance and the more recent proposal for community planning. The driving force of constitutional reform rests on the issue of enhancing the accountability of government to society. This will be achieved in part by the setting up of new arrangements for representative democratic debate over Scottish domestic policies respectively in the Parliament. This forms part of a wider political agenda for change which has already started to address the new social, economic and environmental challenges facing the planning system (Blowers, 1997). The political, managerial and physical decentralisation of local government activities following reorganisation is also part of this modernist tendency in local governance.

There would be a number of benefits arising from the establishment of a national and regional strategic perspective on the planning and development of the Scottish economy. At a time of institutional adjustment and limited resources, coupled with increasing demands on those resources, a national perspective would allow for open, reasoned and logical priorities to be debated and set. An overview of policy priorities of the different organisations involved would pull together their various activities and eradicate overlap and duplication, bringing true efficiency gains in governance. A national strategic perspective would allow for the appropriate decisions to be made about the provision of infrastructure for industrial, commercial and social development. It would also allow for the fuller integration of land use planning with arrangements for economic and social development - something which is lamentably absent at present (Bellini, 1996). It would allow for more effective managerial decision-making by encouraging the integration of the LECs, which in many areas are de facto regional development agencies whose jurisdiction covers several local authorities, with other agencies such as those concerned with infrastructure, environmental protection and natural heritage, as well as the local authorities. Finally, a national perspective would allow a more realistic view to be developed of the interaction of the housing and labour markets that comprise the Scottish economy, rather than being hidebound by administrative boundaries which do not reflect the dynamics of modern day life in Scotland.

9   Implications of the Scottish Parliament for urban regeneration

JOHN McCARTHY

9.1   Introduction

"Urban regeneration policy", or "urban policy", defined in broad terms as the management of urban change, has sought to foster prosperity or moderate the impact of decay since the late 1960s. For much of this period urban policy has been closely associated with economic regeneration, often with property development as a major component, though the emphasis of policy has changed somewhat in the 1990s. While the root causes of urban decline may differ depending on local circumstances, structural factors bound up with broader socio-economic change lie at the heart of the problem, with the frequent result of an increasing incidence of poverty and multiple deprivation or disadvantage. This is manifested by a range of interrelated social and economic symptoms; the social symptoms include increasing income differentials, crime and racial conflict, and the economic symptoms include de-industrialisation, manufacturing decline, increasing unemployment and welfare dependency, and decay of infrastructure (Pacione, 1997a).

While urban policy has sought to address these issues, it has shifted in orientation somewhat. Policy was initially developed as a means of positive discrimination by which funding could be targeted to "areas of special need". However, this approach was later transformed into one geared more to enterprise creation, prioritising the need to secure the local conditions for economic growth; as an important part of this approach, leverage of private sector investment was to be achieved by promoting partnership between business and public sector interests and encouraging community self help. More recently, a strategic approach to policy has been promoted that also allows a greater role for local communities in regeneration activity.

Nevertheless, the persistence since 1968 of broadly the same areas at the head of tables indicating levels of deprivation and disadvantage is an indictment of the effectiveness of such policy in practice (Edwards, 1997). Consequently, many observers have voiced extreme dissatisfaction with the development and application of urban policy. The tendency of policy to avoid articulating basic aims, for instance in relation to meeting needs, is often stressed (Turok and Hopkins, 1997) as is the lack of coherence of policy at the national level, which has constrained the ability of other actors to deliver regeneration outcomes (Pacione, 1997b). It has also been suggested that the frequent prioritisation of property development as a means of regeneration has resulted in a very limited range of interests being served, and there is evidence that such approaches have increased social and economic polarisation (Atkinson and Moon, 1994). While more recent initiatives have avoided this approach, even the most contemporary tenets of regeneration practice, such as the adoption of partnership structures, have been criticised as reflecting a more general obsession with form at the expense of substance (Edwards, 1997), with the effect of distancing policy-makers from underlying urban problems.

More cynically, it may be suggested that the very emphasis on rather marginal urban policy may itself represent an attempt on the part of government to avoid addressing the underlying causes of urban decline, with the implication that glossy, high-profile initiatives are intended primarily for their symbolic value in order to provide a distraction from the process and effects of decline, as well as the meagre and decreasing public resources which are directed to tackling it (Atkinson and Moon, 1994). Meanwhile, areas of multiple disadvantage suffer from increasing marginalisation and residualisation, in the absence of a coherent, national approach which addresses the causes rather than the symptoms of the problem.

A wholesale reformulation of urban policy therefore seems to be necessary. In considering the implications and the opportunities arising from the creation of a Scottish Parliament in this context, section 9.2 will consider first the distinctive approach to urban policy in Scotland, by looking at the specific initiatives that have evolved since the late 1960s, culminating in the present policy regime based on Priority Partnership Areas. This will enable unresolved issues in relation to Scottish urban policy to be identified and discussed. Then, in section 9.3, specific suggestions will be made as to ways in which the new Scottish Parliament can address these issues by increasing the capacity of urban policy to tackle them, and increasing the effectiveness of policy implementation in order to improve the impact or outcomes of such policy.

9.2   Scottish urban policy

In recent times, Scottish urban policy, like that in England and Wales, has developed as a consequence of central government priorities, reflecting a progressive emphasis on market forces and the catalytic effect of regeneration activity on the private sector (Pacione, 1989). However, it has also displayed distinctive characteristics as a result of contextual factors. For instance, the relatively small number of areas in Scotland that suffer from urban decline has allowed a greater degree of co-ordination of policy than could be achieved in England, where urban problems are much more widespread (Keating and Boyle, 1986). Moreover, the smaller size and population of Scotland has allowed the formation of a network of formal and informal links between central and local government and private agencies, which has facilitated the co-ordination of policy (Hayton, 1996; Constitution Unit, 1996). The role of the Scottish Office in carrying out delegated administrative functions has also been significant in this context, since it has allowed a degree of policy independence to be developed within Scotland (Lee, 1995). Furthermore, being relatively small, the Scottish Office has avoided the problems of departmentalism evident in urban policy in England.

These factors have allowed a relatively integrated approach to urban policy within which agencies responsible for policy formulation have co-operated closely with those responsible for policy implementation (Boyle, 1988). Prior to local government reorganisation in 1996, the integration of urban policy with mainstream functions was enhanced by the existence of Regional councils which brought together urban and rural areas and which combined responsibilities for land use planning and provision of major services, as was discussed in chapter 8. Moreover, the experience of the Scottish Development Agency (SDA) illustrates a relatively interventionist approach to urban policy which built on the legacy of municipal action in Scotland (Boyle, 1988), though more recent initiatives have displayed a convergence with practice elsewhere (Ayriss, 1997). It is appropriate to look in more detail at major urban policy initiatives in Scotland, in order to form the basis for suggestions for policy refinement by the Scottish Parliament.

9.2.1 *The Urban Programme in Scotland*

Since 1969 the Urban Programme has been the main source of funding for the improvement of urban areas facing problems of deprivation and social stress in Scotland, with eligible areas being defined by the Scottish Office as those falling within the most deprived 10 per cent of Census Enumeration Districts. Through the Urban Programme, 75 per cent grants for capital and revenue funding were given for approved projects, which had to meet Scottish Office criteria that included demonstration of benefits to deprived areas or groups, creation of a new asset, resource or service, and sponsorship by a local authority (Scottish Office, 1993b). Moreover, projects which were intended to supplement main local authority spending programmes, or which were aimed at fulfilling local authority statutory obligations, were excluded. Applications for funding had to compete for approval at national level, though local authorities had to judge which projects best reflected local needs in order to select which to submit. The emphasis on local needs was also reflected in the Scottish Office's encouragement for projects managed by local community groups and voluntary organisations, and by 1993 around 60 per cent of Urban Programme projects were managed in this way (Scottish Office, 1993b).

Overall, around 600 Urban Programme applications were assessed each year, of which around half would receive funding approval (Scottish Office, 1993b). However, the Scottish Urban Programme was criticised as lacking strategic direction in spite of strong centralised control (Keating and Boyle, 1986). The resulting uncertainty made it difficult for local authorities to incorporate Urban Programme schemes into broader regeneration plans, or to combine Urban Programme resources with other sources of funding, and the consequence was a patchwork effect with the results seen as something of a lottery for local communities. Moreover, the Urban Programme appeared to be marginal or even tokenistic in effect, since it did not address the root causes of poverty (Turok and Hopkins, 1997).

9.2.2 *The Scottish Development Agency*

Turok (1987) emphasises the importance of the SDA in bringing a distinctiveness to Scottish urban policy. In fact the SDA was preceded in 1975 by the Scottish Urban

Renewal Unit, which was intended to "formulate broad urban policy based on co-ordinated, controlled positive discrimination for selected urban renewal schemes, encompassing both socioeconomic and physical change" (Keating and Boyle, 1986, p.6). While the Urban Renewal Unit considered establishing a new agency similar to the Development Corporations in England and Wales, it decided instead to create the SDA with the broader aims of reviving the Scottish economy and co-ordinating industrial and economic development strategy with local environmental improvement (Bailey et al, 1995). Specifically, the SDA, which reported directly to the Secretary of State for Scotland, attempted to attract industry to areas of industrial decline, enable development of public housing, progress the five Scottish new towns and initiate local regeneration projects.

However, the SDA evolved through several phases, the first involving taking control of the Glasgow Eastern Area Renewal (GEAR) scheme, aimed at the economic, social and physical improvement of a large part of the inner area of Glasgow. GEAR represented a shift to a more explicit economic orientation in urban policy, as well as a shift in emphasis from new towns to inner urban areas (Keating and Boyle, 1986; Lawless, 1989). While GEAR appears to illustrate the effective partnership of public agencies in area regeneration, it may be suggested that the SDA largely usurped the role of local government within the GEAR area (Atkinson and Moon, 1994).

The role of the SDA changed significantly in 1978, when it began to emphasise economic intervention, particularly in areas faced with manufacturing plant closures (Boyle, 1988), and after 1981 the SDA's initiatives were targeted on small, concentrated "area projects" attracting 60 per cent of the SDA's targetable funding. Such areas were originally selected on the basis of potential, though this proved to be was contentious, and areas were subsequently selected where there was greatest discrepancy between potential and performance. After 1985, there was a new emphasis on the role of the private sector in business development, and areas were selected that afforded commercially attractive development opportunities; these areas included much of Glasgow city centre since the SDA aimed to improve the city's image in order to attract investment. This illustrates the shift from the SDA's original objectives of employment creation and social regeneration towards a reliance on a "property-led" approach (Keating and Boyle, 1986; Hayton, 1996). However, this strategy of "civic boosterism" led to a marked contrast between the improvements to the city centre and the continued deterioration of the peripheral housing estates (Boyle, 1990).

9.2.3 *"New Life for Urban Scotland"*

The policy document, "New Life for Urban Scotland" (Scottish Office, 1988) provided a review of Scottish urban regeneration policy, and, like the English "Action for Cities" policy statement (Department of the Environment, 1988), it attempted to bring about the more effective use of existing funding by means of greater co-ordination of relevant public sector agencies. In addition, the "New Life" initiative proposed a major shift in emphasis away from inner areas to the peripheral housing estates, since the latter continued to display problems such as high unemployment, limited job prospects, a lack of industrial and commercial activity, a preponderance of run down housing, poor service delivery, environmental blight, crime, poor health and poor education standards. Furthermore, the "New Life" statement addressed the problems of fragmentation of urban policy whereby individual projects were seen as ad hoc and localised (Pacione, 1989), and it sought to encourage inter-agency partnership (Scottish Office, 1988; Lloyd and Newlands, 1989) as well as advocating small business formation, self employment and private sector involvement.

Specifically, "New Life" established four Urban Partnerships in designated localities, incorporating a heightened role for local communities (Bailey et al, 1995) and involving a "holistic", multi-sectoral approach, integrating social, economic and environmental improvements, partly because of the perceived inadequacy of narrowly physical initiatives (McGregor et al, 1995). While there were no new financial resources, "New Life" aimed to make more effective use of Urban Programme funding and to increase the leverage of private sector investment. In comparison to the "Action for Cities" policy statement in England, "New Life" appeared to provide a more systematic review of policy, incorporating a more significant role for local authorities and local communities (Bailey et al, 1995), though, like "Action for Cities", it failed to demonstrate an appreciation of the underlying causes of urban decline (Atkinson and Moon, 1994).

The Urban Partnerships were designated in Castlemilk (Glasgow), Ferguslie Park (Paisley), Wester Hailes (Edinburgh) and Whitfield (Dundee). Construction of these peripheral, public sector housing estates had not been accompanied by economic recovery; moreover, they had been developed quickly in response to urgent housing shortages and the unit cost of development had frequently been minimised, with the result that buildings suffered from early obsolescence (McCrone, 1991). The Urban Partnerships were led by the Scottish Office, but they also involved other agencies such as the (then) SDA, Scottish Homes, Health Boards, the Manpower Services Commission, local authorities, community groups and voluntary bodies, and improvement programmes were phased over a ten-year period to allow a strategic approach (Bailey et al, 1995). Significant achievements were made in terms of housing condition and tenure diversification, and by 1995, in the four Partnerships as a whole, around 30 per cent of the housing stock had been renovated, 6,500 homes had been refurbished and 1,300 new homes had been built (Central Office of Information, 1995). Moreover, by 1995 local authority housing ownership in these areas had declined from 97 per cent to 73 per cent, with a growth in owner-occupation from 2.5 per cent to 10 per cent and an increase in community ownership from 1 per cent to 12 per cent (Central Office of Information, 1995).

However, the social and economic regeneration of these areas proved to be more problematic (Gaster et al, 1995; O'Toole et al, 1995), and McGregor et al (1995) show that in Wester Hailes the proportion of households receiving benefits actually increased between 1988 and 1994. The Urban Partnerships have also been criticised for failing to prioritise economic development by for instance investing in appropriate infrastructure, sites and premises (Turok and Hopkins, 1997). Moreover, while the private sector implemented training initiatives, its input into wider strategy formulation was not significant, and the experience of local communities in the

Partnerships was ambivalent and sometimes unproductive (Hastings et al, 1994; McArthur et al, 1994). Furthermore, in spite of the emphasis on locating local improvements within a wider strategic framework, the Urban Partnerships were rather "inward-looking" in practice (Hall, 1997). The overall achievements of the Urban Partnerships have therefore been mixed, though the fear that they would lead only to the displacement of economic and social problems to other areas does not seem to have been borne out (Kintrea et al, 1995; McGregor et al, 1995), and several lessons from the Urban Partnerships were applied to the "Programme for Partnership" initiative.

9.2.4 *"Programme for Partnership"*

"Programme for Partnership" was in part a response to a review of the Urban Programme carried out by the Government in 1991/92, which recommended a more strategic focus with more local co-ordination and integration of projects (Scottish Office, 1993b). Because the Urban Programme had appeared to work more effectively in the Urban Partnership areas, Programme for Partnership sought to extend the comprehensive, co-ordinated, strategic, inter-agency model by the designation of so-called "Priority Partnership Areas" (PPAs) on which regeneration funding would be targeted (Scottish Office, 1995a). In addition to ensuring explicit links with city-wide urban regeneration strategies, the PPAs emphasised the role of local partnerships which could be developed from existing arrangements or set up specially. Around two-thirds of Urban Programme resources was to be allocated to such Priority Partnership Areas, with selection being competitive and applications having to meet a range of criteria including demonstration of local need and quality of proposals. Funding was to be available for up to ten years, with increased local flexibility in funding allocation (Scottish Office, 1995a), and "Regeneration Programmes" were proposed for areas with lesser concentrations of deprivation, involving a lower level of funding (Scottish Office, 1995a). After the announcement of the proposed implementation timetable in May 1995 (Scottish Office, 1995b), the Scottish Office provided advice on the formation of regeneration strategies and partnerships and on the involvement of local communities (Scottish Office, 1996). No further awards of traditional Urban Programme support were to be made for individual projects, though commitments to previously approved projects were to be met.

Following the submission of 29 applications for PPAs, the Scottish Office announced the designation of 12 PPAs in November 1996, as set out in Table 9.1. In addition, ten Regeneration Programmes were designated in Angus, Dundee, East Renfrewshire, Edinburgh, Falkirk, Glasgow, North Ayrshire, North Lanarkshire, South Lanarkshire and Stirling. In terms of assessing the likely impact of these initiatives, it is significant that they are taking place in the context of overall funding reduction (Turok and Hopkins, 1997). Moreover, a preliminary investigation of the process of bidding, designation funding allocation of PPAs and Regeneration Programmes highlights several areas of concern. First, the bidding process reflected an emphasis on competitive principles that placed considerable strains on local authorities immediately after Scottish local government reorganisation in April 1996. Second, the geographical distribution of PPA funding begs questions concerning equity, since small geographical areas appeared unable to demonstrate required levels of social and economic disadvantage. Third, the relatively small funding levels involved may be insufficient to enable the PPAs to achieve their objectives, particularly within the context of overall funding reductions (Lloyd, McCarthy and Illsley, 1997).

Table 9.1   Designated Priority Partnership Areas (PPAs)

Local Authority	Priority Partnership Area
Aberdeen City	Great Northern
Dundee	Ardler
Edinburgh	(a) Craigmillar (b) North
Glasgow	(a) East End (b) North (c) Easterhouse
Inverclyde	Inverclyde
North Lanarkshire	Motherwell North
Renfrewshire	Paisley
South Ayrshire	North Ayr
West Dunbartonshire	West Dunbartonshire

Turok and Hopkins (1997) identify further shortcomings of the PPA initiative, including a lack of adequate guidance for bidders, resulting in a descriptive approach within funding bids with a consequent lack of attention to the causes of the problems identified. There was also an apparent failure to apply criteria consistently in the selection process, possibly reflecting political priorities such as the need to spread the "winners" geographically. This suggests that any future mechanism for urban regeneration based on competitive bidding must ensure an open selection process that demonstrates clear and consistent application of criteria. In addition, it may be suggested that need should form a more significant criterion for allocation in any future initiative, though it must be acknowledged that the PPA's criterion of need, while limited to a requirement to reach a qualifying standard, was given more emphasis than in the English Single Regeneration Budget (SRB) Challenge Fund. Not only does the latter impose relatively few restrictions in terms of areas eligible to bid, the relationship between local need and allocation of funding under the Challenge Fund was reduced between rounds one and two (Nevin et al, 1996), leading to particular problems in terms of housing, for example (Ewart, 1995).

9.3   Key areas for improvement

Having examined the history of recent urban policy initiatives in Scotland, a number of key aspects of urban regeneration may be suggested in relation to which a Scottish Parliament might concentrate attempts to improve the development and application of policy. First, however, it is appropriate to consider current trends in relation to economic and demographic change which affect urban areas in Scotland.

9.3.1   *Contemporary urban change in Scotland*

In terms of economic change, it may be suggested that Scotland in the late 1990s is experiencing a period of growth and stability, with slowly falling average rates of unemployment. However, this masks severe and persistent inequalities that occur across regions, within regions, within cities and between households. The changing nature of employment is important in this respect, and labour market trends have increased income differentials. Moreover, manufacturing employment is in decline and service sector employment is increasing in importance, with an increasing proportion of employment being part-time or temporary in nature (Scottish Homes, 1997). Such factors have led to declining spending power and increasing concentrations of multiple disadvantage in many areas, and this may be expected to continue.

The nature and pattern of demographic change is also critical to the future of urban problems in Scotland, as explained in more detail in Chapter 11. The Scottish population is expected to fall by 80,000 between 1996 and the year 2013. However, the pattern of predicted population change during this period is very uneven; while many areas are expected to increase in population significantly, such as West Lothian with an 11 per cent increase and Stirling with 7 per cent, many major urban areas are expected to lose population, with Glasgow expected to lose 10 per cent and Dundee 9 per cent. This represents a major migration to rural areas, with growth in dormitory settlements such as Perth at the expense of larger cities such as Dundee (Carrell, 1998). Moreover migration is likely to be selective, with younger, economically active residents more likely to move and older, more disadvantaged residents less able to do so; consequently, Scottish cities will have to cope with ever-greater concentrations of social disadvantage.

Moreover, this decline in population is unlikely to lead to decreased pressure on the housing stock in many areas since it is estimated that the declining size of households will result in an increase in the number of households, possibly to 2.33 million by 2008, representing an increase of 207,000 on the 1995 figure. The implications for regeneration needs are perhaps more serious when this factor is combined with that of the ageing population structure of Scotland, with the number of people under the age of 30 forecast to decrease and the number of people between 35 and 59, and over 75, forecast to increase (Scottish Homes, 1997). Since many of these older people will be concentrated in areas of multiple disadvantage for the reasons outlined above, this will add to the need for local spending on appropriate special needs housing and health facilities in such areas.

These factors serve to underline the urgent need for appropriate urban policy to avoid the entry of disadvantaged urban areas into a "vicious spiral" of cumulative decline. Taking into account the foregoing consideration of policy context, it is now possible to identify key areas in which the Scottish Parliament may increase the capacity of urban policy to address the problems of urban decline. These areas, considered below, comprise the following: the distinctiveness of Scottish urban policy; a strategic approach to policy; the use of partnership; the involvement of local communities; and the use of experimentation for policy development.

9.3.2 *Policy distinctiveness*

Turok (1987) identifies three phases of urban policy which can be discerned in both England and Scotland, namely a social orientation until the mid 1970s, a concentration on economic factors and employment in the late 1970s, and an increasing reliance on the private sector since 1979. Moreover, a degree of convergence with policy in England may be illustrated by the later initiatives of the SDA and the use of competition in the PPA initiative (Ayriss, 1997). Nevertheless, as indicated above, a detailed consideration of policy in Scotland suggests distinctive characteristics including a leading role for local authorities, consensus between national and local government agencies, an emphasis on strategy and, perhaps to a lesser extent, on addressing local needs and involving local communities. These characteristics reflect the historical traditions of corporatism in Scotland which have tempered the market-led ideology that has driven urban policy in England and Wales.

The Scottish Parliament could usefully build on such aspects of distinctiveness by developing urban policy that more directly reflected a Scottish interpretation of needs and opportunities. For this to be effective, however, the aims of urban policy would need to be clarified. Such aims have long been relatively obscure, with little attempt at detailed definition by central Government (Atkinson and Moon, 1994; Blackman, 1995). Even when articulated, policy aims have displayed uncertainty over the relative importance of the need to reduce poverty as compared to the need to encourage economic growth (Edwards, 1997). This has led to confusion between aims and means, with features such as partnership structures being seen as ends in themselves. However, a Scottish Parliament would be in a position to clarify urban policy aims in relation to aspects such as social justice, full employment and the reduction of poverty, and such clarification would offer the opportunity for more effective and sustainable regeneration (Oatley, 1995; Pacione, 1997b).

Such clarification of policy aims could lead for instance to the adoption of need as a central criterion for resource allocation, supported by a more explicit and comprehensive central information base dealing with indicators of deprivation. This could enable the establishment of clear links between levels of disadvantage and resource allocations in specific areas, which could enhance the capacity of initiatives to directly address the most severe urban problems. Furthermore, the abandonment of a rigidly competitive approach could avoid the criticisms of fragmentation, incoherence and indiscriminate grant-chasing that have been applied to the Scottish PPA initiative (Edwards, 1997). Moreover, a clearer definition of urban policy aims could also provide the basis for more effective targeting of resources to those excluded groups in most need of support, such as black/minority ethnic groups. While such groups suffer from disadvantage that is often compounded by personal and institutional discrimination, their needs have been largely ignored by urban policy in Scotland in the past.

9.3.3 *A strategic approach*

There has been an emphasis on strategy, at least in rhetoric, within the Scottish approach to urban regeneration. However, recent initiatives such as the Urban Partnerships have been criticised as "inward-looking", lacking a grounding in a wider strategy, possibly for the city-region, which could help to avoid problems such as employment displacement and which could more directly address the causes rather than the symptoms of urban decline (Hall, 1997). Moreover, while analogous initiatives in England such as City Challenge and the SRB Challenge Fund also emphasised a strategic approach, they lacked a concern for national priorities, for instance in relation to planning and infrastructure provision. However, these aspects could be directly addressed by the Scottish Parliament, with the possibility of a new system of land use planning incorporating a national land use and infrastructure plan, allowing national priorities to be linked directly to resources (Hayton, 1997b).

A framework for land use planning would thus provide the opportunity for a more strategic approach to urban regeneration at all levels, and national priorities in relation to needs could be incorporated within such a framework. The way in which such an approach could lead to the more effective achievement of national priorities may be illustrated by the experience of the Netherlands, where strategic planning at the national level is integrated with national objectives for urban regeneration. The Dutch example also ensures the involvement of all levels of government as well as local communities in decision-making, indicating that such a national policy framework can be combined with a high priority for subsidiarity, a key objective of the Scottish Parliament. Moreover, the Scottish Parliament could also facilitate the local application of land policy as applied in the Netherlands, allowing local authorities to fulfil a role as providers of land for development in order to promote strategic aims.

A more strategic approach could also set the context for funding decisions at national level, allowing a more open and rational approach to funding allocations for policy initiatives. This could also facilitate more effective links between funding for urban regeneration and funding for mainstream services, providing the basis for urban policy that addressed the causes of urban decline rather than merely the symptoms; while such an approach was intended in the 1977 White Paper "Policy for the Inner Cities", these aspirations were never achieved. In addition to more effectively targeting of areas of need, a national strategy could therefore integrate area-based policies with broader social and economic policy. This could address the persistent criticisms of a reliance on area-based initiatives alone, which may result in the marginalisation and residualisation of disadvantaged areas (Atkinson and Moon, 1994). However, such an approach would require a reappraisal of the nature of partnership in urban regeneration, including the contentious role of existing agencies (Lloyd, 1992).

9.3.4 *Partnership*

The issue of partnership has become central to any discussion of urban policy. While it has been criticised for elevating considerations of form and structure over those of substance, it is clear that partnership between relevant agencies will continue to be seen as necessary for the effective delivery of anticipated regeneration outcomes. This is because there is a consensus that, whatever its shortcomings, partnership is likely to be more effective than the conflictual or confrontational relationships that have sometimes dominated regeneration initiatives. However, reform of the relevant agencies is desirable since there are important concerns of accountability and equity. Many so-called partnerships have been characterised by an extremely unequal share of power between the partners, and accountability and inclusiveness might be increased by encouraging more formal, longer-term, collaborative partnerships rather than the pragmatic and temporary alliances that have emerged specifically to lever public sector resources.

In addition, it would seem necessary to reform the most important agencies involved in regeneration. The involvement of the Local Enterprise Companies in economic development is discussed in chapter 6. However, Scottish Homes might also be reformed to increase its accountability, and it may be suggested that such an agency could play a key role in applying national policy for housing regeneration. The development and application of policy in this field is particularly important for the achievement of wider regeneration objectives, not only from the point of view of national priorities, but also within the context of European Union commitments, including a reduction in social exclusion. Specifically, urgent action is necessary to improve the quality, type and choice of housing in areas suffering from disadvantage, as well as to improve housing conditions which continue to seriously affect health in many areas. Improvements in energy efficiency are also necessary, in the context of fuel poverty which is likely to increase given the demographic factors referred to above. The ageing population structure of Scotland also implies the need for the provision of more dwellings suitable for those with mobility and agility difficulties, as well as improved general maintenance in the rented sector (Scottish Homes, 1997). All these areas of action will require co-ordination at the national level, and a central, accountable organisation will be necessary to ensure equity, efficiency and effectiveness in the pursuit of national objectives.

This leads to the issue of accountability and the Scottish Parliament needs to consider how greater inclusiveness in urban regeneration can be encouraged by the formation of appropriate partnerships, for instance by a system of accreditation whereby regeneration partnerships would have to pass a range of tests in relation to aspects such as consultation procedures. The need for greater accountability also has clear implications for bidding processes if a system of competition is retained. For instance, it may be more effective to allow more flexible bidding timescales in order to allow more time for consultation prior to bid submission, as well as to make the process more responsive, though it may be argued that multiple deprivation does not occur suddenly so immediate responsiveness is not an important issue. Alternatively, there may be no bidding rounds, with certain areas being targeted and asked to put forward projects for consideration, possibly on a locally-competitive basis, at any time. This has obvious parallels with the French "Contrat de Ville" approach described below. While the adoption of a similar approach in Scotland would necessitate the retention of a clear leadership role for local authorities in the application of urban policy, it would also seem necessary to ensure the direct involvement of local communities.

9.3.5 *Community involvement*

In addition to a strategic approach, an emphasis on the role of local communities, at least in rhetoric, may be identified within urban policy initiatives such as the Urban Partnerships and the PPAs. However, a focus on local communities may represent an attempt to spread risks, internalise problems and legititimise policies, as opposed to a genuine attempt to increase the involvement of local people in order to ensure more appropriate regeneration activities (Duffy and Hutchinson, 1997). Specifically, evidence from the Urban Partnerships suggests that they sometimes involved a rather coercive approach whereby community aspirations were subservient to the requirements of attracting private investment, leading to the manufacture of consensus and the incorporation of dissent rather than the promotion of "empowerment" (Hastings, 1996). The inadequacy of attempts to involve particularly excluded groups is also seen as a feature of some of the Urban Partnerships. Furthermore, the involvement of local communities has been concentrated on housing-led regeneration schemes in Scotland, and it could usefully be broadened out to cover other aspects of regeneration activity.

The Scottish Parliament could strengthen the role of local communities by the introduction of a national community regeneration agency such as that proposed by Shiner and Nevin (1993). Such an agency could work to assist local authorities and communities in "capacity building" in order to enhance the capability of local people to contribute to regeneration initiatives, and a separate budget could be established for such activity. This agency could be supported by central government aid for aspects such as training initiatives, and it could also assist with the formulation of local community development strategies, avoiding the tokenistic approach to community involvement and the marginalisation of the voluntary sector that was experienced in the English SRB Challenge Fund, for instance. Similarly, in terms of economic development, a national community enterprise corporation could encourage and facilitate local economic initiatives in areas with low activity rates, thereby addressing problems of social exclusion, and local community enterprise agencies could contribute to such initiatives by encouraging the focusing of resources on aspects such as community-based businesses (Lovering, 1997; Pacione, 1997b).

Of course, these provisions would require a greater level of commitment to community involvement in decision-making than was evident in the Urban Partnerships for instance, as well as a reconsideration of the means by which regeneration funding was allocated. In addition, communities would need to be given adequate time and resources to become effectively involved in both strategic and operational aspects of regeneration. Moreover, a broader notion of community "empowerment" leads to wider concerns in relation to the need for accountability in policy formulation and implementation (Hoggart, 1997), as indicated above, and the Scottish Parliament could adopt specific mechanisms to enhance the co-operation of national and local government and other "stakeholders", including the local community. Again, the example of the Netherlands could be instructive in this respect, since it illustrates the application of inclusive and collaborative consensus-building within a strategic approach to policy (Healey et al, 1997).

9.3.6   Policy experimentation

Wilks-Heeg (1996) suggests that urban policy in Britain has progressed largely in a circular fashion, with successive phases of "experimentation" failing to incorporate effective monitoring, with the result that there has been a consistent failure to learn from experience. This may be partly explained by political pragmatism, since such "experiments" have often been small scale but nevertheless highly visible and therefore symbolic. Consequently, they have offered the opportunity for low-cost action that diverts attention from the causes of urban decline, which are much more difficult to address (Atkinson and Moon, 1994). This may be illustrated by the example of enterprise zones, which often appeared to be designated for reasons of political pragmatism, in spite of evidence of their effectiveness. Nevertheless, policy experimentation is particularly necessary in the field of urban regeneration because of the uncertainty that surrounds the long term impact of many initiatives. Again, the operation of the Scottish Parliament would seem to offer several opportunities in this respect; for instance, it could encourage effective monitoring of regeneration initiatives and effective dissemination of the results, thereby increasing the capacity to learn from the effects of previous policy. In addition, it could encourage new experimental regeneration initiatives that could be evaluated and adapted or extended accordingly, allowing the dissemination of "best practice".

Moreover, it may prove useful to consider such "best practice" at a broader level to include experience elsewhere in Europe. In addition to the case of the Netherlands referred to above, the French "Contrat de Ville" initiative may offer a useful example since it applies many of the principles suggested above. For instance, rather than an "all or nothing" bidding process, it involves an initial selection of areas by the government, followed by discussion and negotiation between all the partners, including government, to determine the best options for local regeneration. The Contrat de Ville also gives a high priority to need as a criterion for resource allocation, making use of a series of deprivation indicators to select areas for inclusion, though applicants also have to demonstrate the ability to deliver results as well as the linkage of proposals to a local regeneration strategy. In addition, the Contrat de Ville aims to tackle social exclusion by targeting specific excluded groups such as young people and those excluded from cultural activities (Quaife, 1997).

The process of policy application within the Contrat de Ville would seem to offer several advantages over the PPA approach. Because it proceeds by initial selection prior to detailed discussion between partners, there is more time allowed for community involvement and the building of more genuine partnership between the agencies involved than in the PPA initiative. This enables a potentially more open and inclusive approach, and the close collaboration of central and local government ensures that proposals are in line with strategic regeneration frameworks. Furthermore, the Contrat de Ville retains the possibility of benefits arising from competition since the detailed distribution of local resources can be determined by local competition supervised by government. The Contrat de Ville therefore seems to address many of the shortcomings of present and previous urban policy initiatives in Scotland. Of course, differing contextual factors need to be taken into account before the initiative can be adapted for use, and there are some signs of dissatisfaction with the Contrat de Ville initiative in terms of its narrow, area-based approach. Nevertheless, it retains significant advantages and the Scottish Parliament might usefully initiate an experimental initiative based on this model.

9.4   Conclusions

It is clear that the Scottish Parliament offers a range of opportunities to enhance the effectiveness of urban policy. While it is appropriate to build on aspects of success of previous initiatives, it would seem that a fundamental reformulation of basic policy aims is required, together with a reconsideration of all aspects of policy. This could involve the adoption of a clearer national policy framework as well as the creation of new agencies where necessary, combining a strategic approach with a commitment to local community involvement. Integration of area-based initiatives with mainstream funding programmes could help to avoid the criticisms of tokenism and fragmentation that have been applied to urban policy in the past. Moreover, appropriate experimental initiatives could be encouraged, and a greater emphasis on policy monitoring could facilitate more effective learning from the experience of such initiatives in practice. By such means, a more concerted attempt could be made to address the increasing problems of disadvantage faced by urban communities in Scotland. This is an ambitious agenda, and much will of course depend on political will, but it seems clear that the Scottish Parliament presents a unique opportunity to re-shape urban policy for the twenty first century.

10 The local economic impact of the Scottish Parliament

RONALD W. McQUAID

10.1 Introduction

The Scottish Parliament will have potential economic impacts across the whole of Scotland. This chapter concerns the impacts upon the local economy of locating the Parliament in Edinburgh and considers ways in which some of these benefits might be spread to other local economies in Scotland. The impacts include those directly associated with the Parliament, such as construction of the new Parliament building, the Parliament's operation, other government departments and quangos, associated private and non-governmental organisations, and so on, as well as wider impacts on organisations not directly associated with the Parliament, and wider multiplier and displacement effects. This chapter presents estimates of these various impacts although it should be said at the outset that only very general information on likely impacts was given in the White Paper (Scottish Office, 1997a) and that any estimates will of course depend on the temporal, spatial and sectoral scale of analysis.

The next section briefly sets the analysis within the context of the current distribution of government and quango employment and long term population trends, as the location of the Parliament may directly influence these in the future. Section 10.3 then discusses the possible direct and indirect impacts of the Parliament and discusses some recent detailed studies. Section 10.4 considers some of the policies that may help distribute the benefits to other parts of Scotland.

10.2 The distribution of government and quango employment

There is currently an uneven geographical spread in the location of central government jobs in favour of Edinburgh. With approximately 9 per cent of the Scottish population, Edinburgh city has a much higher share of civil service posts. While this largely reflects the role of the city as the central government administration centre, many of these jobs will be transferred to the control of the Parliament. Consequently, there needs to be a debate on whether the Parliament should seek to influence the location of these jobs. It is useful to start by considering the geographical distribution of government related employment in Scotland.

In Scotland as a whole in April 1996 there were 42,761 permanent civil service posts (full time equivalents, FTEs) in government departments, plus a further 3,827 industrial staff, as shown in Table 10.1 (Scottish Office, 1997e). This compares with some 238,192 local authority employees. Of these civil service FTEs 12,826 (28 per cent) are in government and non-departmental public bodies specifically serving Scotland and which would largely relate to the new Parliament. The Scottish Office, and associated sections dealing with specifically Scottish policies, employs only 5,054 FTE civil servants (including a small number based in London) which is under 11 per cent of the total civil service in Scotland. These are mostly located in Edinburgh (except for some sections, notably Economic and Industry Affairs in Glasgow, some fisheries Research Laboratories in Aberdeen and Pitlochry, the Liaison Office in Dover House in London and some regional HMI Schools offices).

Table 10.1   Civil Service employment in Scotland, 1996, full time equivalents

DEPARTMENT	Permanent Civil Service
Agriculture, Fisheries and Food	283
Cabinet Office (including OPS)	48
Customs and Excise	1,509
Defence	6,168
Education and Employment	3,499
Environment	312
Home Office (including Prison Service)	270
Inland Revenue	5,774
Lord Chancellor's Department	2
National Savings	1,913
Ordinance Survey	65
Scottish Office	4,667
Scottish Prison Service	4,439
Social Security	9,050
Trade and Industry	274
Transport	544
Other Departments	3,948
TOTAL, Civil Service	42,761
	Industrial staff
Defence	3,453
Environment	2
Scottish Office	356
Transport	16
TOTAL, Industrial staff	3,827
TOTAL, Industrial and non-industrial	46,588

Source: Scottish Office (1997e) Mandate and Departmental Returns

The remaining 7,772 FTE Scottish Departmental civil servants are located throughout Scotland, although in institutions that are largely headquartered in Edinburgh. These institutions comprise the Scottish Prison Service (4,439), the Court Service (826), the Record Office (119), the General Register Office (213), the Registers of Scotland

(1,073), the Lord Advocate's Department (20) and the Crown Office and Procurator Fiscal Service (1,082). The number of civil servants has been declining for a number of years (by around 7.5 per cent since 1991) due to contracting out, privatisation (for example, the Insurance Services Group in 1991) and efficiency gains.

The other 72 per cent of FTE civil service posts in Scotland (providing UK wide services or delivering UK services in Scotland) are more geographically spread across various parts of Scotland. Of particular importance are Social Security (9,050 FTEs) and the Inland Revenue (5,774 FTEs, especially the East Kilbride and Cumbernauld offices), and the Ministry of Defence which employed 6,168 non-industrial and 3,453 industrial FTEs at both military bases and support services such as Contracts and Central Purchasing and some Payroll. Other examples are: the UK wide DTI Oil and Gas Directorate in Aberdeen; the Forestry Commission (Edinburgh); the International Development Department (East Kilbride); and various Scottish sections of services such as the Passport Office, Health and Safety Commission, Equal Opportunities Commission, and so on. There are also other major government funded bodies, such as the National Health Service, but these largely follow population distribution, as do, to a lesser degree, Universities and Further Education Colleges, and so on. Hence the over representation of civil service jobs in Edinburgh is particularly clear in those departments servicing the new Parliament.

Also significant is employment in Non-Departmental Public Bodies (or quangos) which serve the whole of Scotland. Their employment is strongly biased towards Edinburgh, despite some decentralisation in recent years, such as the National Gallery annex in Banff and Buchan, the Scottish Enterprise Network and the Further Education Unit in Stirling. Table 10.2 shows the number of FTE posts in 1996 for six of the major centres for such employment; there are relatively few such jobs in other cities such as Paisley, although Scottish National Heritage is headquartered in Perth. One third (2,641) of the national total of 8,102 FTE posts were located in Edinburgh. Glasgow only had 1489 (18 per cent) despite its much larger population. Aberdeen had 764 (9 per cent), Dundee 500 (6 per cent), Stirling 255 (3 per cent) and Inverness 333 (4 per cent). The concentration in Edinburgh is shown by the number of jobs per 10,000 residents. Edinburgh had many more posts per capita than the other cities, except Inverness, with 59, 24, 35, 33, 31, and 51 respectively, as shown in Table 10.3. The high share of jobs in Inverness reflects its role as an administrative centre for the Highlands. These figures do, however, ignore the effect of commuting into the cities. Moreover, most quango headquarters were in Edinburgh, implying better than average jobs and larger multiplier effects in terms of wages, suppliers of services, and so on. It is worth noting that all of these cities have far above the Scottish average of 16 jobs per 10,000 population.

Table 10.2   Employment in quangos (Non-Departmental Public Bodies), employing more than 20 employees, in Scotland

Body	Glas-gow	Edin-burgh	Aber-deen	Dun-dee	Stir-ling	Inver-ness	Total
Accounts Commission for Scotland	20	77	9			11	157
Crofters' Commission						76	76
Highlands and Islands Enterprise						174	350
National Board for Nursing, Midwifery and Health Visiting for Scotland		44					44
National Galleries of Scotland		164					164
National Library of Scotland		217					217
National Museum of Scotland		270					270
Royal Botanic Garden, Edinburgh		202					202
Royal Commission on the Ancient and Historical Monuments of Scotland		65					65
Hannah Research Institute							140
Macaulay Research Institute			260				260
Moredun Research Institute		156					156
Rowett Research Institute			276				276
Scottish Crop Research Institute				343			343
Scottish Arts Council		80					80
Scottish Children's Reporter Administration	66	22	17	18	38	16	327
Scottish Community Education Council		30					30
Scottish Council for Educational Technology	88						88
Scottish Enterprise*	694	114	94	91	79		1,714
Scottish Environment Protection Agency	12	91	64		101		637
Scottish Further Education Unit					28		28
Scottish Higher Education Funding Council		60					60
Scottish Homes	218	310	8	48		17	837
Scottish Legal Aid Board	3	270					273
Scottish Natural Heritage		199	36		9	39	613
Scottish Qualifications Authority	350						350
Scottish Screen	38						38
Scottish Sports Council		150					150
Scottish Tourist Board		120					157
TOTAL	1489	2641	764	500	255	333	8102

* Figures relate to the Highlands and Islands Enterprise and the Scottish Enterprise networks as a whole

There are also 6,616 employees of the three Water Authorities, although these are spread around the country as many are linked to "production" with only 714 employees (11 per cent of the national total) of the East of Scotland Water Authority located in Edinburgh, 1,267 located in Glasgow, and 403, 370, 226 and 253 respectively in the other cities. If Water Authority jobs are added, then the numbers of quango jobs per 10,000 population are 75, 45, 54, 58, 58, and 90 respectively, as shown in Table 10.3.

Table 10.3   Quango employment per 10,000 population, 1996

	Non-Departmental Executive Agency employment per 10,000 residents	Non-Departmental Executive Agency plus Water Authority employment per 10,000 residents
Glasgow	24	45
Edinburgh	59	75
Aberdeen	35	54
Dundee	33	58
Stirling	31	58
Inverness	51	90
SCOTLAND	16	29

Cities are ranked by size; populations based upon GRO(S) 1996 data for Council areas except for Inverness where the former District boundary is used

In addition to the number of jobs in different locations, there may be distinctions between types of jobs or expenditure and between the impacts of expenditure and jobs upon the local economy, with the higher level jobs concentrated in Edinburgh. Expenditure policies in terms of procurement may also be significant, especially with the Ministry of Defence which is the largest customer of British industry. Research suggests that certain expenditure may be heavily geographically biased but also that some of this expenditure may have considerable positive multiplier effects on associated industries, such as the importance of Ministry of Defence expenditure in supporting the growth of "High Tech" firms in the south east and south west of England (Hall et al, 1987).

Even at a more local level, expenditure patterns and policies are important. For instance, Scottish Enterprise National in Glasgow may have greater discretionary expenditure associated with each staff member than other organisations, leading to a greater local multiplier effect and possibly local expenditure (if there is a distance decay in expenditure patterns). Some forms of expenditure may also have greater impact on the local economy than others. For example, funding for a University, Prison or a LEC may have different wider economic impacts for each pound spent. Career prospects and remuneration also vary by job, function and sector, and these aspects may also show an uneven geographical distribution.

There are other differential multiplier effects of this distribution of functions and related jobs. For instance, the Royal Botanical Gardens and the National Library,

Galleries and Museums provide important tourism attractions for Edinburgh. In addition, there may be a substitution effect whereby local government can provide a lower level of facilities and services in these areas; for example, there is no need for a major city library when there is the major National Library. Hence local government expenditure on such services can be relatively lower than in other cities, and indeed Edinburgh does have a low per capita expenditure on Museums. This difference in local expenditure on such services is exacerbated in the case of other major regional cities where such services support a wider hinterland, such as Dundee serving Tayside and North Fife, or Glasgow's Mitchell Library providing specialist books and services for much of the west of Scotland. It is unclear whether government support to local government fully takes these different spending needs into account.

Overall then, when the location of Scottish departments that will be serving the new Parliament is considered, there is a current bias of government and quango employment in favour of Edinburgh. However, when all civil service jobs are considered, this geographical bias is considerably reduced. In the case of quangos, there is a strong concentration in Edinburgh. Hence the distribution and wider impact of expenditure needs to be considered more fully.

The concentration of government employment in Edinburgh could be reinforced by the new Parliament, which could in turn reinforce long term demographic changes. As also discussed in chapter 9, demographic movements in Scotland have shown a relative increase in Edinburgh and many surrounding areas compared to Glasgow and the west of Scotland over a number of decades. From 1971 to 1991, the population of Strathclyde (the industrial west of Scotland) fell by 13.8 per cent compared to a fall of 2.9 per cent in the Lothian region covering Edinburgh and its surrounding areas. The Register General for Scotland estimates that Scotland's population of 5 million will fall slightly (by 80,000) between 1996 and 2013. However, Edinburgh's population is estimated to increase by 2 per cent by 2013 from the 1996 level of 448,850, with two of the three neighbouring areas also rising (West Lothian by 11 per cent from 150,770, East Lothian by 7 per cent from 88,140 people, and Midlothian to remain virtually unchanged from 80,040).

While the wider Edinburgh area grows in population, other areas are expected to decline, in particular the other major cities (the population of Glasgow is estimated to fall by 10 per cent from 615,430, Dundee by 9 per cent from 150,250 and Aberdeen by 3 per cent from 217,260). Most of the west of Scotland is expected to fall in population, although rural areas near Dundee and Aberdeen are estimated to grow. The continued concentration of government related jobs in Edinburgh may exacerbate these employment and population trends, although other factors such as the general economy and demographic structure are likely to be more important. However, it is important to try to understand the political, social and economic pressures reinforcing current and future job and expenditure locations, and these will briefly be considered below.

10.3   Impacts of the Parliament on the local economy

The location of the new Parliament will have many direct and indirect impacts upon Edinburgh and other local economies. These include the jobs and expenditure directly associated with the Parliament and linked industries, wider impacts in terms of the development of the economy and property prices, and multiplier and displacement effects.

Reports on the full range of likely local impacts of the new Parliament have been written by various agencies, although these were carried out before the exact location of the Parliament within the city was known. For instance, the City Council of Edinburgh (1997) estimated that there would be approximately 5,500 new jobs in Edinburgh, of which 600 would be associated with the Parliament, 4,500 with new and relocating businesses and organisations, 200 with business tourism and 200 with construction and refurbishment (see Table 10.4). These figures were based upon an assumed 10 per cent growth in employment in business services, a 25 per cent growth in industry/employer/professional organisation employment, and a 25 per cent growth in media employment, as a result of the Parliament.

Glasgow City Council (1997) and their consultants (Pieda, 1997) estimated that the impacts would around half of those estimated by Edinburgh City Council. These impacts would be predominantly in Edinburgh itself, with 88 per cent of expenditure, 92 per cent of jobs and 88 per cent of construction jobs being located there. Their estimate of the number of direct and indirect jobs was for 2,700 and 417 construction job years (or 41.7 permanent job equivalents assuming 10 years is equivalent to a permanent job), of which 2,500 and 367 respectively would be in Edinburgh.

The variation between these reports reflects different assumptions (for example, concerning the volume of construction compared to refurbishment) and in particular different estimates of growth in associated businesses. The methodology used by each differed, with Edinburgh assuming a certain percentage growth in broad related industries, while Glasgow considered each specific industry and the likely impact upon it. The multipliers used in each study were similar, although the likely displacement effects elsewhere in Scotland (for example, of industry/employer/ professional organisations) is not explicitly considered, perhaps unsurprisingly as the Edinburgh report restricts itself to the impacts upon the city. The timescales for the impacts is important and it is unclear from the reports when the employment figures would be reached, so Edinburgh's figures may reflect a longer timescale than those of Glasgow.

Table 10.4   Estimates of the employment effects on Edinburgh of the Scottish Parliament

	Edinburgh City Council estimates	Glasgow City Council estimates
Employment associated with the Parliament and MSPs	600* (plus 129 MSPs)	575 (plus 129 MSPs)
New and relocating businesses/organisations	4,500*	c. 1,531*
Related tourism	200	96
Construction and refurbishment	200	40
ROUNDED TOTAL**	5,500	2,500
Jobs elsewhere in Scotland	N/A	205

* including multiplier effects.
** rounded totals quoted in the reports referred to
Note that each estimate uses different assumptions and figures are approximate

Sources: Edinburgh Council (1997); Glasgow Council (1997); Pieda (1997)

Finally, the assumptions of the levels of civil service jobs appears to differ, with Pieda suggesting 200 jobs for serving the Parliament (Committee clerks, catering, security, and so on), plus 375 new executive civil service staff and the 129 MSPs, while Edinburgh assume 200 staff for serving the Parliament and 258 support staff for MSPs (a secretary and research assistant each). It is unclear from the reports whether the support staff are equivalent to the executive staff, although they would appear to be different. It must, however, be remembered that these are working reports and were not intended as in-depth definitive studies.

The figures are not insignificant, as the 5,500 estimate represents around 1.6 per cent of the Edinburgh travel to work area workforce (1.9 per cent of the City Council area workforce) and almost half of the registered unemployed in that area (12,786 unemployed claimants in December 1997). Of course, those getting such jobs may commute and the availability of such jobs may increase in-migration but the data show the broad scale of employment. The lower Glasgow estimates still represent close to 1 per cent of the current workforce.

10.3.1 *Jobs and expenditure directly associated with the Parliament*

The White Paper (Scottish Office, 1997a) provides some general estimates of the employment associated with the Parliament, although new proposals for the Parliament may arise and the actual outcomes may be different. The additional running costs of the Parliament are estimated at £20-30 million, including staff and operating costs. This includes the salaries and allowances of the 129 Members of the Scottish Parliament (MSPs). Although MSP and "Cabinet Minister" salaries are yet to be set, the figure may be near the £43,000 per annum for Westminster MPs. The multiplier and displacement effects are considered below. Each MSP will require administration/ secretarial support and possibly other services such as researchers, so it is likely that there could be around 260 such jobs, mostly based in Edinburgh, but some based in constituencies.

These figures assume that the number of new staff required to service the Parliament was estimated at 200, although further new jobs may result from the transfer of other functions currently carried out by the Treasury or Cabinet Office, or to operate new responsibilities (for example, possibly in the areas of policy and taxation by the Parliament). The previous 1977 devolution Bill (HMSO, 1977a) estimated that a higher number of additional civil servants (750) would be needed as a result of devolution. Since then the number of civil servants has decreased due to outsourcing, transfer to quangos, and so on, so posts have already been moved elsewhere.

The full capital costs of the new building and associated infrastructure, including roads is uncertain, although estimates for the building at the chosen Holyrood site are over £50 million (excluding VAT and fees), and a further £3.5-4 million for site purchase (Scottish Office communication, February 1998). Based upon estimates of total construction costs of around £20million, Pieda consultants for Glasgow City Council (1997) estimate that there would be 417 worker years of construction jobs created, of which 88 per cent (367 years) would be spent in Edinburgh. Hence the chosen site at Holyrood would be likely to create from around 770 to 1000 construction job years (assuming the industry average gross output per construction worker), or around an equivalent of 77-100 "permanent" FTEs. In addition, other construction jobs would be created in associated developments, as discussed below.

10.3.2 *Impacts on associated industries*

The new Parliament is likely to attract other organisations which find it advantageous to be nearby. These include those lobbying or seeking to influence the Parliament, consulates, industries associated with the effects of the Parliament such as the media, hotels, firms providing services directly to the Parliament, and local government.

Although many organisations seeking to influence the Parliament are already located in Edinburgh, others such as Trades Unions (for example, the STUC), employers' and voluntary organisations may seek to strengthen their presence there. An important aspect of this will be the dynamic changes over time, in particular those linked to the function of the offices. If the lobbying part of an organisation moves to Edinburgh then, over time, it is likely that further parts of the organisation such as policy making and other functions may then move to join them, thus displacing jobs elsewhere in Scotland. Similarly, private lobbying firms may find it more advantageous to move to Edinburgh, and Pieda (1997) estimated that some 100 additional lobbying posts may be generated, with £3 million in salaries and support costs and a capital expenditure of £1.34 million on offices.

Moreover, there are currently 20 Consular offices listed in Edinburgh; these may be upgraded, and new consulates may be set up or moved from other parts of Scotland. This will depend partly on the perceived significance of the Parliament and its expanding role in dealing with the EU and elsewhere, which may be aided by a wider and higher profile of the Scotland Europa office in Brussels.

In addition, other important associated industries likely to show growth include the various parts of the media industry. The number of new media jobs is uncertain and will depend upon the organisation of the firms involved. Some may expand or create new Edinburgh offices, while others may predominantly use existing staff based elsewhere or may "outsource" to independent firms in Edinburgh. The Edinburgh Council report estimated an increase of 25 per cent (75 jobs) in broadcast, media and news agency activity, somewhat higher than the Pieda figure of 50. Moreover, the Parliament may require specialist legal and professional services such as accounting, and these may be concentrated in Edinburgh. Pieda estimate that there could be up to 500 such jobs supported by the Parliament.

Further impacts will be upon services used by those working in, or with, or visiting the Parliament, especially restaurants, hotels, speciality shops, and so on. Some 2,000 extra hotel rooms are expected to be developed in the next few years, partly due to the extra business and tourism travel linked to the Parliament and the associated organisations around it. Edinburgh estimated a resulting 200 jobs in business tourism, although there could be some growth in other tourism due to the city's higher profile. Pieda estimated a more modest 96 jobs and £865,000 expenditure per annum. Improvements to transport (for example, air travel) may also result from higher travel to the city, although the scale of this effect may be relatively small, at least in the short run.

Finally, there will be additional expenditure by the local authority for services such as police security, environmental improvements, and so on. This may also result in a greater level of central government grant support for the local authority in Edinburgh.

10.3.3 *Multiplier effects*

The employment and expenditure discussed above will have multiplier (indirect and induced effects) and displacement effects. Most studies of the multiplier effects have concentrated upon impacts of private investment with multiplier effects spreading to the public and private sectors (for example, Greig, 1971), although others (such as Ashcroft and Swales, 1982 and Brownrigg, 1973) have also considered public sector investment or moves. The income and employment multiplier effects include first round effects of additional salary and other income from those not previously resident in Edinburgh, or extra income for existing residents and further jobs in public services, such as schools and health services (although some of these may be provided in the private sector). This first round effect will be the equivalent of the average propensity to consume based upon average post tax income. The first round effects will also include the initial investment injection (for example, the construction of the Parliament building). Subsequent rounds of the multiplier will be based upon the marginal propensities to create income in the public sector and the marginal propensities to consume, pay tax, give up state benefit and import (Harris et al, 1987). Ashcroft and Swales (1982) estimate that the local employment multiplier of moving civil service jobs (Property Services and Ministry of Defence) from London to West Glamorgan and Cleveland were 1.09 and 1.14 respectively, while the income multipliers were 1.71 and 1.66.

The studies of the Scottish Parliament did not estimate new specific multipliers but used generally accepted estimates of likely multiplier effects. Using a multiplier figure of 1.32, Pieda (1997) estimated the income multiplier effects to be 861 FTEs, plus 96 FTEs in tourism and 40 FTEs in construction. Edinburgh City Council (1997) used an income multiplier of 1.2 and supplier multiplier of 1.1. These figures appear to be for the multiplier effects within Edinburgh, although it is important to distinguish these from the wider multiplier effects on the rest of Scotland and beyond. For some expenditure it may differ (for example, Mackay Consultants, 1995, use a multiplier of 1.75 for the media industry in Scotland). These broad figures seem reasonable, although detailed study would be required to estimate more precise figures. However, the geographical distribution of this multiplier effect within Scotland is less certain although the effects would be concentrated in Edinburgh. The detailed effects will depend on issues such as the level of commuting by MSPs and additional workers linked to the Parliament (or existing government staff who choose to stop commuting and move to Edinburgh to live). Similarly, the purchasing policies of the Parliament and other (for example, the construction firms) will affect the distribution of the multipliers.

10.3.4 *Wider impacts*

In the longer term the Parliament, particularly if it is seen as a constructive forward looking body, may improve the perception of Edinburgh as a major European city and an attractive residential and industrial location. This may be important for certain industries such as finance, if the Parliament is seen as demonstrating integrity and prudence, and electronics. Some of these impacts may be captured in the multiplier effects, as they relate to future potential rather than existing economic relationships covered by usual multiplier estimates. In California's Silicon Valley some 40 per cent of the staff are non-US (in a wide range of jobs) and relatively few of the rest were born in the greater central California area, so the attractiveness of the location to potential workers can be important, although obviously many other factors are more fundamental to the development of electronics (see for instance Hall et al, 1987). It is not possible to accurately estimate these effects, particularly as so many other factors are more influential, including the future policies of the Parliament, but the effects should be positive unless the Parliament is perceived by decision makers and others in a negative light. A key policy will, no doubt, be to use the new Parliament to support development across Scotland and not just around Edinburgh.

In addition, commercial and residential property prices will increase although it is uncertain by how much. This will lead to some displacement as firms move or perhaps even close but should conversely also increase pressure for new developments. Some estimates of the impact on property prices immediately beside the location of the new Parliament have indicated that prices will rise by 30 per cent over what would reasonably have been expected before the site of the Parliament was announced, particularly for offices, restaurants, and so on (*Scotland on Sunday*, 1998). The Edinburgh study estimated an increase in demand for office space of 63,000 sq.m. while the Glasgow study estimated around 30,000 sq.m., (reflecting the lower overall employment impact estimates) but both estimates were made before the government's choice of the Holyrood site.

However, the geographical distribution of these impacts within Edinburgh will vary, and in the long run the impacts on the city as a whole will depend upon many other factors such as the general economic health of the local and national economies, and of course the availability of existing space (such as the city centre offices recently released after local government reorganisation). The existence of the Parliament may also help create opportunities for specialist property areas, such as a "media district", although these would need to be based on more than just the work associated with the Parliament.

10.3.5 *Displacement and other potentially negative impacts*

There will, of course, be some negative impacts of the Parliament upon Edinburgh and the rest of Scotland, such as displacement effects and the impacts of rising commercial property prices. For Edinburgh, the additional traffic congestion and pollution (especially due to cars) will adversely affect the city as a whole and especially around the Holyrood site chosen for the Parliament (although any city centre site would have similar problems).

Moreover, residential prices in the city are already amongst the highest in Scotland, and the increased incomes and employment, plus some increase in "weekday" accommodation for Parliamentarians and others should raise prices further. The impacts near the Parliament and in the city centre are likely to be greatest, and this may result in many low income residents (including the large student population) having to move from these areas. In addition, generally higher property prices may lead to labour market pressures in terms of difficulties in attracting people to the area and higher wage demands. However, other factors affecting property prices are likely to be much more important; furthermore, Edinburgh is by no means a "closed economy" and it is likely that higher prices may result in greater commuting.

As with the multiplier effects, displacement effects will be dynamic and change over time. However, within Edinburgh, there may also be displacement as some organisations move out due to higher rents, congestion, difficulty or expense in staffing, which may benefit some other areas unless the organisations contract or close. Harris et al (1987) found that the growth of the oil sector in Aberdeen led to displacement (of jobs to other sectors) as well as deterrence (that is, firms decided not to come to the city due to the impacts of the oil company growth on labour and property prices for instance). These effects amounted to eight jobs lost in the non-oil sectors for every 100 jobs created in the oil sector. The extent of these effects depends upon the demands and characteristics of the relevant industries as well as the characteristics and responses of the local economy. In the case of the Parliament, the opening of development opportunities (near the Parliament but also in the wider city and surrounding areas) by the City Council, the responses of the labour market (for example, through training schemes for lower skilled jobs and the attraction of new workers or retention of graduates for higher skilled jobs) will influence the impacts.

Displacement effects are particularly important for the rest of Scotland. Expenditure on the Parliament and any additional support for local authorities may result in lower government expenditure in other parts of Scotland. Indeed, if the Parliament is funded from areas employing staff with a high propensity to spend (for example, low paid NHS workers) then the multiplier effects could be lower than for these alternatives. In such a case, if expenditure on the Parliament is substituted totally for expenditure elsewhere (as will be the case if tax raising powers are not used during the first Parliament, as promised by the main political parties, and debt is not increased) there could be a decline in total jobs as higher paid MSPs and officials replace lower paid workers elsewhere, who have a higher propensity to spend. Even if the Scottish Block grant is increased to reflect the cost of the Parliament, this means that the displacement will be more widely spread across the UK.

To illustrate the scale of this, a senior official or MSP on a salary of £43,000 is equivalent to three fully qualified Grade D registered nurses near the top of their pay scale. Of course, to counter this, the Parliament may increase overall economic growth and GDP, but that is a different issue from that discussed here. In addition, the transfer of some lobbying and media jobs based elsewhere in Scotland represent displacement.

This is not to argue that MSPs or staff at the Parliament should be poorly paid. Their costs are a legitimate cost of democracy. It does, however, indicate that there will be real costs to the whole of the country, and that the Parliament should seek to redistribute the benefits of the Parliament across the country where this is possible and practical, as discussed further in the next section, as well as seeking to increase development outside Scotland beyond that which would occur without its existence. Of course, efficiencies that could be gained even without the Parliament could not reasonably be counted as "covering" the costs of the Parliament and any associated displacement effects.

In summary, a range of industries will be significantly affected directly or indirectly, although the impacts will depend upon the time and spatial scales chosen for analysis, and the policies of the Parliament, local government and firms.

10.4   Ways to spread the benefits

The employment and expenditure benefits of the Parliament could potentially be spread by: ensuring easy access to information and dialogue with the Parliament for all parts of Scotland (where possible without having to travel to the Parliament); easing access for those from other parts of Scotland who need to visit or work at or near the Parliament; decentralising civil servant posts; and supporting the potential development of the wider economy.

10.4.1 *Why develop policies to spread the benefits beyond Edinburgh?*

Before discussing ways of spreading the impact of the Parliament to other parts of Scotland, it is worth asking why this should be considered. The first reason is that Edinburgh is one of the most prosperous local economies in Scotland, and has a per capita GDP 10 per cent above the UK average. Although there are difficulties with the definitions of unemployment in official statistics, the percentage unemployed (unadjusted claimant count, December 1997) in the Edinburgh travel-to-work area was only 3.8 per cent of the workforce, well below the 5.7 per cent figure for Scotland as a whole and the figure for Glasgow (6.4 per cent). Consequently, on equity grounds, other parts of the country should benefit where possible. Moreover, on efficiency grounds, the Edinburgh local economy may "overheat" leading to difficulties getting suitable employees for all organisations in or near the city, as well as congestion and inflationary pressures.

The scope for those outside Edinburgh and its contiguous areas to take up the new employment opportunities by commuting are limited, unless there are improvements in infrastructure and services. Edinburgh has a high level of commuting with a third of all employees (69,400 out of 215,470) commuting into Edinburgh, as shown in Table 10.5. However, the vast majority of these (32,190) come from the three surrounding Council areas in the former Lothian Region and a further 7,390 from neighbouring Fife. Consequently, only 12,050 of Edinburgh employees (5.6 per cent of the total) came from elsewhere in Scotland, including 1,110 from Glasgow; hence the great majority of new employment opportunities resulting from the new Parliament are likely to remain in Edinburgh and contiguous areas.

In addition, some of the jobs resulting from the Parliament will be for self-employed people. There are even fewer (490 or 4.8 per cent) of the 10,230 self-employed currently commuting from outside Edinburgh and its contiguous areas, with 80 per cent of the total living and working in the city. Again, therefore, this indicates that the benefits are unlikely to be spread widely.

Table 10.5   Travel to work origins of all employees in Edinburgh, 1991

Origin	Employees	Self-employed	Total
Edinburgh	146,070	8,140	154,210
East Lothian	13,480	440	13,920
Mid Lothian	16,890	430	17,320
West Lothian	18,220	440	18,660
Fife	7,390	240	7,630
Central	3,980	120	4,100
Borders	1,990	120	2,110
Glasgow	1,110	60	1,170
Rest of Strathclyde	3,250	110	3,360
Rest of Scotland	1,720	80	1,800
England and Wales	950	40	990
Outside UK/Offshore	420	10	430
TOTAL	215,470	10,230	225,700

Source: Census of Population, 1991; areas are based upon local authority boundaries; figures have been grossed up from the 10 per cent sample

However, there are a number of barriers to spreading the benefits of the Parliament beyond Edinburgh City and its travel-to-work area. In the case of decentralising more government employment, potential barriers include the implications for efficiency of administration and the difficulties of interactions between the networks of public bodies and government departments and others. In addition, the equity arguments are not all "one-sided" as there are parts of Edinburgh and surrounding areas with significant unemployment and it is important to integrate disadvantaged groups in these areas who are sometimes on the margins of the economy. There is also a danger of reducing the wider agglomeration effects on the economy if there are major relocations of civil servants from Edinburgh.

The debate over benefits should not be seen as an "Edinburgh versus the rest of Scotland" fight or "zero sum game" of expenditure or jobs. The impact of the Parliament should be seen as a means of expanding the economy of the entire region so that policies to spread the impacts reinforce other policies to promote the development of Scotland as a whole. Indeed, a parochial Parliament more concerned with one geographical area or group fighting against another could be greatly damaging to the whole of Scotland.

10.4.2 *How to spread the benefits*

The first issue in spreading the benefits of the Parliament is how to reduce the "drag of distance", whereby those located outside the city may be at a disadvantage. In this respect, questions of physical infrastructure, organisational structures and public policies need to be considered, and benefits may be spread by improved communications (both physical, such as rail and bus links, and information technology) from the Parliament and civil service to businesses, households and others throughout Scotland. The choice of a site relatively close to the city centre and the main rail station should aid this to some degree, although the transportation links for the specific Holyrood site chosen will need major improvement both in local terms and in terms of access to the rest of the country.

Information technology presents considerable scope for improvement. To indicate the scale of improvements required, the Internet capability from houses and offices in most of Scotland is limited. Even in small US States such as West Virginia new infrastructure investment is rapidly increasing the capacity and characteristics of information technology links. There the speed of downloading a 17 volume encyclopaedia is expected to fall from around 28 hours to 13 seconds as a result of the installation of new infrastructure. Such technological networks need to be supplemented by other institutional and policy support so that the benefits may be reaped by all parts of society and the economy. For instance, the growth of networks of small firms can be aided by such policies and support from economic development agencies such as Local Enterprise Companies and others.

Moreover, organisational issues may also be important. For example the Parliament could hold some meetings (for example, Committee meetings) outside Edinburgh, and it could organise the Parliamentary day and week to suit those having to travel to the city and to restrict the number of visits and amount of time having to be spent there.

The second issue is whether many more civil servants can be decentralised from Edinburgh. As noted above, there are a large number of UK civil service jobs carried out throughout Scotland, but those most directly related to (and controlled by) the Scottish Parliament, together with many quangos, are concentrated in Edinburgh. The Hardman Report (1973) considered decentralising civil service jobs from London and some of the issues remain similar. The potential benefits include reduced congestion (although clearly the congestion and other costs in London cited by Hardman may have been greater), easier access to labour and lower labour costs such as labour turnover, property cost savings, and greater effectiveness by increased proximity. However, there are likely to be problems of decentralisation in terms of communications, travel costs (especially time), shared facilities with other departments, the need to be close to decision makers and the possibility of losing economies of scale in services (see McQuaid, 1993, for a discussion relating to economies of scale).

Nevertheless, most of the Scottish population are roughly an hour and a half's travel from the Parliament (particularly as it is relatively close to the main rail station), so there should be scope for dispersal of more jobs at all levels including support or clerical jobs. Suitable planning of working days by the Parliament (for the benefit of MSPs) should also help this process if attendance in Edinburgh by officials can be more effectively planned. This may also imply the need for a network organisational structure for the civil service, at least in location and communication terms, which may include sub-regional centres outside Edinburgh, possibly based upon more appropriate locations for the specific functions (for instance, and as a precedent, the former Industry Department was located in the main industrial city of Glasgow).

Third, purchasing policies of the new Parliament should also seek to ensure that there is no local geographical bias. This requires mechanisms to ensure that firms throughout Scotland have equal access to tender information and that they are not put at a disadvantage due to geography. Even the European Commission can be parochial, and it has been accused of geographical bias when seeking tenders in 1996 for MEP offices with 22 out of the 46 "invited" firms being based in Belgium. However, procurement of all government departments, not just the Parliament, should seek to support the long term competitiveness of regional or UK firms (for instance Porter, 1990, considered how the national health service in Denmark supported innovative products and treatments through support for testing).

The first major contracts will be for the construction of the new Parliament buildings, and the firms gaining, as well as the location of their workforces, will be important. In the longer term, great efforts must be made to ensure that suppliers of goods and services, including specialist legal or financial advice from throughout Scotland are given equal opportunities. This should involve the monitoring of the location of firms and workforces carrying out contracts and ensuring that formal and informal information on tendering is equally available to all.

Finally, it is crucial that the many impacts upon the wider economy are spread throughout Scotland by firms and support agencies seeking to grasp the opportunities presented. Greater tourism and media interest in Edinburgh will present opportunities for other areas to build upon. Moreover, the Parliament may raise Edinburgh's (and Scotland's) profile as an attractive European city for new firms and workers, in addition to helping to retain existing workers (partly through reducing out-migration) and to aid the development of existing firms. It is strongly in the interest of all of Scotland for these wider economic impacts to be developed, even if most were located in or near Edinburgh, as these in themselves will increase the market for other Scottish firms. Edinburgh needs be seen as a part of the wider Scottish (or at least Central Scotland) economy, rather than as a self contained entity. Hence, reducing development opportunities in Edinburgh may reduce overall development in Scotland as a whole. The higher international profile of Scotland and Edinburgh, and the possible increase in consulates, may further help increase international trade for firms across the country.

At the micro-level, it will also be important for Edinburgh itself to maximise the opportunities to revitalise areas of the city and to use the increased demand for uses such as offices and restaurants to upgrade the quality of development and the environment in different parts of the city. As discussed earlier, effort will also be needed to ensure that all residents in and around the city get access to the new employment opportunities that will arise.

10.5 Conclusions

This chapter has considered the wide range of impacts of the Scottish Parliament upon the local economy in Edinburgh. The positive impacts, particularly direct and indirect employment and expenditure, have been identified and discussed. There will also be some negative impacts such as congestion, labour market pressure, rising house prices, and displacement of employment elsewhere. The current geographical distribution of civil service and quango employment has been analysed, and Edinburgh appears to be over represented, although by less than at first appears when only Scottish Office jobs are considered. The actual impact of the Parliament will also depend on the wider policies of the Parliament itself, as the use of tax varying powers for instance may lead to different growth rates in employment, property prices, and so on.

Some ways in which the employment and expenditure benefits of the Parliament could potentially be spread across Scotland have also been considered, particularly by ensuring easy access to information and dialogue with the Parliament from all parts of Scotland, easing access for those from other parts of Scotland who need to visit or work at or near the Parliament, by decentralising civil service and quango posts (including higher level posts), and supporting the potential development of the wider economy. This will require greater transport and information technology infrastructure, organisational change and the responsive organisation of the Parliament. While the full costs as well as benefits need to be considered, a positive scenario would be for the Parliament to act as a catalyst for wider economic and social benefits across Scotland.

Acknowledgements

Thanks are given to those who provided help and information, including Cathy Craig, George Sneddon and Martin Wight. All views and errors are, of course, the responsibility of the author.

11 A policy agenda for the Scottish Parliament

JOHN McCARTHY and DAVID NEWLANDS

This book has noted the various economic constraints, problems and risks which will confront the Scottish Parliament. The freedom of action of a Scottish Parliament, as of any regional government anywhere in the world, is limited. Nevertheless, the book has also sought to identify the opportunities which the Scottish Parliament offers to improve the governance of Scotland and of the UK. The individual chapters of this book contain a large number of ideas as to what the Scottish Parliament might attempt in the area of economic policy.

The following are a number of proposals which seek to contribute to the emerging economic policy agenda for the Scottish Parliament in the first years of the twenty first century. They reflect the views of the editors rather than of the authors of the individual chapters. While there is a consensus among the authors on a wide range of issues, there are some areas of disagreement. An example is whether tax varying powers should be used and, if used, what effects they might have.

- **Lower expectations of what the Scottish Parliament can achieve**

At least in the first few years, there are severe limits as to what the Parliament can realistically hope to achieve. There are a whole variety of ways in which the Parliament can aspire to increase the competitiveness and rate of growth of the Scottish economy. However, these require changes to business and institutional conditions which inevitably take a long time. The immediate future does not offer any prospect of significant economic gains. Indeed, if the creation of the Scottish Parliament coincides with the onset of a world recession, the first few years may be ones of rising unemployment and falling incomes.

- **Do not use tax varying powers, at least in the Parliament's first term**

Tax varying powers are a distraction. While there are a number of administrative and economic difficulties with the use of tax varying powers, the major problem again is the burden of public expectation which is so great that even the maximum additional revenue of £450 million could not begin to meet the competing demands upon it. The best course of action is for the Parliament to place a self imposed embargo upon the exercise of its tax varying powers until such time as it has proven its ability to put existing resources to creative and efficient use.

- **Push for a Territorial Exchequer Board and a new Needs Assessment**

Disputes about the allocation of public finances across the constituent parts of the UK are not going to go away. As David Heald and Neal Geaughan make clear in chapter 4, the arrangements for financing the work of the Scottish Parliament do not constitute an enduring fiscal settlement. The Barnett formula is not a statutory mechanism. Therefore, in the absence of an independent Territorial Exchequer Board or a new UK wide Needs Assessment, the assigned budget of the Scottish Parliament will remain politically vulnerable. In any case, the Scottish Parliament may have less to fear from a scrutiny of the territorial allocation of public spending across the UK than many might think because, while Scotland may receive an above average share of identifiable public expenditure, its share of non identifiable public spending appears to be below average.

- **Strengthen European partnerships and networks**

As Peter Roberts explains in chapter 3, European partnerships generally work better already in Scotland than the somewhat fragmented arrangements found in many English regions. Nevertheless, the Scottish Parliament could strengthen European partnerships further. It should bring in those social partners, such as trade unions and local authority members, which have generally been excluded to date. It should also seek to broaden the European networks of which Scotland is part, including the formal structures of the European Union but also the many specific transnational projects and informal bodies. On many occasions, this will simply involve giving encouragement and support to local authorities and other organisations which are already part of such networks.

- **Broaden the remit of Scottish Enterprise**

The remit of Scottish Enterprise should be broadened to encompass the social dimension of development, as Highlands and Islands Enterprise is already charged to do. The Local Enterprise Companies should survive but their activity should be less focused on business development. Scottish Enterprise and Highlands and Islands Enterprise should be required to devote more effort to the promotion of partnerships, between local authorities, the Local Enterprise Companies, Scottish Homes, employers, trades unions and local communities.

- **Change the remit and focus of Locate in Scotland**

The Scottish Parliament should re-examine the role which inward investment plays in the development of the Scottish economy. The benefits are considerable in terms of the acquisition of new investment, technology and management skills as well as additional employment. However, external ownership also has a number of adverse impacts which Locate in Scotland could do more to acknowledge and address. Thus, it should seek stronger commitments from potential inward investors on such issues as the location of higher corporate and research functions, technology transfer, and corporate recruitment, sales and purchasing policies.

- **Support the Scottish financial sector**

The Scottish financial sector makes an important contribution to income and employment in its own right. However, it also has a role to play in improving the availability and terms of investment resources in Scotland. The Scottish Parliament should examine the model of regional investment banks which in countries such as Germany and Spain have been successful in plugging some of the gaps left by the conventional banking system.

- **Raise the level of skills in the Scottish economy**

A major concern of the Scottish Parliament will be levels of education and skills. Its powers encompass the whole formal education sector, from nurseries through to universities, and the Parliament will be acutely aware of its responsibilities to maintain the distinctive Scottish tradition in education. However, the Parliament will also have the opportunity to improve the provision of industrial training in Scotland. It should encourage businesses to recognise their interest in a better trained workforce but it might also consider more interventionist measures - including the imposition of a training levy on Scottish employers.

- **Enhance the economic development responsibilities of local authorities**

Scottish local authorities have a legitimate role in the pursuit of economic development which the Parliament should encourage. The Parliament should ensure that local authorities are adequately funded so that they are not reluctantly squeezed out of, or tempted to withdraw from, the economic development field. Councils should be given a "power of general competence" which would permit the more rapid development of projects where competence was in doubt. Closer relationships between local authorities and Local Enterprise Companies should be encouraged.

- **Recreate the Scottish tradition of innovation in planning**

As Greg Lloyd demonstrates in chapter 8, there has been a loss of strategic overview within the planning process in Scotland. The Parliament should seek to address this "strategic deficit" and regain a long Scottish tradition of innovation in planning policy and practice. Specifically, it should establish a strategic planning structure which would create the framework for decisions about the provision of infrastructure for industrial and commercial development. This structure would also permit the fuller integration of land use planning with economic and social development, and of local housing and labour markets in Scotland.

- **Reinvigorate urban policy in Scotland**

By comparison with England and Wales, there has been a relatively integrated approach to urban policy in Scotland for some years. However, there is scope for further improvement. The Parliament could adopt a clearer policy framework, combining a strategic approach with a commitment to local community involvement. Area based initiatives could be better integrated with mainstream funding programmes. The Parliament could encourage appropriate experimental initiatives while a greater emphasis on policy monitoring would facilitate more effective learning from the experience of such initiatives in practice.

- **Spread the employment and expenditure benefits of the Parliament**

The Scottish Parliament will have positive net income and employment effects on the economy of Edinburgh but these are likely to be at the expense of other parts of Scotland. There should be attempts therefore to spread the benefits of the Parliament. Among the possibilities identified by Ron McQuaid in chapter 10 are ensuring easy access to information and dialogue with the Parliament from all parts of Scotland, easing access for those from other parts of Scotland who need to visit or work at or near the Parliament, and decentralising civil service and quango posts.

- **Ensure that the policy making process is open, inclusive and well resourced**

The argument for clarity, transparency and accessibility made by David Heald and Neal Geaughan in chapter 4 in the specific context of budgetary decisions is of more general applicability. It also accords with the general thrust of the policy recommendations made in this chapter. The Scottish Parliament should seek to ensure that the economic policy making process is as open as possible so that people know what decisions have been made and why. This is the best hope of ensuring the accountability of all agencies involved in economic development, including the Parliament itself. Partnership between all the different actors should be encouraged where possible although the ultimate decision making responsibility rests with the Parliament. It is important that the policy making process is well resourced. The relevant committees of the Parliament should have the appropriate administrative support and be able to call upon a wide range of economic advisers, from within the civil service, the Scottish universities and thinktanks, local government and business. Finally, the Parliament could significantly improve the quality of the decision making process by devoting comparatively modest sums to the collection of better data about the structure and performance of the Scottish economy.

Bibliography

Adonis, A. (1998) "The Fabian Column: Blair not Bossi is the third way", *Fabian Review*, 101(1), p.7.

Alden, J. (1996) "Regional development strategies in the EU: Europe 2000+" in Alden, J. and Boland, P. (eds) *Regional Development Strategies: A European Perspective*, Jessica Kingsley, London, pp.1-13.

Allmendinger, P. and Tewdwr-Jones, M. (1997) "Post-Thatcherite urban planning and politics: a major change?", *International Journal of Urban and Regional Research*, 21, pp.100-116.

Ancram, M. (1997) *House of Commons Debates*, vol. 304, 13 January 1998, c.247.

Anderson, J.E. and van den Berg, H. (1998) "Fiscal decentralization and government size: an international test for Leviathan accounting for unmeasured economic activity", *International Tax and Public Finance*, 5, pp.171-186.

Archer, J. and Livingstone, K. (1998) "Notes in capital letters", *Guardian*, 2 May.

Armstrong, H. (1997) "Regional-level jurisdictions and economic regeneration initiatives" in Danson, M., Lloyd, G. and Hill, S. (eds) *Regional Governance and Economic Development*, Pion, London, pp.26-46.

Ashcroft, B. and J.K. Swales (1982) "The importance of the first round in the multiplier process: the impact of Civil Service dispersal", *Environment and Planning A*, 14(4), pp.429-444.

Ashcroft, B., Love, J. and Schouller, J. (1987) *The Economic Effects of Inward Acquisition of Scottish Manufacturing Companies 1965-1980*, Industry Department for Scotland, Glasgow.

Atkinson, A.B. and Stiglitz, J.E. (1980) *Lectures on Public Economics*, McGraw-Hill, London.

Atkinson, R. and Moon, G. (1994) *Urban Policy In Britain*, Macmillan, London.

Ayriss, L. (1997) "Reforming the patchwork quilt - a comparison of national regeneration programmes", *Welsh Housing Quarterly*, 26, pp.7-8.

Bachtler, J. and Turok, I. (1997) "Conclusions: an agenda for reform" in Bachtler, J. and Turok, I. (eds) *The Coherence of EU Regional Policy*, Jessica Kingsley, London.

Bailey, A., Barker, A. and MacDonald, K. (1995) *Partnership Agencies in British Urban Policy*, UCL Press, London.

Balcells, A. (1996) *Catalan Nationalism Past and Present*, Macmillan, Basingstoke.

Barnes, W.R. and Ledebur, L.C. (1998) *The New Regional Economies: The US Common Market and the Global Economy*, Sage, London.

Barnett, J. (1982) *Inside the Treasury*, André Deutsch, London.

Begg, I., Lansbury, M. and Mayes, D. (1995) "The case for decentralised industry policy" in Cheshire, P. and Gordon, I. (eds) *Territorial Competition in an Integrating Europe*, Avebury, Aldershot, pp.179-205.

Bell, D. and Dow, S. (1995) "Economic policy options for a Scottish Parliament", *Scottish Affairs*, Autumn.

Bell, D., Dow, S., King, D. and Massie, N. (1996) *Financing Devolution*, Hume Papers on Public Policy, 4(2), Edinburgh University Press, Edinburgh.

Bellini, N. (1996) "Regional economic policies and the non-linearity of history", *European Planning Studies*, 4, pp.63-73.

Bennett, R. (1982) *Central Grants to Local Governments: The Political and Economic Impact of the Rate Support Grant in England and Wales*, Cambridge University Press, Cambridge.

Bennett, R. (1990) "Decentralisation and local economic development" in Bennett, R. (ed) *Decentralisation, Governments and Markets*, Clarendon Press, Oxford, pp.221-244.

Bennett, R. and Krebs, G. (1991) *Local Economic Development*, Belhaven Press, London.

Bentley, G. and Shutt, J. (1997) "European regional policy in the English regions: the West Midlands and Yorkshire and Humberside" in Bachtler, J. and Turok, I. (eds) *The Coherence of EU Regional Policy*, Jessica Kingsley, London.

Blackman, T. (1995) *Urban Policy in Practice*, Routledge, London.

Blow, L., Hall, J., and Smith, S. (1996) *Financing Regional Government in Britain*, IFS Commentary No. 54, Institute for Fiscal Studies, London.

Blowers, A. (1997) "Society and sustainability. The context of change for planning" in Blowers, A. and Evans, B. (eds) *Town Planning into the 21st Century*, Routledge, London, pp.153-168.

Booth, J. (1997) "Anger at Bill's plan for place in Europe", *The Scotsman*, 19 December 1997.

Botham, R.W. (1997) *Inward Investment, Scotland and the Electronic Industries*, paper presented to the Regional Science Association (British and Irish Section) Annual Conference, Falmouth, September 10-12.

Boyle, R. (1988) "Private sector urban regeneration: the Scottish experience" in Parkinson, M. and Foley, B. (eds) *Regenerating the cities: the UK crisis and the US experience*, Manchester University Press, Manchester, pp.74-92.

Boyle, R. (1990) "Regeneration in Glasgow: stability, collaboration and inequity" in Judd, D. and Parkinson, M. (eds) *Leadership and Urban Regeneration*, Sage, London.

Bradbury, J. and Mawson, J. (1997) "Conclusion: the changing politics and governance of British regionalism" in Bradbury, J. and Mawson, J. (eds) *British Regionalism and Devolution*, Jessica Kingsley, London.

Brownrigg, M. (1973) "The economic impact of a new university", *Scottish Journal of Political Economy*, 20, pp.123-139.

Bruton, M.J. and Nicholson, D. (1985) "Strategic land use planning and the British development plan system", *Town Planning Review*, 56, pp.21-40.

Bryden, J. (1997) "The implementation of Objective I in the Highlands and Islands of Scotland" in Bachtler, J. and Turok, I. (eds) *The Coherence of EU Regional Policy*, Jessica Kingsley, London.

Budd, L. (1997) "Regional government and performance in France", *Regional Studies*, 31(2), pp.187-192.

Carrell, S. (1998) "Financing crisis as Scotland's population set to drop", *Scotland on Sunday*, 25 January, p.8.

Castells, A. (1990) "Financing regional government and regional income distribution in Spain" in Bennett, R. (ed) *Decentralisation, Governments and Markets*, Clarendon Press, Oxford, pp.282-294.

Central Office of Information (COI) (1995) *Aspects of Britain: Urban Regeneration*, HMSO, London.

Colwell, A. (1997) *Devolution, Scottish Local Authorities and Europe*, Convention of Scottish Local Authorities, Edinburgh.

Commission of the European Communities (1991) *Europe 2000*, CEC, Brussels.

Commission of the European Communities (1994) *Study of Prospects in the Atlantic Regions*, CEC, Brussels.

Commission of the European Communities (1996) *Structural Funds and Cohesion Funds 1994-1999: Regulations and Commentary*, CEC, Brussels.

Commission of the European Communities (1997a) *Structural Funds: The United Kingdom Within the European Context*, CEC, Brussels.

Commission of the European Communities (1997b) *Agenda 2000*, CEC, Brussels.

Commission on Local Government and the Scottish Parliament (1998) *Consultation Paper 1*, Scottish Office, Edinburgh.

Constitution Unit (1996) *Scotland's Parliament: Fundamentals for a New Scotland Act*, University College London.

Coopers & Lybrand and Pieda (1997) *Comparative Study of Local Authority Current Expenditure in Scotland, England and Wales: Report*, Scottish Office Central Research Unit, Edinburgh.

Council of Europe (1990) *The Impact of the Completion of the Internal Market on Local and Regional Autonomy*, Council of Europe, Strasbourg.

Crick, B. (1995) "Ambushes and advances: the Scottish Act 1998", *Political Quarterly*, 66, pp.237-249.

Cullingworth, J.B. (1994) "Fifty years of post war planning", *Town Planning Review*, 65, pp.277-290.

Cullingworth, J.B. and Nadin, V. (1994) *Town and Country Planning in Britain*, Allen and Unwin, London.

Danson, M. (1995) "New firm formation and regional economic development: an introduction and review of the Scottish Experience", *Small Business Economics*, 7, pp.81-87.

Danson, M. (ed) (1996) *Small Firm Formation and Regional Economic Development*, Routledge, London.

Danson, M. (1997) "Scotland and Wales in Europe" in Macdonald, R. and Thomas, H. (eds) *Nationality and Planning in Scotland and Wales*, University of Wales Press, Cardiff.

Danson, M., Fairley, J., Lloyd, M.G. and Newlands, D. (1990) "Scottish Enterprise: an evolving approach to integrating economic development in Scotland" in Brown, A. and Parry, R. (eds) *The Scottish Government Yearbook 1990*, Unit for the Study of Government in Scotland, Edinburgh, pp.168-194.

Danson, M., Fairley, J., Lloyd, G. and Turok, I. (1997) *The Governance of European Structural Funds: The Experience of the Scottish Regional Partnerships*, Scotland Europa Paper 10, Brussels.

Danson, M., Halkier, H. and Damborg, C. (1998) "Regional development agencies in Europe: an introduction and framework for analysis" in Danson, M., Halkier, H. and Damborg, C. (eds) *Regional Development Agencies in Europe*, Jessica Kingsley, London.

Danson, M., Lloyd, M.G. and Newlands, D. (1990) "The Scottish Development Agency, economic development and technology policy" in Ter Heide, H. (ed) *Technological Change and Spatial Policy*, Royal Netherlands Geographical Society, Amsterdam, pp.179-190.

Danson, M. and Whittam, G. (1998) "Networks, innovation and industrial districts: the case of Scotland" in Steiner, M. (ed) *From Agglomeration Economies to Innovative Clusters*, Pion, London.

Darling, A. (1997) *Hansard*, 9 December, cols.510-13W.

Davidson, K. and Fairley, J. (1998) *Running the Granite City - Local Government in Aberdeen 1975-96*, Scottish Cultural Press, Edinburgh.

de Roo, G. (1993) "Environmental zoning: the Dutch struggle towards integration" *European Planning Studies,* 1, pp.367-378.

Dehousse, R. and Christiansen, T. (1995) *What Model for the Committee of the Regions?*, European University Institute, Florence.

Department of the Environment (1988) *Action for Cities*, HMSO, London.

Department of Transport, Environment and the Regions (1998) *Building Partnerships for Prosperity: Sustainable Growth, Competitiveness and Employment for the English Regions*, HMSO, London.

Diamond, D. (1979) "The uses of strategic planning: the example of the National Planning Guidelines in Scotland", *Town Planning Review,* 50, pp.18-25.

Dinwoodie, R. (1998) "Kilted out for the long game", *Herald*, 30 May.

Doeringer, P., Terkla, D. and Topakian, G. (1987) *Invisible Factors in Local Economic Development*, Oxford University Press, New York.

Dow, S. (1997) "Scottish devolution and the financial sector" in Danson, M., Lloyd, G. and Hill, S. (eds) *Regional Governance and Economic Development*, Pion, London, pp.229-241.

Duffy, K. and Hutchinson, J. (1997) "Urban policy and the turn to community", *Town Planning Review*, 68, pp.347-362.

Edinburgh City Council (1997) *Implications for Edinburgh of a Scottish Parliament*, Report to the Economic Development Committee, 9 June.

Edwards, J. (1997) "Urban policy: the victory of form over substance", *Urban Studies*, 34, pp.825-843.

Eichengreen, B. (1997) *European Monetary Unification: Theory, Practice and Analysis*, MIT Press, Cambridge, Massachusetts.

Emmerson, C. and Hall, J. (1998) *Modernising Local Democracy: A Response to the Government's Consultation Process on Local Government*, Commentary 70, Institute for Fiscal Studies, London.

Ewart, A. (1995) "Regenerating communities into the 90s: a case of 'back to the future?'", *Housing Review*, 44, pp.10-12.

Fairley, J. (1992a) "Local authorities and Local Enterprise Companies - a developing relationship?", *Regional Studies*, 26(2), May.

Fairley, J. (1992b) "Local authorities and Local Enterprise Companies - strategic issues", *Local Government Policy Making*, 19(1), July.

Fairley, J. (1995) "The changing politics of local government in Scotland", *Scottish Affairs*, 10, Winter.

Fairley, J. (1996a) "Scotland's new local authorities and economic development", *Scottish Affairs*, 15, Spring.

Fairley, J. (1996b) "Vocational education and training in Scotland - towards a strategic approach?", *Scottish Educational Review*, 28(1), May.

Fairley, J. (1997) *Future Directions for Local Economic Development in Scotland*, Scottish Local Government Information Unit, Occasional Paper 3, Glasgow.

Fairley, J. and Lloyd, M.G. (1995a) "Scottish Enterprise and Highlands and Islands Enterprise: a preliminary assessment and some critical questions for the future", *Regional Studies*, 29(8), pp.785-790.

Fairley, J. and Lloyd, M.G. (1995b) *Economic Development and Training in Scotland - the Roles of Scottish Enterprise, Highlands and Islands Enterprise and the Local Enterprise Companies*, June.

Fairley, J. and Lloyd, M.G. (1998) "Enterprise in Scotland - a mid-term assessment of an institutional innovation for economic development" in Danson, M., Halkier, H. and Damborg, C. (eds) *Regional Development Agencies in Europe*, Jessica Kingsley, London.

Fletcher, J. (1998) "You want £2bn from Scotland? Get lost!", *Scottish Mirror*, 15 April.

Galbraith, R. (1995) *Without Quarter, a Biography of Tom Johnston*, Mainstream, Edinburgh.

Gamble, A. (1994) *The Free Economy and the Strong State: The Politics of Thatcherism*, Second Edition, Macmillan, Basingstoke.

Gaster, L., Smart, G. and Stewart, M. (1995) *Interim Evaluation of the Ferguslie Partnership*, Scottish Office Central Research Unit, Edinburgh.

Gibson, H., Riddington, G., Whigham, D. and Whyte, J. (1997) *Caledonian Blue Book 1997: National Accounts for Scotland 1951-96*, Glasgow Caledonian University, Glasgow.

Gibson, N. (1996) "Northern Ireland and Westminster: fiscal decentralisation - a public economics perspective" in Northern Ireland Economic Council, *Decentralised Government and Economic Performance in Northern Ireland*, Occasional Paper 7, Northern Ireland Economic Council, Belfast, pp.10-89.

Gieve, J. (1997) Oral evidence, in Treasury Committee, *The Barnett Formula*, Second Report of Session 1997-98, HC 341, HMSO, London, Q.160.

Glasgow City Council (1997) *Potential Impact of a Scottish Parliament on Glasgow's Economy*, Report to the Policy Formulation and Monitoring Subcommittee.

Glasson, J. (1992) "The fall and rise of regional planning in the economically advanced nations", *Urban Studies*, 29, pp.505-531.

Goetz, K.M. (1993) *German Federalism and European Integration: Compatibility and Adjustment*, paper presented at the ESRC Research Seminar on "Intergovernmental Relations in the European Union", London School of Economics, London, December.

Goodhart, C.A.E. and Smith, S. (1993) "Stabilization" in *The Economics of Community Public Finance, European Economy: Reports and Studies No. 5*, pp.417-443.

Government of Ireland Act 1920, Chapter 67, HMSO, London.

Greater London Council (1985a) *The London Industrial Strategy*, GLC, London.

Greater London Council (1985b) *The London Labour Plan*, GLC, London.

Greig, M. (1971) "The regional income and employment multiplier effects of a pulp and paper mill", *Scottish Journal of Political Economy*, 18, pp.31-48.

Group of Lisbon (1995), *Limits to Competition*, MIT Press, Massachusetts.

Hague, C. (1996) "Spatial planning in Europe: the issues for planning in Britain", *Town Planning Review,* 67.

Halkier, H. and Danson, M. (1995) *Regional Development Agencies in Western Europe*, European Studies Working Papers, University of Paisley.

Halkier, H. and Danson, M. (1997) "Regional development agencies in Western Europe: a survey of key characteristics and trends", *European Urban and Regional Studies*, 4(3), pp.243-256.

Hall, P. (1997) "Regeneration policies for peripheral housing estates: inward and outward looking approaches", *Urban Studies*, 34, pp.873-890.

Hall, P., Breheny, M., McQuaid, R.W. and Hart, D. (1987) *Western Sunrise - The Genesis and Growth of Britain's Major High-Tech Corridor*, Routledge, London.

Hansen, N.M. (1968) *French Regional Planning,* Edinburgh University Press, Edinburgh.

Harding, A., Evans, R., Parkinson, M. and Garside, P. (1997) *Regional Government in Britain - an Economic Solution?*, Policy Press, Bristol.

Hardman Report (1973) *The Dispersal of Government Work from London*, Cmnd 5322, HMSO, London.

Harris, A., Lloyd, M.G., McGuire, A., and Newlands, D. (1987) "Incoming industry and structural change: oil and the Aberdeen economy", *Scottish Journal of Political Economy,* 34(1), pp.69-90.

Harvie, C. (1994) *The Rise of Regional Europe*, Routledge, London.

Hastings, A. (1996) "Unravelling the process of 'partnership' in urban regeneration policy", *Urban Studies*, 33, pp.253-268.

Hastings, A., McArthur, A. and McGregor, A. (1994) *Community Involvement in Wester Hailes*, Training and Employment Research Unit, University of Glasgow.

Haughton, G. and Peck, J. (1991) "Evaluating TECs as effective labour market institutions" in Hardy, S. and Lloyd, M.G. (eds) *Business Development and Training: An Integrated Approach to Regional Policy*, Regional Studies Association, London.

Haynes, K., Maas, G, Stough, R. and Riggle, J. (1991) "Regional governance and economic development: lessons from federal states" in Danson, M. (ed) *Regional Governance and Economic Development*, Pion, London, pp.68-84.

Hayton, K. (1994a) "Economic development in a unitary local government system", *Quarterly Economic Commentary*, Fraser of Allander Institute, 20(1), University of Strathclyde, Glasgow.

Hayton, K. (1994b) "Planning and Scottish local government reform", *Planning Practice and Research,* 9, pp.55-62.

Hayton, K. (1995) "Taking the structure out of Scottish planning", *Town and Country Planning,* 64, pp.45-47.

Hayton, K. (1996) "Planning policy in Scotland" in Tewdwr-Jones, M. (ed) *British Planning Policy in Transition,* UCL Press, London, pp.78-97.

Hayton, K. (1997a) "Planning in a Scottish Parliament", *Town and Country Planning,* 66, pp.208-209.

Hayton, K. (1997b) *The W(h)ithering of Scottish Development Planning? The impact of a Scottish Parliament upon Development Planning*, University of Strathclyde, Strathclyde Papers on Planning.

Heald, D.A. (1990) *Financing a Scottish Parliament: Options for Debate*, Scottish Foundation for Economic Research, Glasgow.

Heald, D.A. (1992) *Formula-based Territorial Public Expenditure in the United Kingdom*, Aberdeen Papers in Accountancy, Finance and Management, Department of Accountancy, University of Aberdeen, Aberdeen.

Heald, D.A. (1994) "Territorial public expenditure in the United Kingdom", *Public Administration*, 72, pp.147-176.

Heald, D.A. (1995) "Steering public expenditure with defective maps", *Public Administration*, 73, pp.213-40.

Heald, D.A. (1998) "Transparency about public expenditure numbers" in Treasury Committee, *Pre-Budget Report*, HC 420-i & ii, Session 1997-98, HMSO, London, pp.38-44.

Heald, D.A. and Geaughan, N. (1996), "Financing a Scottish Parliament" in Tindale, S. (ed) *The State and the Nations: The Politics of UK Devolution*, Institute for Public Policy Research, London, pp.167-183.

Heald, D.A. and Geaughan, N. (1997) "The tartan tax: devolved variation in income tax rates", *British Tax Review*, 5, pp.337-348.

Heald, D.A. and Geaughan, N. (1998) "Fiscal consequences" in Norton, P. (ed) *The Consequences of Devolution*, Hansard Society, London.

Heald, D.A., Geaughan, N. and Robb, C. (1998) "Financial arrangements for UK devolution", *Regional & Federal Studies*, 8, pp.23-52.

Healey, P. (1994) "Development plans: new approaches to making frameworks for land use regulation", *European Planning Studies*, 2, pp.39-57.

Healey, P. (1997) "The revival of strategic spatial planning in Europe" in Healey, P., Khakee, A., Motte, A. and Needham, B. (eds) *Making Strategic Spatial Plans*, UCL Press, London, pp.3-19.

Healey, P., Khakee, A., Motte, A. and Needham, B. (1997) "Strategic plan-making and building institutional capacity" in Healey, P., Khakee, A., Motte, A. and Needham, B. (eds) *Making Strategic Spatial Plans: Innovation in Europe*, UCL Press London, pp.283-296.

Healey, P., McNamara, P., Elson, M. and Doak, J. (1988) *Land Use Planning and the Mediation of Urban Change*, Cambridge University Press, Cambridge.

Helm, D. and Smith, S. (1989) "The decentralised state: the economic borders of local government" in Helm, D. (ed) *The Economic Borders of the State*, Oxford University Press, Oxford, pp.275-296.

Henig, S. (1997) *The Uniting of Europe*, Routledge, London.

Hesse, J.J. and Wright, V. (eds) (1996) *Federalizing Europe: The Costs, Benefits, and Preconditions of Federal Political Systems*, Oxford University Press, Oxford, pp.2-24.

Highlands and Islands Enterprise (1997) *Welfare to Work*, Submission to the Scottish Affairs Select Committee, HIE, Inverness.

Hill, S. and Munday, M. (1992) "The UK regional distribution of foreign direct investment: analysis and determinants", *Regional Studies*, 26, pp.535-544.

HMSO (1972) *Land Resource Use in Scotland: Volume 1*, Select Committee on Scottish Affairs, House of Commons Papers 511-i, 1971-1972.

HMSO (1977a) *Scotland Bill*, HMSO, Edinburgh.

HMSO (1977b) *Devolution: Financing the Devolved Services*, HMSO, London.

Hodgson, G. (1989) "Institutional rigidities and economic growth", *Cambridge Journal of Economics*, 13, pp.79-101.

Hoggart, P. (1997) *Contested Communities: Experiences, Struggles, Policies*, Policy Press, Bristol.

Hood, N. (1995) "Inward investment and Scottish devolution: towards a balanced view" *Fraser of Allander Quarterly Economic Commentary*, 20(4), pp.67-78.

House of Lords (1997) Select Committee on the European Communities, Session 1996-97, 11th Report: *Reducing Disparities Within the European Union* (H L Paper 64), HMSO, London.

International Monetary Fund (1998) *Code of Good Practices on Fiscal Transparency: Declaration on Principles*, published in *IMF Survey*, 27, pp.122-124.

Jackson, A. and Roberts, P.W. (1997) "Greening the Fife economy: ecological modernisation as a pathway for local economic development", *Journal of Environmental Planning and Management*, 40, pp.615-629.

Jackson, A. (1989) "The Scottish client group approach: indicators of need or discretionary variations in expenditure?", *Public Policy and Administration*, 4(2), pp.35-47.

Jeffrey, C. (1997) "The decentralisation debate in the UK: Role-modell Deutschland?", *Scottish Affairs*, 19, pp.42-54.

Jenkins, S. (1995) *Accountable to None: The Tory Nationalization of Britain*, Hamish Hamilton, London.

Jha, R. (1998) *Modern Public Economics*, Routledge, London.

Johnston, T. (1952) *Memories*, Collins, Glasgow.

Keating, M. (1988) *The City that Refused to Die; Glasgow: the Politics of Urban Regeneration*, Aberdeen University Press, Aberdeen.

Keating, M. (1995) "Europeanism and regionalism" in Jones, B. and Keating, M. (eds) *The European Union and the Regions*, Clarendon Press, Oxford.

Keating, M. (1998) "Book Review of Tindale, S. (ed) The State and the Nations: The Politics of Devolution", *Public Administration*, 76, pp.184-185.

Keating, M. and Boyle, R. (1986) *Remaking Urban Scotland: Strategies for Local Economic Development*, Edinburgh University Press, Edinburgh.

Keeble, D., Bryson, J. and Wood, P. (1991) "Small firms, business service growth and regional development in the United Kingdom: some empirical findings", *Regional Studies*, 25(5), pp.439-457.

Kellas, J.G. (1991) "The Scottish and Welsh Offices as territorial managers", *Regional Politics and Policy*, 1, pp.87-100.

Kennedy, C. (1989) "The Highland Question" in Edwards, O.D. (ed) *A Claim of Right for Scotland*, Polygon, Edinburgh.

Kerremans, B. and Beyers, J. (1997) "The Belgian sub-national entities in the European Union: second or third level players?" in Jeffery, C. (ed) *The Regional Dimension of the European Union*, Frank Cass, London.

Khatami, S. (1991) "Decentralisation: a comparative study of France and Spain since the 1970s", *Regional Politics and Policy*, 1, pp.161-181.

Kilbrandon (The Royal Commission on the Constitution) (1973) *Report*, Cm5460, HMSO, London.

King, D. (1984) *Fiscal Tiers: The Economics of Multi Level Government*, George Allen and Unwin, London.

Kintrea, K., McGregor, A., McConnachie, M. and Urquhart, A. (1995) *Interim Evaluation of the Whitfield Partnership*, Scottish Office Central Research Unit, Edinburgh.

Kopits, G. and Craig, J. (1998) *Transparency in Government Operations*, Occasional Paper 158, International Monetary Fund, Washington DC.

Kornai, J. (1980) "The soft budget constraint", *Kyklos*, 39, pp.3-30.

Lang, I. (1994) "Local government reform: change for the better", *Scottish Affairs*, 6, Winter.

Lawless, P. (1989) *Britain's Inner Cities*, Paul Chapman, London.

Lawrence, R.J. (1965) *The Government of Northern Ireland: Public Finance and Public Services 1921-64*, Clarendon Press, Oxford.

Lee, C. H. (1995) *Scotland and the United Kingdom*, Manchester University Press, Manchester.

Levitt, I. (1996) "The origins of the Scottish Development Department, 1943-62", *Scottish Affairs*, 14, Winter.

Levitt, I. (1998) "Britain, the Scottish Covenant movement and devolution, 1946-50", *Scottish Affairs*, 22, Winter.

Lloyd, M. G. and Newlands, D. (1989) "Recent urban policy development in Scotland: the rediscovery of peripheral housing estates", *Scottish Geographical Magazine*,105, pp.116-119.

Lloyd, M.G. (1992) "Property-led partnership arrangements in Scotland: the private sector domain" in Healey, P., Davoudi, S., O'Toole, M., Tavsanoglu, S. and Usher, D. (eds) *Rebuilding the City: Property-led Urban Regeneration*, E and F N Spon, London, pp.233-244.

Lloyd, M.G. (1994) "Innovative strategic land use planning: National Planning Guidelines in Scotland", *Scottish Affairs*, 6, pp.84-100.

Lloyd, M.G. (1996) "Local government reorganisation and the strategic planning lottery in Scotland", *Town Planning Review,* 67, pp.v -viii.

Lloyd, M.G. and Rowan-Robinson, J. (1988) "Local authority responses to economic uncertainty in Scotland" in McCrone, D. and Brown, A. (eds) *The Scottish Government Yearbook 1988*, University of Edinburgh, Edinburgh.

Lloyd, M.G., McCarthy, J. and Illsley, B. (1997) "Priority Partnership Areas in Scotland", *Town and Country Planning*, 66, pp.60-62.

Lovering, J. (1997) "Global restructuring and local impact" in Pacione, M. (ed) *Britain's Cities: Geographies of Division in Urban Britain*, Routledge, London, pp.63-87.

Lynch, P. (1996) "The Scottish Constitutional Convention, 1992-5", *Scottish Affairs*, 15, pp.1-16.

Lythe, C. and Gilbert, A. (1996) "Are there local labour markets in Scotland?", *Fraser of Allander Quarterly Economic Commentary*, 21, pp.78-84.

McArthur, A., Hastings, A. and McGregor, A. (1994) *An Evaluation of Community Involvement in the Whitfield Partnership*, Scottish Office Central Research Unit, Edinburgh.

McCaffer, J. (1995) "Re-organisation and economic development" in Black, S. (ed) *The Impact of Re-organisation on Particular Services*, Unit for the Study of Government in Scotland, Edinburgh University, Edinburgh.

McCrone, D. (1992) *Understanding Scotland: The Sociology of a Stateless Nation*, Routledge, London.

McCrone, G. (1991) "Urban renewal: the Scottish experience", *Urban Studies*, 28, pp. 919-938.

MacDougall, D. (Chair) (1977) *Report of the Study Group on the Role of Public Finance in European Integration*, Volume I: *Report*; Volume II: *Individual Contributions and Working Papers*, Commission of the European Communities, Collection Studies, Economic and Financial Series, No. B13, European Commission, Luxembourg.

McFadden, J. (1997) *A Power of General Competence - the Time has Come*, Scottish Local Government Information Unit, January.

MacGregor, B. and Ross, A. (1995) "Master or servant? The changing role of the development plan in the British planning system", *Town Planning Review*, 66, pp.41-59.

McGregor, A., Kintrea, K., Fitzpatrick, I. and Urquhart, A. (1995) *Interim Evaluation of the Wester Hailes Partnership*, Scottish Office Central Research Unit, Edinburgh.

McGregor, P., Stevens, J., Swales, J.K. and Yin, Y.P. (1997) "The economics of the 'tartan tax'", *Fraser of Allander Quarterly Economic Commentary*, 22, pp.72-87.

McGregor, P.G., Stevens, J., Swales, J.K. and Yin, Y.P. (1997) "Some simple macroeconomics of Scottish devolution" in Danson, M., Lloyd, G. and Hill, S. (eds) *Regional Governance and Economic Development*, Pion, London, pp.187-209.

Mackay Consultants (1995) *The Initial Economic Impact of an Independent Scotland in Europe*, Mackay Consultants, Inverness.

Mackay, E. (1996) "Public expenditure in Scotland", *SEC(96)2*, Scottish Economic Council, mimeo.

McLean, I. (1997) "Previous convictions", *Prospect*, May, p.80.

McLeish, H. (1998) House of Commons Debates, vol. 304, 13 January 1998, c.248-249.

MacMahon, P., Duncan, G. and Wilson, G. (1998) "£2bn windfall for Dewar in cash shake-up: Treasury review will boost devolution spending", *Scotsman*, 28 May.

McQuaid, R. (1992) *Local Authorities and Economic Development in Scotland*, Report prepared for the Convention of Scottish Local Authorities, COSLA, Edinburgh.

McQuaid, R.W. (1993) "Costing local government reform", *Local Government Studies*, 19(4), pp.477-486.

Malecki, E. and Nijkamp, P. (1988) "Technology and regional development: some thoughts on policy", *Environment and Planning C*, 6, pp.383-399.

Marr, A. (1998) "On remaking Britain: Scotland's Parliament must deliver before demanding more power", *Independent*, 15 April.

Martin, R. and Tyler, P. (1994) "Real wage rigidity at the local level in Great Britain", *Regional Studies*, 28(8), pp.833-842.

Maxwell, S. (1989) "The MSC and the voluntary sector" in Brown, A. and Fairley, J. (eds) *The Manpower Services Commission in Scotland*, Edinburgh University Press, Edinburgh.

Midwinter, A. (1993) "Local government reform: taking stock of the Conservative approach", *Scottish Affairs*, 5, Autumn.

Midwinter, A. (1993) "The review of local government in Scotland - a critical perspective", *Local Government Studies*, 18, pp.44-54.

Midwinter, A. (1995) *Local Government in Scotland - Reform or Decline?*, Macmillan, Basingstoke.

Midwinter, A. (1997) "The Barnett formula and Scotland's public expenditure needs" in Treasury Committee, *The Barnett Formula*, Second Report of Session 1997-98, HC 341, HMSO, London, Appendix 1, pp.29-32.

Midwinter, A. and McGarvey, N. (1995) *From Accountability to Control? The New Council Tax in Practice*, Certified Accountants Educational Trust, London.

Midwinter, A. and McVicar, M. (1996) "The devolution proposals for Scotland: an assessment and critique", *Public Money and Management*, 16, pp.13-20.

Midwinter, A., Keating, M. and Mitchell, J. (1991) *Politics and Public Policy in Scotland*, Macmillan, Basingstoke.

Ministers Responsible for Spatial Planning (1997) *European Spatial Development Perspectives,* Ministers Responsible for Spatial Planning, Noordwijk.

Moore, C. and Booth, S. (1986) "Unlocking enterprise: the search for synergy" in Lever, W. and Moore, C. (eds) *The City in Transition: Policies and Agendas for the Economic Regeneration of Clydeside*, Clarendon Press, Oxford.

Morata, F. (1992) "Regions and the European Community: a comparative analysis of four Spanish regions", *Regional Politics and Policy*, 2, pp.187-216.

Morgan, K. (1995) *Institutions, Innovation and Regional Renewal: The Development Agency as Animateur*, University of Wales, Cardiff.

Musgrave, R. (1959) *The Theory of Public Finance*, McGraw Hill, New York.

Musgrave, R. (1961) "Approaches to a fiscal theory of political federalism" in National Bureau of Economic Research, *Public Finances: Needs, Sources and Utilisation*, NBER, New York, pp.97-133.

Neil, A. (1997a) "Sleep-walk to devolution", *Scotsman*, 18 April.

Neil, A. (1997b) "We are moving on up: our Parliament will be a wake-up call to a reality few Scots have yet grasped", *Scotsman*, 12 December.

Neil, A. (1998) "Out of step with Scotland", *Scotsman*, 27 February.

Nevin, B., Loftman, P. and Beazley, M. (1996) "Cities in crisis - is growth the answer?", *Town Planning Review*, 68, pp.145-164.

Newlands, D. (1992) "A 'Europe of the Regions'? The economic functions of regional government in the European Community", *Current Politics and Economics of Europe*, 2(3), pp.187-202.

Newlands, D. (1995) "The economic role of regional governments in the European Community" in Hardy, S. et al (eds) *An Enlarged Europe: Regions in the Competition?*, Jessica Kingsley Publishing, London, pp.70-80.

Newlands, D. (1997) "The economic powers and potential of a devolved Scottish Parliament" in Danson, M., Lloyd, G. and Hill, S. (eds) *Regional Governance and Economic Development*, Pion, London, pp.109-127.

Newlands, D. and Parker, M. (1997) "The prospects and potential of a new university in the Highlands and Islands", *Scottish Affairs*, 21, Autumn.

Newman, P. and Thornley, A. (1996) *Urban Planning in Europe. International Competition, National Systems and Planning Prospects,* Routledge, London.

North, D. (1994) "Economic performance through time", *American Economic Review*, 84(3), pp.359-368.

Northern Ireland Information Service (1998a) *Northern Ireland: Towards a Prosperous Future - Chancellor Announces £315m Economic Strategy*, Press Release 98/0512c, 12 May, Northern Ireland Office, Belfast.

Northern Ireland Information Service (1998b) *Virgin boss joins Secretary of State to urge 'Yes' vote*, Press Release 98/0520b, 20 May, Northern Ireland Office, Belfast.

Northern Ireland Office (1995) *Frameworks for the Future*, HMSO, Belfast.

Nye, R. (1997) "Wrestling blancmange", *Prospect,* 21, pp.8-9.

Oates, W.E. (1972) *Fiscal Federalism*, Harcourt Brace Jovanovich, New York.

Oates, W.E. (1977) *The Political Economy of Fiscal Federalism*, D.C. Heath, Lexington Mass.

Oatley, N. (1995) "Urban regeneration", *Planning Practice and Research*, 10, pp.261-269.

O'Farrell, P.N., Hitchens, D.M.W.N. and Moffat, L.A.R. (1992) "The competitiveness of business service firms: a matched comparison between Scotland and the South East of England", *Regional Studies*, 26(6), pp.519-533.

Osborne, D. and Gaebler, T. (1993) *Reinventing Government - How the Entrepreneurial Spirit is Transforming the Public Sector*, Plume.

O'Toole, M., Snape, D. and Stewart, M. (1995) *Interim Evaluation of the Castlemilk Partnership*, Scottish Office Central Research Unit, Edinburgh.

O'Tuathail, G., Herod, A. and Roberts, S. (1998) "Negotiating unruly problematics" in Herod, A., O'Tuathail, G. and Roberts, S. (eds) *Unruly World. Globalisation, Governance and Geography,* Routledge, London, pp.1-24.

Pacione, M. (1989) "The urban crisis: poverty and deprivation in the Scottish city", *Scottish Geographical Magazine*, 105, pp.101-115.

Pacione, M. (1997a) "Urban restructuring and the reproduction of inequality in Britain's cities: an overview" in Pacione, M. (ed) *Britain's Cities: Geographies of Division in Urban Britain*, Routledge, London, pp.7-62.

Pacione, M. (1997b) "The urban challenge: how to bridge the great divide" in Pacione, M. (ed) *Britain's Cities: Geographies of Division in Urban Britain*, Routledge, London, pp.335-348.

Paddison, R. (1997) "The restructuring of local government in Scotland" in Bradbury, J. and Mawson, J. (eds) *British Regionalism and Devolution. The Challenges of State Reform and European Integration,* Jessica Kingsley, London, pp.99-117.

Paterson, L. (1994) *The Autonomy of Modern Scotland*, Edinburgh University Press, Edinburgh.

Peacock, P. (1997) *Developing the Economy of the Highlands and Islands*, Highland Council, Inverness, April.

Pearce, D. (1977) "Justifiable government intervention in preserving the quality of life" in Wingo, L. and Evans, A. (eds) *Public Economics and the Quality of Life*, Johns Hopkins University Press, Baltimore.

Perroux, F. (1950) "Economic space: theory and applications", *Quarterly Journal of Economics*.

PIEDA (1993) *Strathclyde IDO: Interim Evaluation*, Industry Department of Scotland, Glasgow.

PIEDA (1997) *The Potential Impact of a Scottish Parliament on the Glasgow Economy*, Pieda, Edinburgh.

Porter, M. (1990) *The Competitive Advantage of Nations*, Macmillan, London.

Pottinger, G. (1979) *The Secretaries of State for Scotland*, Scottish Academic Press, Edinburgh.

Prud'homme, R. (1990) "Decentralisation of expenditure or taxes: the case of France" in Bennett, R. (ed) *Decentralisation, Governments and Markets*, Clarendon Press, Oxford, pp.116-130.

Quaife, P. (1997) *The French Connection: Regeneration Lessons from "Contrats de Ville"*, London Housing Unit, London.

Quigley, G. (1996) "Opening remarks" in Northern Ireland Economic Council, *Decentralised Government and Economic Performance in Northern Ireland*, Occasional Paper 7, Northern Ireland Economic Council, Belfast, pp.1-9.

Quintin, J.M. (1974) *European Co-operation in Frontier Regions: Background Study*, Council of Europe, Strasbourg.

Ramsdale, P. and Capon, S. (1986) "An analysis of local authority discretionary expenditure" in Cmnd 9801, *The Conduct of Local Authority Business, Research Volume I: Aspects of Local Democracy*, HMSO, London.

Riker, W.H. (1996) "European federalism: the lessons of past experience" in Hesse, J.J. and Wright, V. (eds) *Federalizing Europe: The Costs, Benefits, and Preconditions of Federal Political Systems*, Oxford University Press, Oxford, pp.2-24.

Ritchie, A. (1997) Oral evidence, in Treasury Committee, *The Barnett Formula*, Second Report of Session 1997-98, HC 341, HMSO, London, Q.162.

Roberts, P.W. (1993) "Managing the strategic planning and development of regions: lessons from an European perspective", *Regional Studies, 27*, pp.759-768.

Roberts, P.W. (1996a) "Ecological modernisation strategies for regional development in Europe", paper presented at the 17th Conference "Europe of Regions", Odessa, September.

Roberts, P.W. (1996b) "Regional planning guidance in England and Wales. Back to the future?", *Town Planning Review, 67*, pp.97-110.

Roberts, P.W. (1997a) "Strategies for the stateless nation: sustainable policies for the regions in Europe", *Regional Studies, 31*, pp.875-882.

Roberts, P.W. (1997b) "Whitehall et la désert anglais: managing and representing the UK regions in Europe" in Bradbury, J. and Mawson, J. (eds) *British Regionalism and Devolution*, Jessica Kingsley, London.

Roberts, P.W. and Hart, T. (1996) *Regional Strategy and Partnership in European Programmes*, Joseph Rowntree Foundation, York.

Roberts, P.W. and Hart, T. (1997) "The design and implementation of European programmes for regional development in the UK: a comparative review" in Bachtler, J. and Turok, I. (eds) *The Coherence of EU Regional Policy*, Jessica Kingsley, London.

Roberts, P.W. et al (1997) "One Union, fifteen systems", paper presented at the European Urban and Regional Research Network Conference on "Regional Frontiers", Frankfurt am Oder, September.

Rothenburg, J. (1970) "Local decentralisation and the theory of political federalism" in Margolis, J. (ed) *The Analysis of Public Output*, National Bureau of Economic Research, New York, pp.31-68.

Rowan-Robinson, J. (1997) "The organisation and effectiveness of the Scottish planning system" in Macdonald, R. and Thomas, H. (eds) *Nationality and Planning in Scotland and Wales*, University of Wales Press, Cardiff, pp.32-53.

Rowett, B. (1980) "Statistics for policy: needs assessment in the Rate Support Grant", *Public Administration*, 59, pp.173-186.

Savy, R. (1996) *Regions and Territories in Europe,* Assembly of European Regions, Limoges.

Scotland Bill, Session 1997-98, Bill 104, HMSO, London.

Scotland on Sunday (1998) "Holyrood making waves in property", 25 January, p.4.

Scotsman (1998) "Dewar gets his fighting fund", 28 May.

Scottish Constitutional Convention (1989) *Towards a Scottish Parliament*, SCC, Edinburgh.

Scottish Constitutional Convention (1990) *Towards Scotland's Parliament*, SCC, Edinburgh.

Scottish Constitutional Convention (1995) *Scotland's Parliament, Scotland's Right*, SCC, Edinburgh.

Scottish Council Development and Industry (1995) *Exports Survey*, SCDI, Edinburgh.

Scottish Council Development and Industry (1997) *Economic Development and the Scottish Constitutional Convention Blueprint for a Scottish Parliament*, SCDI, Edinburgh.

Scottish Government Yearbook (1979) "Referendum results" in Drucker, H. and Drucker, N. (eds), *The Scottish Government Yearbook 1980*, Paul Harris Publishing, Edinburgh, p.231.

Scottish Homes (1997) *Scotland's Housing into the 21st Century*, Scottish Homes, Edinburgh.

Scottish Local Government Information Unit (1995) *The Guide to Scottish Local Government*, SLGIU, Glasgow.

Scottish Office (1983) *Public Expenditure to 1985-86: A Commentary on the Scotland Programme*, Scottish Office, Edinburgh.

Scottish Office (1988), *New Life for Urban Scotland*, HMSO, Edinburgh.

Scottish Office (1993a), *Progress in Partnership: a Consultation Paper on the Future of Urban Regeneration Policy in Scotland*, Scottish Office, Edinburgh.

Scottish Office (1993b) *Scotland in the Union*, Cm2225, HMSO, Edinburgh.

Scottish Office (1995a), *Programme for Partnership: Announcement of the Outcome of the Scottish Office Review of Urban Regeneration Policy*, Scottish Office, Edinburgh.

Scottish Office (1995b) *Programme for Partnership: Consultation Paper on Implementation Arrangements*, Scottish Office, Edinburgh.

Scottish Office (1995c) *Overseas Ownership in Scottish Manufacturing Industry 1994*, Scottish Office Statistical Bulletin, Industry Series, Edinburgh.

Scottish Office (1996) *Programme for Partnership: Guidance for Applying for Urban Programme Funding*, Scottish Office, Edinburgh.

Scottish Office (1997a) *Scotland's Parliament*, Cm3658, HMSO, Edinburgh.

Scottish Office (1997b) *Government Expenditure and Revenue in Scotland, 1995-96*, Scottish Office, Glasgow.

Scottish Office (1997c) *Towards a Development Strategy for Rural Scotland*, A Discussion Paper, Edinburgh.

Scottish Office (1997d) *Scottish Local Government Financial Statistics 1994-95*, HMSO, Edinburgh.

Scottish Office (1997e) *Civil Service Yearbook 1997*, HMSO, Edinburgh.

Scottish Office (1998) *Serving Scotland's Needs: Departments of the Secretary of State for Scotland and the Forestry Commission - The Government's Expenditure Plans, 1998-99*, HMSO, London.

Scottish Trades Union Congress (1992) *Power for Change: The Agenda for a Scottish Parliament*, STUC, Glasgow.

Seabright, P. (1996) "Accountability and decentralisation in government: an incomplete contracts model", *European Economic Review*, 40, pp.61-89.

Sedgemore, B. (1997) Oral Question 7, in Treasury Committee (1997) *The Barnett Formula*, Second Report of Session 1997-98, HC 341, HMSO, London.

Seely, A. (1998) "The Scotland Bill - tax raising powers", *House of Commons Research Paper 98/4*, House of Commons Library, London.

Select Committee on Relations between Central and Local Government (1996) *Rebuilding Trust*, Volume I - Oral Evidence and Associated Memoranda, HL Paper 97-I, HMSO, London.

Sharpe, L.J. (1993) "The European meso: an appraisal" in Sharpe, L.J. (ed) *The Rise of Meso Government in Europe*, Sage, London.

Shiner, P. and Nevin, B. (1993) "Helping the community take the driving seat in renewal", *Planning*, 12 January, pp.22-23.

Sinclair, D. (1997) "Local government and a Scottish Parliament", *Scottish Affairs*, 19, pp.14-21.

Smith, D. (1997), "Can the Assembly fill the strategic vacuum?", *Town and Country Planning*, October.

Smith, S. (1996) "Regional government, fiscal and financial management in Northern Ireland" in Northern Ireland Economic Council, *Decentralised Government and Economic Performance in Northern Ireland*, Occasional Paper 7, Northern Ireland Economic Council, Belfast, pp.90-146.

Solow, R. (1970) *Growth Theory*, Oxford University Press, Oxford.

Standing Commission on the Scottish Economy (1989) *Final Report*, Glasgow.

Stewart, M. (1997) "The shifting institutional framework of the English regions: the role of Conservative policy" in Bradbury, J. and Mawson, J. (eds) *British Regionalism and Devolution. The Challenges of State Reform and European Integration*, Jessica Kingsley, London, pp.137-157.

Stohr, W. (1989) "Regional policy at the crossroads: an overview" in Albrechts, L. et al (eds) *Regional Policy at the Crossroads - European Perspectives*, Jessica Kingsley, London.

Storey, D. (1984) "Small firms in regional economic development", *Regional Studies*, 18.

Strassoldo, R. (1973) *Frontier Regions: An Analytical Study*, Council of Europe, Strasbourg.

Sutcliffe, J.B. (1997) "Local government in Scotland: re-organisation and the European Union", *Regional and Federal Studies*, 7, pp.42-69.

Talbot, S. and Reeves, A.C. (1997) "Boosting the business birth rate in Scotland: evidence from the Lanarkshire Development Agency's entrepreneurship programme", *Fraser of Allander Quarterly Economic Review*,22, pp.26-35.

Tanzi, V. (1996) "Fiscal federalism and decentralization: a review of some efficiency and macroeconomic aspects", in Bruno, M. and Pleskovic, B. (eds) *Annual World Bank Conference on Development Economics 1995*, World Bank, Washington DC, pp.295-316.

Taylor, P. (1988) "The Urban Programme in Scotland", *Local Economy*, 3, pp.208-218.

Ter-Minassian, T. (1997) *Fiscal Federalism in Theory and Practice*, International Monetary Fund, Washington DC.

Thornley, A. (1993) *Urban Planning under Thatcherism. The Challenge of the Market,* Routledge, London.

Tiebout, C. (1956) "A pure theory of local government", *Journal of Political Economy*, 64, pp.416-424.

Tiebout, C. (1961) "An economic theory of fiscal decentralisation" in National Bureau of Economic Research, *Public Finances: Needs, Sources and Utilisation*, NBER, New York, pp.79-96.

Tirole, J. (1994) "On the internal organization of government", *Oxford Economic Papers*, 46, pp.1-29.

Toothill Lord (1961) *Inquiry into the Scottish Economy*, SCDI, Edinburgh.

Treasury (1997a) *Fiscal Policy: Lessons from the Last Economic Cycle,* Pre-Budget Report Publications, HM Treasury, London.

Treasury (1997b) "Memorandum submitted by HM Treasury" in Treasury Committee, *The Barnett Formula*, Second Report of Session 1997-98, HC 341, HMSO, London, pp.12-13.

Treasury (1997c) "Supplementary memorandum submitted by HM Treasury on Tuesday 16 December 1997" in Treasury Committee, *The Barnett Formula*, Second Report of Session 1997-98, HC 341, HMSO, London, pp.36-39.

Treasury (1998a) "Barnett formula: impact on relative public spending per head in England, Scotland, Wales and Northern Ireland" in Treasury Committee, *The Barnett Formula: The Government's Response to the Committee's Second Report of Session 1997-98*, Fourth Special Report of Session 1997-98, HC 619, HMSO, London, Appendix 2, pp.v-vii.

Treasury (1998b) *The Code for Fiscal Stability*, HM Treasury, London.

Treasury (1998c) *Stability and Investment for the Long Term: Economic and Fiscal Strategy Report 1998*, Cm 3978, HMSO, London.

Treasury (1998d) *Fiscal Policy: Current and Capital Spending*, HM Treasury, London.

Treasury Committee (1997) *The Barnett Formula*, Second Report of Session 1997-98, HC 341, HMSO, London.

Turok, I. (1987) "Continuity, change and contradiction in urban policy" in Donnison, D. and Middleton, A. (eds) *Regenerating the Inner City: Glasgow's Experience*, Routledge and Kegan Paul, London, pp.34-60.

Turok, I. (1997) "Inserting a local dimension into regional programmes: the experience of Western Scotland" in Bachtler, J. and Turok, I. (eds) *The Coherence of EU Regional Policy*, Jessica Kingsley, London.

Turok, I. and Hopkins, N. (1997) *Picking Winners or Passing the Buck? Competition and Area Selection in Scotland's New Urban Policy*, Department of Urban Studies Occasional Paper, University of Glasgow.

Turok, I., Gray, J., Hayton, K., Raines, P., Clement, K. and McBride, G. (1994) *ERDF Business Development Evaluation*, University of Strathclyde, Glasgow.

Twigger, R. (1998) *The Barnett Formula*, Research Paper 98/8, House of Commons Library, London.

Vaessen, P. and Keeble, D. (1995) "Growth-oriented SMEs in unfavourable regional environments", *Regional Studies*, 29, pp.489-506.

Ventura, J. (1963) *Les Llengues Europeens*, Edicons D'Abortacio Catalana, Barcelona.

Wannop, U. (1995) *The Regional Imperative*, Jessica Kingsley, London.

Wannop, U. and Cherry, G.E. (1994) "The development of regional planning in the United Kingdom", *Planning Perspectives*, 9, pp.34-53.

Weir, S. and Hall, W. (1994) *Extra-governmental Organisations in the United Kingdom and their Accountability*, Charter 88 Trust, London.

Welsh Office (1997) *An Economic Strategy for Wales,* Cardiff.

Welsh Office (1997) *Goverment Expenditure and Revenue - Wales, 1994-95*, Welsh Office, Cardiff.

Wheatley Rt Hon Lord (1969) *Report of the Royal Commission on Local Government in Scotland 1966-1969*, Cmnd.4150, HMSO, Edinburgh.

Wiehler, F. and Stumm, T. (1995) "The powers of regional and local authorities and their role in the European Union", *European Planning Studies*, 3, pp.227-250.

Wilks-Heeg, S. (1996) "Urban experiments limited revisited: urban policy comes full circle?", *Urban Studies*, 33, pp.1263-1279.

Wright, A. (1995) "The Scottish Office and the European Union", in Hardy, S., Hebbert, M. and Malbon, B. (eds) *Region Building,* Regional Studies Association, London, pp.82-85.

Young, R. (1983) "A little local inequality" in Brown, G. and Cook, R. (eds) *Scotland - The Real Divide: Poverty and Deprivation in Scotland*, Mainstream, Edinburgh.

Zimmerman, H. (1990) "Fiscal federalism and regional growth" in Bennett, R. (ed) *Decentralisation, Governments and Markets*, Clarendon Press, Oxford, pp.245-264.